ODINISM

present, past and future

by

Osred

Renewal Publications, PO Box 4333, University of Melbourne, 3052, Australia

Printed in the USA by Lulu Press, Inc

© 2010 by Osred
ISBN 978-1-4457-6816-8

All rights reserved. Without limiting the rights under copyright above, no part of this publication shall be reproduced, stored in or introduced into a retrieval system, or transmitted in any form or by any means (electronic, mechanical, photocopying, recording or otherwise), without the prior permission of both the copyright owner and the publisher of this book.

"I know you're out there. I can feel you now. I know that you're afraid ... you're afraid of *us*. You're afraid of change. I don't know the future. I didn't come here to tell you how this is going to end. I came here to tell you how it's going to begin. I'm going to hang up this phone, and then I'm going to show these people what you don't want them to see. I'm going to show them a world without you. A world without rules and controls, without borders or boundaries. A world where anything is possible. Where we go from there is a choice I leave to you."

- Neo, in the 1999 film, *The Matrix*

CONTENTS

1	Time to reclaim our religious heritage	1
2	What is Odinism?	4
3	Ancestor worship	9
4	Our ancestors in prehistoric times	12
5	The Indo-Europeans	17
6	Three lost Indo-European tribes	22
7	Divine blood: The nation of Odin	31
8	What is religion? What is mythology? What are gods?	34
9	Odin	40
10	"Pagan", "heathen" and "cretin"	44
11	The Germanic concept of evolution	46
12	Odinist cosmology	55
13	The Odinist soul	60
14	The pagan afterlife	67
15	The clash of values	70
16	The rise of intolerance	78
17	Heathen victims of Christianity	81
18	Æthelfrith	84
19	Destruction of the Continental Saxons	90
20	Odinist vengeance	96
21	The fall of Scandinavia	101
22	Þorgeir's terrible choice	108
23	Odinism on the Borders	111
24	The Christian economic strategy	121
25	Odinism in Christian churches	126
26	The Period of Dual Faith: Women	133
27	The Period of Dual Faith: Chartres Cathedral	138
28	Folk customs: Yule	146
29	Anglo-Saxondom and cognitive dissonance	150
30	A proto-Odinist President: Thomas Jefferson	155

31	A proto-Odinist Poet: Algernon Charles Swinburne	160
32	A proto-Odinist Scholar: James Murray	169
33	A proto-Odinist Composer: Richard Wagner	174
34	A proto-Odinist art movement: Australian "paganism"	179
35	The limits of proto-Odinism	183
36	Odinist pioneers: Rud Mills	188
37	Odinist pioneers: Evelyn Price	193
38	Odinist pioneers: Ann Lennon, rebel with a cause	196
39	Odinist pioneers: Else Christensen, "The Folkmother"	203
40	Odinist pioneers: Alec Christensen: an unsung hero	206
41	The limits of early modern Odinism	210
42	The Odinist transvaluation of values	214
43	Toward tomorrow	226

1

TIME TO RECLAIM OUR RELIGIOUS HERITAGE

> Christianity, as a sort of backdrop to people's lives and moral decisions – and to the Government, the social life of the country – has now almost been vanquished.
>
> - Cardinal Cormac Murphy-O'Connor,
> Archbishop of Westminster, 2001

> Christianity for a large part of our history was the whole formal basis of our entire culture, the absolute from which were deduced our moral codes, our laws, and our political systems; it largely informed our art, inspired our literature, animated our music, and sustained our men of science. The void that has been left is so great that few can peer into the dark abyss without vertigo.
>
> - Revilo P. Oliver, *Christianity and the Survival of the West*

Professor Oliver was correct in at least one respect. Very few people can face "the dark abyss" that has been left by the passing of Christianity as a coherent way of viewing the world. Many Westerners seem to have no soul left in them anymore. Instead, they have a sterile, materialistic attitude to life. The still-controversial 1991 novel, *American Psycho* [1], was a satirical exploration of how that ethos debauches the individual. Self-destructive consumerism, it implied, can only lead to a world in which nothing has any intrinsic value, in which great art is almost impossible, "style" is everything, and people are so interchangeable that even "thrill-killing" is scarcely more remarkable than any other hobby.

Some Westerners still feel spiritual yearnings, but often they turn in despair to foreign beliefs that are alien to their own cultural and spiritual needs, or to new pseudo-religions and cults. Most of them probably settle for an anemic form of secularized Christianity – the comfortable repetition of platitudes that are now little more than verbal reflexes.

Even more notably, Westerners today seem like the decaying 20th century English working classes of whom Richard Hoggart [2] wrote:

> This regular, increasing and almost entirely unvaried diet of sensation without commitment is likely to help render its

consumers less capable of responding openly and responsibly to life, is likely to induce an underlying sense of purposeless in existence outside the range of a few immediate appetites.

Hoggart had in mind the British working class of the 1950s, but the condition he observed appears now to have spread to nearly all levels of Western society. Like the uprooted working classes he described, our society as a whole has been uprooted from its cultural soil. The comfortable values of the past, many of them once considered to be Christian, have vanished, and "a great many [suffer] from the hypnosis of immature emotional satisfactions". Hence the wine, restaurant and film reviews that take up increasing space in our "quality" media, the "food pornography" of popular television, the reduction of national politics to the personal and trivial.

Even worse, prominent intellectuals have convinced many people that Western cultural traditions, and even Western people themselves, are so intrinsically bad that the world would be a better place without either. As the French writer Pascal Bruckner summed up their views:

> The whole world hates us, and we deserve it: that is what most Europeans think, at least in Western Europe. Since 1945 our continent has been obsessed by torments of repentance. Ruminating on its past abominations ... it views its history as nothing more than a long series of massacres and sackings that led to two world wars, that is, to an enthusiastic suicide. [3]

Apathetic, docile, immature, uninformed, crassly materialistic, consumed by consumerism, suicidal, addicted to the cult of personality, most people in the West no longer *care* about very much at all – except when whipped up into periodic and hysterical bouts of self-righteousness by the media and the politicians, often on issues that are ultimately to our own detriment. This is understandable, now that the religion that claimed to inspire the old Western system of values has largely been swept away.

Yet a small minority of Westerners believes that the end of any coherent or intelligent form of Christianity presents us with wonderful opportunities – spiritual, cultural and artistic, even scientific. These are the people who dare to "peer into the dark abyss", and find that beyond the chasm there is a world of brilliant light. Carefully examining all the evidence, they conclude that although Christianity was for many centuries *part* of the cultural mortar of Western civilization, it was, at best, an interruption of our spiritual tradition and a drag on our progress.

They cite the fact that people of European descent have our own religious traditions. The Christian period occupied less than 4% of our history – even if we begin the count no earlier than the Cro-Magnon period. It changed us when we adopted it, in most cases under duress, just as we adapted it to try to make it closer to our old morality. Perhaps this led to an uneasy compromise that was, ultimately, unhealthy for us.

Was Christianity, at its core, fundamentally incompatible with the intrinsic values of people of European origin? Despite "all our pomp of yesterday" when Christianity was our official faith, were we perhaps nurturing a spiritual sickness that would eventually destroy us?

Many of us are coming to believe that the demise of Christianity gives us an opportunity to start afresh, to return to our own traditional ways, our own spiritual roots, to reclaim our own religious heritage. These people are often called "pagans" or "heathens", just as we were all "pagan" or "heathen" for at least 96% of our people's history.

In the main English-speaking countries the majority of the population originated in the British Isles and neighboring parts of northern Europe. The indigenous faith of these people is today called Odinism, which is defined in law as "the organic spiritual beliefs and religion of the indigenous peoples of northern Europe as embodied in the Eddas and as they have found expression in the wisdom and in the historic expression of these peoples." [4] (This will be discussed further in Chapter 2.)

The modern revival of Odinism began in Australia in the 1920s and 1930s, but went underground from 1942 as a result of state persecution (see Chapter 36). Finally, in 1972, the Australian Attorney General officially confirmed that there were no constitutional or legal impediments to the practice of Odinism in that continent.

Today, a new generation of Westerners around the world is discovering that Odinism's ancient truths are as relevant today as they were in the springtime of our people. If you dare to "peer into the dark abyss", if your mind is truly open, if you can seriously consider the idea that were it not for Christianity we would be far more advanced in every respect than we are today, then you are well and truly on the path to Odinism. If so, then this book may help you on your spiritual quest.

First, though, you will need to get over the preconceptions some of us have formed about the nature of religion and its role in the history of our people and culture. Most of those preconceptions can only bind us to a moribund past. They can never be a basis for the Odinist transvaluation of residual Christian values that has already begun and is gathering pace from day to day. Therefore if you are not yet ready to open your mind fully to the future and its glorious promise, you may wish to wait before considering Odinism any further.

If you *are* ready, please take the time to work through Chapter 2. It is largely about the meaning of words, which may seem to be a "dry" topic. But in any field of knowledge, the student needs to understand some essential terms. A student of music needs to know words like "clef", "key", "chord", "octave", "scale" and so on. In the same way, a student of Odinism needs to understand the basic terms involved. It isn't hard.

2

WHAT IS ODINISM?

Origin of the word

The word *Odinism* seems to have been first used in 1848 by the writer Orestes Brownson, who wrote of "A revival of Odinism, or the old Scandinavian heathenism".

Brownson was wrong to limit the origin of Odinism to Scandinavia. Odinism is – at the very least – the ancestral religion of all the Germanic peoples prior to their forced, and only partial, conversion to Christianity. It is therefore the indigenous spirituality of many or most of the people living in what are now Norway, Sweden, Denmark, Iceland, England, Scotland, Ireland, Wales, France, Belgium, the Netherlands, Germany, Russia, Austria, Italy and Spain. All of these regions (and many others) were inhabited by Germanic tribes and groups, such as the Goths, Anglo-Saxons, Lombards, Franks, Visigoths, Rus, and so on.

In more recent times emigrants from these lands have made large contributions to the population of many "New World" countries. Odinism is therefore also the spiritual heritage of millions of people in Canada, the United States, Australia and New Zealand. In many other countries the ancestors of a significant minority of the population were also Odinists. This applies to many South American states and to South Africa.

Hence, all people around the world whose ancestors were Odinists are today known collectively as "the Nation of Odin".

Some of us may regret Brownson's choice of the word *Odinism*. It can seem to be misleading, at least superficially, and this will be examined in Chapter 9. Even so, the word is firmly established in the English language, and recent attempts to coin more "inclusive" names for the faith of our forebears have met with limited success.

The dictionary definition

The *Oxford English Dictionary* defines Odinism as follows: "The worship of Odin, called the *All-father*, the chief deity of Norse mythology, corresponding to the OE [i.e. Old English] Woden, from whom most of the kingly lines of the Angles and Saxons reckoned their descent; the mythology and religious doctrine of the ancient Scandinavian people before the introduction of Christianity." It defines an "Odinist" as: "a votary of Odin; a student of Odinism".

Citing no authority at all, the dictionary implies that our ancestors were practically monotheists – believers in one god, or in one main god. This is incorrect, even though it is possible to view Odin as emblematic in some respects of all the gods and goddesses of our ancestors.

The legal definition

Readers will recall that Odinism is legally defined as: "the continuation of ... the organic spiritual beliefs and religion of the indigenous peoples of northern Europe as embodied in the Edda and as they have found expression in the wisdom and in the historical experience of these peoples". While this is an accepted legal definition, there are five aspects of it that need to be clarified.

(1) First, "the indigenous peoples of northern Europe" is a vague description. For much of human history, northern Europe was buried under the glaciers of the Ice Ages, and was as uninhabitable as today's Antarctica. Early forms of *homo sapiens* (modern humans) seem to have drifted into northern Europe during the warm periods between the Ice Ages, then wandered off pursuing their food supplies during the cold interludes, returning again when the climate improved. It follows that, for much of our history, our ancestors were not in northern Europe at all. As we will see later, in prehistoric times they spread far and wide, from Europe to Africa, from modern Russia to modern China and Afghanistan.

For the purposes of this book, "the indigenous peoples of northern Europe" will be taken to mean: *everyone who has or had a primary genetic relationship to the modern forms of humans who intermittently colonized northern Europe during the times when that region was inhabitable, prior to the last few decades of mass-immigration.*

(2) "The indigenous peoples of northern Europe" therefore include many cultural groups who did not speak Germanic languages or participate in Germanic culture. The speakers of ancient Greek, Latin and the Celtic languages are obvious examples. Even before their time, we could trace our ancestral lineage back to people who did not even speak Indo-European languages. Many of us will have inherited genes from the builders of Stonehenge, who spoke a language that is now long-forgotten, and most of us are probably descended from the Cro-Magnons who created unsurpassed artworks at the height of the last Ice Age, but whose language is irretrievable. (This will be examined in Chapter 3.)

(3) The term "organic spiritual beliefs and religion" is another tricky phrase, since the words "spiritual" and "religion" are notoriously difficult to define. For simplicity, at this stage we will take *religion* to mean a set of beliefs concerned with the nature and purpose of the universe and life itself, with the spiritual nature of humans and with the

role in life of "supernatural" powers such as the gods. (This will be further examined in Chapter 8.)

(4) The phrase, "as embodied in the Edda", does *not* imply that the Edda is the sole or even the prime source of information on our ancestors' religious or spiritual beliefs.

The *Poetic Edda* (also called the *Elder Edda* and *Sæmundar Edda* and the *Codex Regius*) is a manuscript collection of Icelandic poems. It was written down in the second half of the thirteenth century and discovered on a farm at Skálholt in 1643. It contains most but not all of the surviving poetry from the pre-Christian period in Iceland. We have no precise dates for the composition of the individual poems, and some show obvious Christian influence or interference. Furthermore, there are many gaps in the picture the Edda gives of Icelandic heathen belief, presumably because other important poems from that time have been lost.

The Edda is therefore not in any way a "Bible" for Odinists. It is useful in that it gives us a very good idea of how *some* Odinists in Iceland at a particular time expressed their religious beliefs, and it is the most recent systematic collection of European religious poetry to have survived from pre-Christian times. Since it is an ordered account of our ancestors' beliefs, Odinists honor both the Edda itself and those Icelandic Odinists who resisted conversion long enough to compose its poems – about six centuries after paganism became punishable by death in the Roman Empire.

Yet despite the honor due to the Edda and its authors, a full understanding of our ancestral beliefs requires far more evidence. Fortunately for us, this is available in abundance. Many great literary works from the pagan periods in Greece and Rome have survived, as have works that our ancestors composed outside Europe itself, such as the Vedas of India. We have many authentic Odinist poems that were written or transcribed long before the Edda, as well as the evidence of art, music, legal codes, linguistics, science and technology, folklore, and the wonderful achievements of modern archaeology. (This topic will be further examined in future chapters, especially Chapter 14.)

(5) The phrase "…as they have found expression in the wisdom and in the historical experience of these peoples" is a *crucial* part of the legal definition of Odinism and must not be forgotten or downplayed. Modern Odinism is not by any means the reconstruction of a world-view that ceased to exist when the leaders of our different tribes and nations officially embraced alien religions.

What usually happened after the "conversion" of such peoples is that their rulers tried to enforce the new and "official" religion, while at the same time the majority tried to ensure the survival of their old customs, beliefs and values. This led to a *Period of Dual Faith,* in which the two religions, the old and the new, co-existed. Sometimes they clashed violently, sometimes compromises were reached. The faith of our European forebears was officially driven underground. But in return, particularly in northern Europe, we managed to heathenize Christianity in innumerable ways, to the point that it was not recognizable as the faith that the Popes in Rome had originally exported to the north. Despite all the legal sanctions against it, Odinism survived within the official faith remarkably well. Or to put that another way, if Odinism failed to survive in its original purity, so too did Christianity. The two had fused in a very uncomfortable union. If we can say that one "died out", we have to say the same of the other. (This will be further examined in Chapters 26, 27 and 28.)

By the 19th century the shackles that bound the two faiths together were rusting. The Period of Dual Faith was coming to an end. Since then, Christianity has largely collapsed, both intellectually and morally. Among the Germanic-speaking nations it seems to be hanging on, and then often merely in its most bizarre forms, only in the USA. Yet at the same time, Odinism has gained greatly in moral and intellectual integrity, not to mention numbers, and our society as a whole is taking on many core Odinist values without even knowing their origin.

Odinism now seems to have been the stronger partner in what amounted to a "forced marriage" of faiths. We shall see later that this was only possible because Odinist values continued to find expression in the wisdom and in the historical experience of our people.

The word "Odinism" in this book

We saw above that Odinism has at least two recognized definitions. The dictionary definition is inadequate and misleading, while the legal definition, although adequate for its purpose, needs to be used with care.

It is not the intention of this book to provide a better or more complete definition of Odinism. Religions are impossible to define in secular language, and their inner propositions are only meaningful to those who immerse themselves in that discipline. There is nothing mysterious about this. Religion is one of several ways of apprehending the reality of the world in which we humans find ourselves. Other ways include mathematics, literature and art, science, the human sciences and history, and philosophy. Each discipline has its own logical structure, which conveys both meaning and validity. The logical structure of one form of human inquiry does not apply to the others, although there are of course areas of overlap. (This will be discussed further in Chapter 25.)

In this book the word Odinism will be used mainly in the sense of its legal definition, with the qualifications mentioned above. Where necessary, it will be clarified further by using phrases such as "modern Odinism", or "Odinism in the pre-Christian period". Otherwise, the context should indicate the intended meaning.

The name "Odin"

Odin is a name used only in the present stage of the English language. Our pre-Christian ancestors did not speak modern English, and the god we know today as Odin was called by them Wóden (in Old English), Wuotan (in Old High German), Wódan (in Old Low German) and Óðinn (in Old Norse). It is standard modern practice to refer to the god as Odin except where an historical context is required. So when quoting from Old English sources the spelling used here will be Wóden, from Icelandic sources Óðinn, and so on. This is in keeping with the way we spell the modern day of the week named after this god "Wednesday", retaining the original Wódnesdæg for Old English contexts. (It is a rough and ready system, which sometimes breaks down.)

In all religions the attributes of a god or goddess that are most valued, or regarded as most typical, vary from period to period, often reflecting social change, and sometimes from region to region. The many attributes of Odin will be discussed in later chapters, but it will help if the reader bears in mind that gods resembling Odin in some non-Germanic religious traditions of our ancestors include: Hermes (the Greek guide of souls), Mercury (Roman), Teutates (Celtic), Radigast (Slavonic) and Brahma (Vedic). It should also be remembered that, like other deities of our people, Odin has also been known by many other by-names, usually reflecting different aspects of his nature and functions.

The etymology of Odin's name has often been misrepresented. The 11th century Christian writer, Adam of Bremen, infamously wrote: "Wodan, id est furor": "Wodan, that is fury." Adam was probably thinking of the adjective that survived in Old Norse as "óðr", and in Middle English as "wood". The Norse adjective has several related meanings. These include: mad, frantic, furious, vehement, eager, fast and rapid. An identical Icelandic word is the noun "óðr", meaning mind, wit, soul, sense, song and poetry.

The English word "wood", which was used by Chaucer and Spencer, is explained by the *Oxford English Dictionary* as follows:

> OE. *wód* = OHG. *wuot* (in *ferwuot* raging, frantic), ON. *óðr*, Goth. *wôl-*, **wōþs* possessed (cf OHG., MHG., *wuot*, G. *wut* rage) f. Teut. wōð- (to which belong also OE. *wōþ* song, sound, ON. *oðr* poetry, and WODEN): - Indo-Eur. *wāt-*, represented by L. *vātēs* seer, poet, OIr. *fáith* poet, W. *gwawd* song of praise, the fundamental meaning being 'to be excited or inspired'.

In short, then, the name Odin means something akin to "excitement, inspiration". From what we know of other branches of our people's ancient religion, related terms in modern English probably include: ecstasy, exuberance, passion, fervor, ardor, rapture, delight, bliss, and the imported but almost naturalized term, nirvana. As long ago as 1899 the great Cambridge scholar H. M. Chadwick wrote: "The word **wōðanaz-**wōðenaz* seems to be participial in form and may originally have denoted 'inspired'." [5]

3

ANCESTOR WORSHIP

... in the days of our ancestors, it was these [death masks] that were to be seen in their halls, and not statues made by foreign artists, or works in bronze or marble: portraits modeled in wax were arranged, each in its separate niche, to be always in readiness to accompany the funeral processions of the family; occasions on which every member of the family that had ever existed was always present. The pedigree, too, of the individual was traced in lines upon each of these colored portraits. Their muniment-rooms, too, were filled with archives and memoirs, stating what each had done when holding the magistracy. On the outside, again, of their houses, and around the thresholds of their doors, were placed other statues of those mighty spirits, in the spoils of the enemy there affixed, memorials which a purchaser even was not allowed to displace; so that the very house continued to triumph even after it had changed its master. A powerful stimulus to emulation this, when the walls each day reproached an unwarlike owner for having thus intruded upon the triumphs of another!

- Pliny the Elder (23-79 CE), *Naturalis Historia*

> Lo, there do I see my father.
> Lo, there do I see my mother, and my sisters, and my brothers.
> Lo, there do I see the line of my people
> Back to the beginning.
> Lo, they do call to me.
> They bid me take my place among them,
> In the halls of Valhalla,
> Where the brave may live... forever.

- 1999 film, *The Thirteenth Warrior*, by John McTiernan

When one religion is repressed by another, those aspects of the older faith that were dearest to the hearts of its adherents are the most likely to survive. Sometimes this happens in a modified form, such as the continuing worship of the pre-Christian English goddess *Ēostre* (West Saxon *Ēastre*, Old High German *Ostara*) under her modern name of Easter. The survival of our veneration of Easter indicates that she was too popular for the church to suppress entirely, so her beloved rites were clumsily grafted on to the Christian festival that bears her heathen name. (This process will be discussed further, with regard to Yule or "Christmas", in Chapter 28.)

Since the most beloved aspects of the older faith will be usually the ones that survive best, it would seem that ancestor-worship was the most popular element of our ancestors' religion.

A visitor to many a stately home in Britain will see a hall that is decorated with the portraits of ancestors of the family that has lived there for generations, together with curiosities such as weapons or other trophies that individual ancestors have brought back from foreign expeditions. Pliny would have had no trouble in recognizing this as a continuation of the Roman ancestor-worship customs that he described. In Roman times only those of noble birth were permitted to worship their ancestors in this way, and until the Industrial Revolution only the land-based aristocracy in Britain could afford stately homes and family portraits. Yet today this veneration of our ancestors is growing at all levels of Western society, with the computerization of government records fuelling a massive growth in the study of genealogy.

Furthermore, the veneration of those of our ancestors who are perceived to have heroically defended our way of life is increasingly celebrated, particularly by younger members of our folk. In Australia, for instance, growing numbers of young people are visiting Anzac Cove, walking the Kokoda Track, and attending the dawn service at Villers-Bretonneux. Equally, many people from the "New World" countries now go on personal pilgrimages to the places in the British Isles and Europe from which their families emigrated – just as others visit the place in New England where the Pilgrims landed.

So *was* ancestor-worship really one of the most popular of our religious customs in pre-Christian times? The Western literary evidence suggests so. The Ancient Greeks were so fiercely proud of their lineage that many royal clans traced their origins back to Herakles, a son of Zeus. According to two different Roman traditions, true Romans were descended either from Romulus, a son of Mars, or from Aeneas, a son of Venus. The family trees of the rulers of the Anglo-Saxon kingdoms exult in their descent from Wóden. (This will be discussed further in Chapter 7.) Other than that, the official records shed almost no light on pre-Christian religious beliefs in England, so divine descent was clearly a very important matter. The heathen Norwegians and Swedes believed that their early kings were descended from the god Yngvi-Frey, while the Danish monarchy claimed descent from Frey's son Skjöld. This is not the place to investigate the traditions of every tribe in our family tree, but it is fair to say that wherever sufficient literary evidence survives, the most obvious belief they all had in common was ancestor-worship.

The phrase "ancestor-worship" may seem a little strange to some modern readers, perhaps recalling the un-Western activities of "primitive" tribes. It should not. Our modern word "worship" is derived from a good Old English word (*weorðscipe*) that means, quite simply: "The condition ... of deserving, or being held in, esteem or repute; honor, distinction, renown; good name, credit".

The term does, however, suggest that our ancestors are still with us in some way, rather than simply having vanished without trace, and also that they can affect the fortune of their descendants. (A possible scientific basis for this belief will be discussed further in Chapter 13.)

We are only in the early stages of our journey into Odinism, and the concepts raised so far will be amplified and clarified in subsequent chapters. One thing is clear, though, already. Given that ancestor-worship is central to modern Odinism, we need to know who "our ancestors" were – and who they were not. In Chapter 4 we will survey what is currently known about our ancestors in prehistoric times – the times before "history" was written. In Chapter 5 we will look at what seems to have been the last period during which most of our ancestors were united in culture, religion and language. In Chapter 6 we will look at some tribal branches of our family tree that have become extinct. In Chapter 7 we will examine the divine blood of the Nation of Odin.

4

OUR ANCESTORS IN PREHISTORIC TIMES

Hardly any animal or plant species is really "indigenous" to anywhere. The earth's climate has changed so often, and so drastically, that plants and animals – including humans – have had to migrate from zone to zone to find conditions that suit them.

Four times in the last million years, much of Europe was in the grip of Ice Ages. During these four cold periods glaciers a mile deep covered much of what is currently fertile land. Most of Europe was a howling wilderness of ice. Very few forms of life could survive there.

Between the Ice Ages there were warm periods, which allowed all sorts of species that would seem "exotic" today to thrive. Over 100,000 years ago, during a period a bit warmer than today, hippopotamuses swam in the Thames, where London now stands. They had to move out of Europe as the last Ice Age set in, and some of their direct descendants may possibly be seen in the Zambezi River today.

As it was with hippopotamuses, so it was with humans. Our ancestors ventured into Europe in eras when the ice was melting, stayed for as long as humans could, then moved on to more suitable climes when the ice started to build up again. Eventually, many thousands of years later, there would be another thaw in the ice, an "inter-glacial" as it is called, and some of our ancestors would drift back into Europe.

Let's summarize those four Ice Ages:

Günz: c. 680,000 to 620,000 years ago
Mindel: c. 455,000 to 340,000 years ago
Riss: c. 200,000 to 130,000 years ago
Würm: c. 110,000 to 12,000 years ago

These dates are obviously approximate. Still, the time-scale is about as accurate as current science allows.

Now, let's consider the evidence for human beings during the interglacial periods, bearing in mind that the further back we delve in time, the sparser the archaeological record. What follows is necessarily only a brief summary:

(1) **Günz-Mindel interglacial**, perhaps about 500,000 years ago. A few remains of a tall human named Boxgrove Man have been found in what is now England We cannot reconstruct what he looked like.

(2)   **Mindel-Riss interglacial**, perhaps about 300,000 years ago. A young woman died beside England's River Thames in an area now known as Swanscombe. The great 20th century anthropologist, Carleton Coon, speculating on her relics, said they were undeniably human: *Homo sapiens*. A scientific conference held in 1962 officially concluded that she was a modern human. A cast of the impressions made by her brain on the inside of her skull proved that her brain was indistinguishable in that respect from our more recent British and northern European ancestors. Her brain capacity was at least 1,270 cc: close to average for a modern European woman. The retrieved parts of her skull suggest that she looked like the more recent, and thoroughly modern-looking, Cro-Magnons.

(3)   **Riss-Würm interglacial**. Very few physical remains of the people who lived and died in Europe during this period have been discovered. In 1947, G. Henri-Martin excavated a cave in the French valley of Fontéchevade. There he found fragments of two human skulls, covered by a layer of stalagmite. H. V. Vallois, the anthropologist who studied these relics most thoroughly, concluded that there is no difference between them and modern humans. [6] He was also certain that they are part of the same branch of humanity as Swanscombe. The cranial capacity of Fontéchevade was about 1460 cc., and the cephalic index was 79. These measurements correspond closely with the modern north Germans. In recent years, Vallois' conclusions have been disputed, but if he was correct, there is a continuity from Swanscombe through Fontéchevade and Cro-Magnon to recent northern Europeans, one that suggests direct ancestry.

(4)   **Modern period**. The people known as Cro-Magnons began to enter Europe during a warmer break in the last ice age, maybe as early as 80,000 years ago, probably trekking after game animals like the woolly mammoth and rhinoceros.

The definitive Cro-Magnon "was nearly six foot tall, powerfully built, with a narrow, craggy skull, wide face, square jaw, strong chin and high-bridged nose" [7] They have been described as "strikingly handsome, fully human, physically superior to most human beings of modern times. The men were well over six feet in height. They had high foreheads, prominent cheekbones, firm chins. Tall, powerful, splendidly shaped, these ancestral figures seemed like titans out of some forgotten golden age of mankind." [8] Less romantically, perhaps, "a Cro-Magnon man from Europe might well be mistaken for a modern Swede if he walked down the street in Stockholm today." [9]

Psychologist Stan Gooch wrote extensively on early humans, arguing that Cro-Magnons must have had fair hair and light eyes. [10] We have no direct evidence of Swanscombe's skin color, but it is known that pale skin helps to synthesize vitamin D at high latitudes, and for this reason Roger Lewin summed up the prevailing view when he wrote that "long

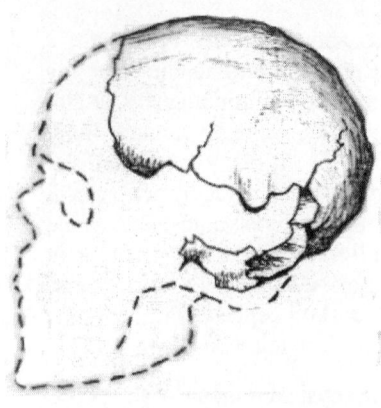
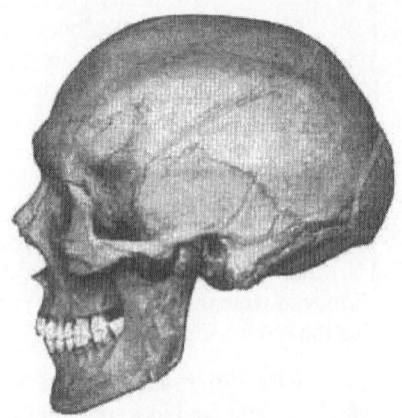

The retrieved pieces of Swanscombe woman's skull, c. 300,000 years ago

A typical Cro-Magnon skull, c. 30,000 years ago

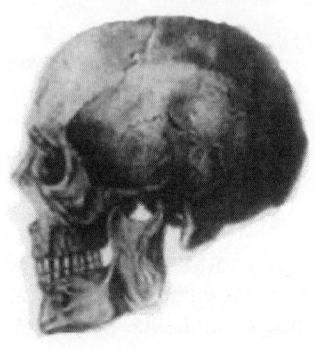
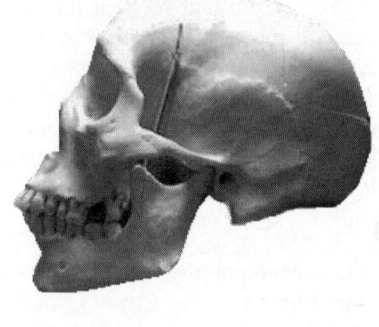

Skull of a Roman officer, from York, England

A very different skull-type, frequently encountered in modern East Asia

before [Cro-Magnon] times, all European populations would have been white." [11] The genes for light pigmentation in modern northern Europeans would then have been passed down to us from our Cro-Magnon ancestors, who in turn presumably received them from their own forebears – perhaps including Swanscombe Woman's people.

By 23,000 years ago, a boomerang made from mammoth tusk was in use near what is now Cracow in Poland [12] Bows and arrows were to follow, invented by some unsung genius in Germany to bring down reindeer. Bone flutes and whistles appeared from France across to Russia between 20,000 and 30,000 years ago. During this period the human population of Europe may have been about 350,000, plus another 80,000 for Russia. After another twelve millennia, the total perhaps climbed to 950,000, plus another 15,000 in Scandinavia.[13] Therefore the population of the whole of Europe was only a little more than the present population of the US city of Detroit.

None of the sites mentioned above are in the areas that were usually covered by glaciers, for the simple reason that humans could not live there. Even today, few of us could survive in the British Isles or Scandinavia if our modern technological civilization were to break down. Yet by about 8,000 years ago, the glaciers were melting, causing sea water to rise. Despite the melting of the ice, the old glacial areas were still extremely inhospitable – rather like tundra today.

Before the seas rose and covered it, the best real estate in this region was the low-lying area that is now the North Sea. Known to modern archaeologists as "Doggerland", this was a huge area of rich fenland, abounding in wildfowl, deer, aurochs, fish and shellfish. This region of plenty was the heartland of our most linear ancestors, a genuine European "Garden of Eden" surrounded by the then-marginal lands that are now France, Holland, Germany, Scandinavia and the British Isles.

Gradually the waters rose, sometimes by scarcely noticeable amounts, sometimes in huge tsunamis, until the North Sea and the English Channel were flooded. Our ancestors were forced out of their easy-living paradise and the ocean covered their traces there for 8,000 years. Occasionally, fishing boats dragged up an ancient tool. In 1936 the great Cambridge scholar Grahame Clark named this lost culture "Maglemosian", but archaeology was clearly impossible under more than 50 meters of water and millennia of sludge.

Luckily, the North Sea is now economically important, not least for its oil and gas. In the last few years maritime geophysics companies have carried out massive mapping of the seabed. They have discovered the ancient rivers, lakes, hills and coastlines of our forebears, using modern seismic technology that can "see" through the more recent layers of sediment. One of these surveying companies, Petroleum Geo-Services, has donated its survey of over 22,000 sq km to Birmingham University, where a team led by Professor Vincent Gaffney is compiling 3D stereo maps. These will soon lead to Virtual Reality reconstructions of the landscapes of our most direct ancestors. [14] This is magnificent progress, and everyone who has been involved in rediscovering and reconstructing these aspects of our ancestral past deserves the greatest of possible praise.

Yet despite the superb progress that is being made, especially over the last decade or so, we should not lose sight of the fact that our ancestors were never confined to NW Europe. Families, branches, whole tribes of

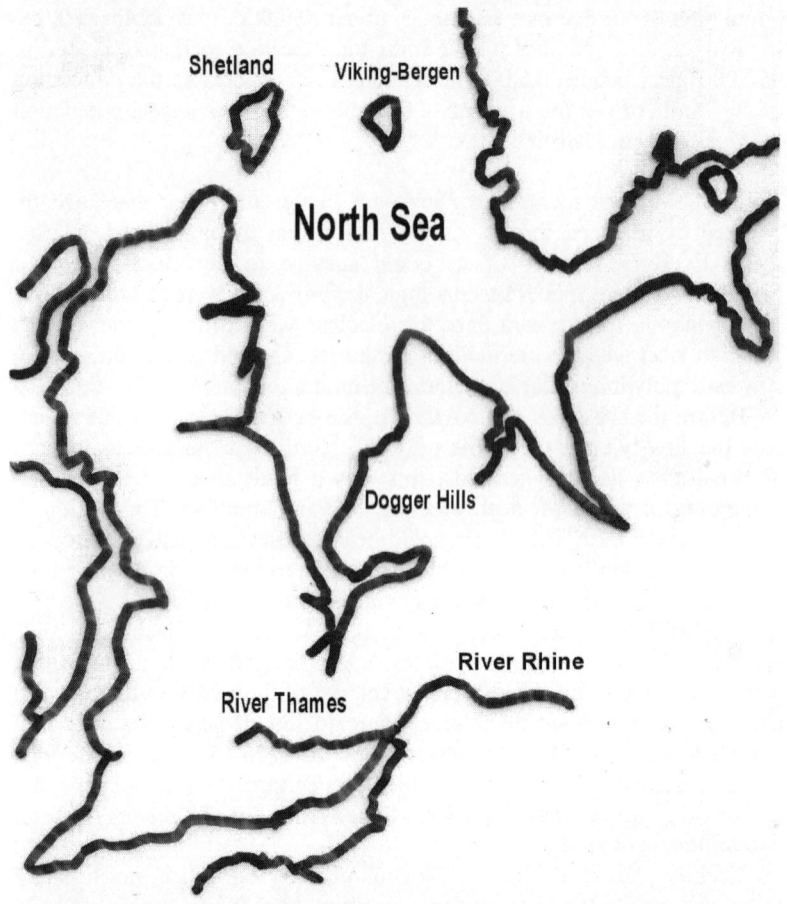

North-west Europe about 8,000 years ago. The water that had been locked up in glaciers had not yet melted enough to inundate the North Sea.

our people moved east, through what are now Turkey and Lebanon as far as Russia, Afghanistan, China and India. Others headed north and west, through Scandinavia to Iceland, Greenland and America. Still others moved south, founding or playing a major role in the civilizations of ancient Persia, Greece, Rome, Egypt and elsewhere.

All of these are also our ancestors. Although their physical type may have been "indigenous" to the North Sea area since the last ice age, we shall soon see that a modern person from, say, Afghanistan, who looks like us is indeed our kith and kin. His or her ancestors are also ours.

5

THE INDO-EUROPEANS

> Once we acknowledge that the historically attested Indo-European languages must derive from an earlier common or Proto-Indo-European language, logic also requires us to accept the existence of prehistoric communities which spoke that language. We may, of course, question the validity of the precise forms of our linguistic reconstructions and whether they represent exactly, or even approximately, the actual speech of the Proto-Indo-Europeans. We may also dismiss a wholly uniform dialectless proto-language as extremely improbable, and admit that there must have been considerable linguistic differences throughout the Proto-Indo-European speech community. But the actual existence of these Proto-Indo-European speakers, who must have left traces in the archaeological record of Eurasia, cannot be denied.
>
> - J. P. Mallory, *In Search of the Indo-Europeans*

When Christianity was the official faith of the ruling classes of Europe, it was generally thought that all existing languages must be descended from Hebrew. This derived from the belief that all humans other than Noah and his family died in a flood described in the Biblical book of *Genesis*. Since Noah presumably spoke Hebrew, and since only people on his ship lived to re-populate the earth after the flood, there could not be a living language that was not somehow derived from Hebrew.

In 1796 Sir William Jones, a Chief Justice of British India, noted that Greek, Latin, the Germanic and Celtic languages, Old Persian and Sanskrit had so many features in common that they must all be derived from a common source – an earlier language that is now extinct. Many scholars have investigated this field since Jones' day, and there is no essential disagreement.

For the benefit of readers who are not familiar with linguistics it may be helpful to present the word for "three" in various Indo-European languages, to show the similarities. In Gaelic it is "tri"; in Welsh, "tri"; in Greek, "treis"; in Latin, "tres"; in modern Italian, "tre"; in Spanish, "tres"; in French, "trois"; in Old English, "thrie"; in German, "drei"; in

Dutch, "drie"; in Swedish, "tre", in Danish, "tre"; in Polish, "trzy"; in Russian, "tri"; in Sanskrit, "tri"; in Bengali, "tri"; in Lithuanian, "trys"; in Albanian, "tre"; in Tocharian, "tre". By contrast, here is the number "three" in some non-Indo-European languages: in Turkish, "ukh", in Malay, "tiga"; in Japanese, both "mitsu" and "san"; in Swahili, "tatu"; in Aranda "taramananinta"; in Mongolian, "dolo"; in Hebrew, "shlosha". It is clear from these examples that the Indo-European languages form a single family group, from which the others must be excluded. However, it is important to understand that this is not merely a matter of individual words with closely resembling sounds. Far more importantly, the underlying structure and grammar of the related languages point clearly to their common origin.

It may be helpful to have, at this stage, a list of the main groups of the Indo-European languages, if only to gain a broad idea of their geographical distribution. In the list that follows, languages that are now extinct are marked with an asterisk (*).

Anatolian group – from what is now Turkey, including Old Assyrian*, Hittite*, Luwian *, Lycian*
Greek – both ancient* and modern
Indo-Aryan group – Sanskrit*, Hindi, Bengali, etc
Iranian group – Old Persian*, Avestan*, Persian, Kurdish, Ossete, etc
Dardic group – Kashmiri, etc
Nuristani group – Bashgali, etc – all of them currently endangered
Italic group – Latin*, Dalmatian*, Italian, French, Spanish, Portuguese, Rumanian
Celtic group – Gaulish*, Welsh, Breton, Cornish*, Irish, Scots Gaelic, Manx*
Germanic group – Gothic*, Burgundian*, Vandalic*, Old Norse*, Danish, Swedish, Norwegian, Icelandic, Faeroese, German, Langobardic*, Old English*, English, Frisian, Flemish, Dutch, Afrikaans
Armenian group – many dialects
Tocharian* group – two languages, both extinct
Slavic group – Russian, Ukrainian, Czech, Slovak, Slovenian, Serbo-Croat, Macedonian, Bulgarian, etc
Baltic group – Old Prussian*, Lithuanian, Latvian
Albanian – Albanian, perhaps Illyrian*

At one stage there was a single language which has since split up into the mutually unintelligible yet closely related Indo-European languages listed above, and we call it Proto-Indo-European. It follows that there must have been an identifiable group of people who once spoke Proto-Indo-European. Furthermore, they must have lived at one time in a definable area, and shared a mutual culture and religion. We do not know what they called themselves, but most scholars today call them the Indo-Europeans.

Nor do we know where their homeland at that time was, but most think it was somewhere between the Baltic and Black Seas, or else in the area north of the Black Sea and the Caspian. A few suggest Anatolia. The evidence for these assumed homelands is both archaeological and linguistic – the latter involving shared words for certain plants, animals and scenery that together have a limited geographical spread.

As bands, tribes or even nations of the Indo-Europeans migrated away from their homeland, their dialects developed into separate languages. Sometimes these tribes ended up dominating unrelated peoples who then came to speak the language of their new rulers, just as French is still the first language of over a hundred million African people whose ancestors were ruled by the French. Equally, it has sometimes happened that Indo-Europeans adopted the language of the people among whom they settled. Therefore we must be careful not to assume that individual speakers of an Indo-European language in more recent times are genetically descended from the people who originally spoke Proto-Indo-European. Equally, the fact that a tribe or nation spoke a *non*-Indo-European language when they first emerged into history does not mean that they are not descended from the people of the Proto-Indo-European homeland.

Fortunately, there are other forms of evidence that we can use to establish the appearance of the Indo-Europeans. Today we can see at a glance that a native of Senegal or Congo who happens to speak French is not a descendant of the Franks, the Germanic tribe from which France derives its name. We cannot quite "see at a glance" what the original speakers of Indo-European languages looked like, but we have three no less compelling forms of evidence available to us. These are:

(1) Skeletal remains. Today, if someone discovers a skeleton or even just a skull, forensic specialists aid the police investigation by identifying the race to which the deceased belonged. This can be done by measuring those aspects of the remains that differ from one race to another. The same procedure can be applied to human remains found in classically Indo-European cultural sites. Many of these people cremated their dead, but one group that lived between the Dnieper and Donets rivers in the 5th millennium BCE has left us over 800 burials. "They are predominantly characterized as late Cro-Magnons with more massive and robust features than the gracile Mediterranean peoples of the Balkan Neolithic. With males averaging about 172 centimeters (nearly 5'8") in height they are a fairly tall people within the context of Neolithic populations" [15] Given the very early period in which these individuals died and were buried, and also their geographic location, they are prime candidates to represent the Proto-Indo-European peoples. As we have seen above (Chapter 4) they would have looked "at home" in modern northern Europe.

(2) Another source is self-descriptions of Indo-Europeans, whether in their own literature or their artwork. Perhaps the most comprehensive evidence of this sort is from ancient Greece. We know from the sculpture

surviving from Classical Greece that those remarkable people could have walked the streets of Shakespeare's London without being seen as foreigners. (The Greek statues are so realistic that we can even observe the gradual incursion of alien genes and features, as in a statue of Socrates, now in the Vatican.) As to their hair color, Homer in the *Iliad* specifically states that Aphrodite, Demeter, Rhadamanthus, Aurora, Agamede, Herakles, Harmonia, Lyksos, Achilles, Menelaus, Meleager, Helen and Briseis all had fair hair. [16] "Similarly, Pindar and Theocritus both speak of fair-haired gods. Thus Athene, described by Pindar as the 'blonde blue-eyed goddess', is probably typical of the Greek concept of noble physiology, and where coloring has survived on terra cotta figurines, this also reflects light hair and blue eyes in almost all cases, except those which are intended to represent grotesque caricatures." [17]

As to self-descriptions in literature, another example may suffice. The earliest poem in Scottish Gaelic, the *Duan Albanach* [18], begins:

> O all ye learned ones of Alba [Scotland],
> O stately yellow-haired company ...

(3) There are also descriptions of these tribes or nations by others – again, in either literature or artwork. To return to the Greeks for a moment, the Jewish writer Adamantius wrote as late as the 5th century CE that: "wherever the Hellenic and Ionic race has been kept pure, we see proper, tall men of fairly broad and straight build, neatly made, of fairly light skin and blond". Similarly, old Chinese writers described light-eyed blond tribes as a threat to the Chinese borders. (These were presumably related to the Tocharians, whom we shall meet properly in Chapter 6.)

As far as artistic depictions by others are concerned, a good example is ancient Egyptian art, which although often stylized is also at times so realistic that modern racial types can be recognized instantly. One tribe with whom the Egyptians came into contact was the Amorites, who lived in and around what is now Palestine. "What the Amorite was like we know from the portraits of him which have been left to us by the artists of Egypt. His features were handsome and regular, his cheek-bones high, his jaws orthognathous, and his eyebrows well defined. His skull is apparently dolicocephalic ... At Abu Simbel his skin is painted a pale yellow, his eye blue, and his eyebrows and beard red." [19] The Amorites are interesting in that, although they were clearly related to us, at some stage they had adopted a Semitic language.

This book is about Odinism, not race. Yet since ancestor-worship is fundamental to Odinism, we need to know a little more about the appearance of our ancestors than the glimpses given so far. The German-born American anthropologist Theodor Poesche did most of the necessary literary spadework in 1878, when he collected as many references as he could to early Indo-European peoples and found that they were usually described as being blond-haired and light-eyed. [20] This does not necessarily mean that every single member of every Indo-European tribe had that coloration. It need only mean that light hair and eyes were common enough to be seen as typical – just as we might observe today that most Japanese people are comparatively short.

In very simple terms, the genes for fair hair and light eyes are both "recessive". In effect, someone born with one gene for brown eyes and one for blue eyes will have brown eyes. Only a person born with two "blue-eye genes" will have blue eyes. If your parents are both blue-eyed you are guaranteed to inherit that trait, but the odds in a general population decline – eventually to zero – as people with different eye colors mingle their genes. So, once darker genes are added to a blue-eyed population, fewer and fewer blue-eyed children will be born down through the generations, until eventually blue eyes are eliminated from that gene-pool. The same equation applies to fair hair.

So if light hair and eyes were common enough to be seen as typical of Indo-Europeans in historical times, and given that the genes for these traits are recessive, it follows that earlier generations of those tribes or nations *must* have had a higher proportion of these genes. If we could trace our family tree back far enough, we would eventually arrive at a population that was entirely blue-eyed and blond-haired. Since all humans are derived from some earlier ancestral population, and since in our own case that population appears to be the Cro-Magnons of Ice-Age Europe, logic impels us to accept that Cro-Magnons were more blond and blue-eyed than most northern Europeans today. Yet the Cro-Magnons themselves also had ancestors, which possibly takes us all the way back to Swanscombe Woman of maybe 300,000 years ago. The point is that, if we could "see" far enough back in time, at some stage all of our ancestors in the Cro-Magnon line must have been blond and blue-eyed.

Given the fact that these "marker-genes" are recessive, other non-Indo-European tribal groups who look generally like us and still have a significant percentage of light hair or eyes in their population must be assumed, in most cases, to have split off from our family tree before our more direct ancestors spoke Proto-Indo-European. There are a few possible exceptions, such as the occasionally light-haired Aborigines of the central desert area of Australia, which might be due to more recent genetic mutations. Yet the Berbers of the Atlas Mountains in northern Africa, and the Ainu descendants of the original population of Japan, have enough of our other genetic traits to indicate that we share some common ancestors. On the evolutionary time-scale, we are cousins.

6

THREE LOST INDO-EUROPEAN TRIBES

Some early 20th century writers portrayed our ancestors as all-conquering warriors. Those writers were wrong. Time after time, tribes and even whole nations of our folk have been defeated in battle by unrelated peoples. One need only recall the invasion of Europe by the Huns, before whom many of our proudest nations fell, fled or submitted. These include the Goths, the Alans, the Vandals, the Suevi and the Gepids. Under their leader Attila, the Huns controlled the valleys of the Danube, Dnieper, Don and Volga – probably the old Indo-European heartland – and nearly conquered Rome in 452 CE.

Far from being invincible, many of our ancestral tribes are now extinct. People who might be described in a modern police report as being "of Anglo appearance" – in the traditional British policing Identity Code, "IC 1" – made up at least the ruling classes of the Hittites, the "Aryans" who brought the Vedas to India, and the ancient Persians, Greeks, Phoenicians and Romans, to name only a few. While some of them may have bequeathed a sprinkling of their genes to those who survive today where they once ruled, they would not have recognized most modern inhabitants of these areas as kin.

In some cases our lost ancestors were defeated in battle. Sometimes they formed a dominant minority ruling over a vastly greater number of unrelated people, and were eventually genetically absorbed into the majority. Sometimes they imported slaves who ended up genetically swamping them. For instance, it has been estimated that during the reign of Augustus (who passed various laws in an attempt to reverse the process), 85% of the workers employed in Roman shops, factories and households were descended from slaves taken mainly from Africa, the Middle East, and beyond. [21]

The rest of this chapter will examine three specific groups who, after their conversion from Odinism, became extinct – or worse – in different ways. These are the Tocharians, who converted to Buddhism; the Kafirs of Afghanistan, who were defeated in battle and converted to Islam on pain of death; and the Visigoths, who submitted to a form of Christianity. Their stories are far from unique, and they are presented only as examples.

The Tocharians

In the mid-1990s a temporary Chinese museum exhibition was installed in the "Melbourne Central" shopping complex in Victoria, Australia. On display were several naturally mummified human bodies. Those who had died most recently were typically Chinese in appearance, while the earlier ones had white skin, Nordic-looking faces, and blond hair.

A young Chinese official spoke to the audience, referring to the blond mummies as "Caucasoids". When this author asked her precisely what she meant by that term, the official's command of English, which had previously been very good, suddenly deteriorated dramatically. It was clear that she had been instructed not to discuss this particular issue, leaving one to ask the inevitable question: Why?

Now we know why, thanks to a very comprehensive book on the topic [22]. The authors of this study were Victor Mair, the U.S. academic who first drew western journalists' attention to the blond mummies, and J. P. Mallory whose earlier work, *In Search of the Indo-Europeans*, has already been mentioned.

From perhaps 2,000 BCE down to historical times, white people occupied East Central Asia. In one part of this region, the Tarim River Basin, there is scarcely any rainfall. The land is a desert, with huge amounts of salt in the sand. Bodies buried in such arid, saline conditions mummify naturally. Some of these mummies are as well preserved, after 4,000 years, as if they had been bottled in formaldehyde only recently.

This region was combed over by European explorers in the period from about 1890 to 1920. Several of them encountered European-looking mummies which had often been flung around graveyards by modern looters. None of the explorers had the wherewithal to transport mummies back to European museums, so although many photos were taken, few among the general public were aware of these discoveries.

In 1988 an American academic, Victor Mair, visited the museum in Urumchi, the capital of China's Xinjiang Province. A new gallery had recently opened, and it was dedicated to the naturally mummified bodies found in the region. The American was particularly taken with one of them, a tall blond man who looked very like his own brother. From that moment Victor Mair began to spread knowledge of these Asian Europeans in the West.

Prior to Mair we knew of the existence of white people in this area from a number of sources. These included written accounts from ancient Greece, Rome, India and China, paintings of blond and blue-eyed people in Buddhist shrines, and a few other Asian images showing Western facial features.

We also had the evidence provided by the two Tocharian languages, known as Tocharian A and B. Documents in these dead tongues first came to light in 1892, and many more have been recovered since then from the oasis towns of the Tarim Basin. These languages, presumably once very widespread, are members of the Indo-European family group, and thus related to English. (Compare, for instance, these words in Tocharian B – *keu, okso, āu* and *suwo* – with their English equivalents in "cow", "ox", "ewe" and "sow".)

Mair and Mallory concluded that the mummies from the eastern sites probably spoke Tocharian languages, with those from the western side of the range speaking Iranian languages. The names of some Iranian-speaking tribes will be familiar to readers, names like Scythians, Sarmatians, Alans and Bactrians. According to Pliny (*Natural History*, XXIV), one of these groups, the Serai, were "more than normal height, and have flaxen hair and blue eyes, and they speak in harsh tones".

Mair and Mallory give various reasons to think that in about 2,000 BCE the Tocharians arrived in the region from the north-east. If the suggested date and the direction are correct (and there is no reason to doubt it on the available evidence), then they would presumably have been offshoots of the Afanasevo culture, which flourished near the Altai Mountains from about 3,500 to 2,500 BCE. While the Afanasevo people left no mummies, their skeletal remains show that they looked like traditional northern Europeans, and there are clear parallels between their culture and that of the Tarim Basin.

A Chinese physical anthropologist, Han Kangxin, has suggested on the basis of cranial measurements that the earlier mummies comprised three sub-racial groups, which resemble the Nordics, Alpines and Mediterraneans of early 20th-century textbooks. The Nordic group was the earliest. According to the Australian geographer, Griffith Taylor, the average cephalic index of the Indo-European speakers was 76.

It helps to get a sense of the land that these people occupied. A dreary, salty desert, locked in by mountains, with an oasis here and there, the region is important because it is the natural conduit between East and West. This area is the most difficult part of what was to become famed as the "Silk Road". Furthermore, the land is rich in minerals. The mountains to the north provided copper, iron, tin, lead, gold, coal, sal ammoniac, copper oxide, sulfur and other valuable items. Salt was and still is abundant. Whoever controlled the Tarim Basin was therefore guaranteed a materially high standard of living. For that reason the Han Chinese invaded it, then the Tibetans, then the Uighurs, and the Chinese in turn are now dispossessing the Uighurs. As we would imagine, then, the Tarim mummies are magnificently dressed in expensive clothes made of felt, leather, and wool woven into striking tartan-like patterns.

Through the land they controlled passed Chinese inventions and goods; but, crucially, the flow of ideas also went in the other direction. Chinese culture did not grow in splendid isolation from the rest of the world, and Mair and Mallory give several examples.

China had acquired domestic horses and wheeled chariots from the West at an early date. Donkeys, sheep and wool were also introduced to China from the west.

During the very first Chinese dynasty, the Shang, China was importing Iranian-speaking priests. So much so that the modern Mandarin word for a magician is derived from the Old Persian *magus*. Some carvings depicting these Magi have survived, and they are clearly of Caucasoid appearance. The province of Yunnan in southwest China has also yielded bronze figures with Caucasoid facial features. They wear clothing identical to that of the Tarim mummies.

Bronze metallurgy, and later iron casting, probably also arrived in China along a similar route, originating with the Iranian-speaking tribes of the steppelands. Chemical testing has shown that the jade objects of the Shang dynasty were probably supplied by the Tarim Basin people. At a very late date they even had a major influence on Chinese music. The town of Kucha was noted for the great talent of its musicians. The Emperor Xuanzong (8th century CE) was so impressed by Kuchean music that he "completely reorganized the instrumentation of China to accommodate Kuchean music". (Incidentally, the name Kucha might be an ethnonym meaning "the white people".)

Given the huge impact that the Tarim people had on the development of Chinese culture, it is tragic to read that their mummies are now treated with very little respect. As Mair and Mallory wrote: "The overwhelming majority of the Tarim mummies either have been or are currently in the process of being destroyed. In some instances, ripped from their graves and strewn over the ground like grotesque props from George Romero's *Dawn of the Dead*, literally hundreds of corpses could be found rotting in the sun ..." Even the few mummies that find their way to museums fare little better, often being dumped in damp cellars to rot. The Chinese claim a lack of funds to look after them properly, but funds raised overseas have not resulted in any better treatment for the mummies.

Choosing their words carefully, Mair and Mallory wrote: "It is suspected that in some cases certain archaeologists and officials with their own political or racial agenda have been blatantly hostile to the discovery and preservation of these ancient 'foreign devils' ... [W]e should hardly be surprised when *some* Chinese officials appear to prefer that the mummies of these troublesome foreigners dissolve under conditions of not-so-benign neglect. From their viewpoint, these were *hu*, 'barbarians' ..."

So, because of Chinese refusal to acknowledge the massive impact of Indo-Europeans on their civilization, the mummies are being allowed to rot away. Priceless evidence of *our* people's history is being destroyed to prop up the official Chinese propaganda line that *their* people's culture is indigenous. Yet nothing can alter the fact that the Tocharians are extinct. When the last Tocharian died is anyone's guess; perhaps a few of their genes have been inherited by the Uighurs. We know that prior to their extinction they forsook their native religion and adopted Buddhism, as attested by the surviving documents in their language.

The Kafirs

Rudyard Kipling's short story, *The Man Who Would Be King*, tells of two nineteenth century British redcoats who venture across the Hindu Kush in order to rule a tribe of "white people" thought to live in that region. The "white people" who inspired Kipling's story were the Kafirs, an Arabic word for heathens, hailing from north-eastern Afghanistan.

Between 1895 and 1898, Abdur Rahman Kahn, Emir of Afghanistan, waged a jihad against the Kafirs, and forcibly converted them to Islam. It is fortunate for us today that Sir George Scott Robinson visited the region in 1889 and 1890-91, and recorded as much information about this people as he could. [23] Sir George failed to record many fascinating things that he must have seen. Nevertheless, his is the most valuable account of these people before their tragic demise.

With regard to their appearance Sir George stated unequivocally: "Their features are Aryan". There seems to be no doubt that they were the remnants of a branch of our people that strayed into this part of Asia four to five millennia ago. Quintus Rufus and Arrian are among the Classical scholars who knew of the existence of the Kafirs. Possibly our lost kinfolk, too, had some idea of their distant ethnic origins. Just as the later Romans liked to wear blond wigs in memory of their fairer ancestors, so: "The Kafirs admire beards, and love to dye them red as soon as they begin to get grey".

By the time of Sir George's visit, they were racially mixed and had only a vague idea of their own history. "That they came from the west, at least the great majority of them, is their own fixed idea and is more than probable". One clan told him: "They came from the west, and were once part of a numerous tribe which divided into two parties. One division, consisting of all the wealthy and other notable persons, went to London, while the other, comprising menials only, settled in Kafiristan".

The Kafirs were then at the end of a long struggle for survival which they lacked the numbers to win, and Sir George was well aware of the essence of their struggle: "Even in times far remote, it may be doubted if race antagonism was not at least as strong as difference of creed in keeping Afghan and Kafir at bitter feud". They were also by that time partly but not entirely miscegenated: "[In 1890] when strolling through the village, I was riveted with astonishment to see at a spring a short distance from me a perfectly white-skinned woman with golden hair".

She was a rare sight by then. But although their genes had been mixed, the Kafirs still maintained their ancestral folkways. Their domestic furniture included un-Asiatic tables, stools and cupboards, and they used planks as communal feasting benches, all unlike their Muslim neighbors. Sir George found in them a "wonderful dignity". They had unalterable laws of hospitality that are reminiscent of Eddaic values. Sir George also noted their high degree of family affection, their lack of cruelty to animals, and a tendency to indulge their children. Again unlike their neighbors, they brewed mead and wine. All Kafirs were theoretically equal. In defining their ideal of a "fine manly character" the Kafirs volunteered the following attributes: "... he must be a successful homicide, a good hill-man, ever ready to quarrel, and of an amorous disposition. If he is also a good dancer, a good shot with bow and arrow or matchlock, and a good 'aluts' or stone-quoit player, so much the better". Placed beside the list of personal accomplishments of which Rognvald Kali boasted in *Orkneyinga Saga* the Kafir account is culturally threadbare, but still strikingly similar.

What should be of most interest to modern Odinists, however, is that the Kafirs were able to communicate something of their ancient and cognate religion to Sir George. The principal god was Imra, The Creator, who was sacrificed to very often, particularly with cows. His temples stood in every village, and usually contained a wooden or stone idol. Although his popularity was waning, one fascinating story concerned his Thor-like slaying of an enormous serpent that had wrapped itself around the head of the Bashgul Valley. The very spot where this mighty struggle took place was pointed out to Sir George.

The most popular Kafir god was Gish, who was always called Great Gish. "He was first and foremost a warrior, a man with iron nerves, fierce and sudden in his terrible onslaughts ... He is the Kafir type of a true man, and can never be sufficiently honored. Fabulous numbers of enemies felt the weight of his fateful hand. He killed Hazrat Ali; he killed Hasan and Husain; in short, he killed nearly every famous Musalman [Muslim] the Kafirs ever heard of." He was sacrificed to with male goats and bulls.

There was a separate war-god, called Moni, but by the 1890s he was regarded with "more respect than enthusiasm". It is not difficult to trace in the popular fates of Gish and Moni the confusion of roles apparent in Snorri's account of Thor and Tyr. The relative lack of Tyr-elements in Viking Age personal and place names seems to mirror Moni's decline.

Dizanne was clearly the most popular Goddess. To her was devoted the new year festival, celebrated with the sacrifice of female goats. In return, Dizanne saw to the productivity of the wheat fields. Her son Bagisht was another fertility figure, presiding over natural resources and helping good men become rich and powerful. The Kafirs pointed out that he was the only god whose birth was not attributed to Imra, which suggests a comparison with the Vanir of the northern pantheon.

Kafir cosmology divided the universe into Urdesh, the abode of the gods; Michdesh, the earth; and Yurdesh, a nether world. (Clearly Asgard and Midgard; and perhaps Jotunheim.) Unfortunately for us, language difficulties prevented Sir George from obtaining a fuller exposition of this cosmology. (But Georges Dumézil's *Les trois fonctions dans la panthéon des Kafirs* provides some further details.)

Summarizing the social aspects of their culture, Sir George wrote: "Kafirs have no intense fear of death, although they cannot understand the idea of suicide. The idea of a man killing himself strikes them as inexplicable. They are never melancholy. The gods are worshipped by sacrifices, by dances, by singing hymns and by uttering invocations."

He also picked up a tantalizingly vague tidbit about a sacred world tree, "whose branches were seven families of brothers, each seven in number, while the trunk was Dizanne and the roots Nirmali [a goddess who protected women in childbirth] but the record of this story was lost in a mountain torrent".

A 12 year-old Afghan girl famously featured on a 1985 *National Geographic* cover. She is clearly white, and descended from the Kafirs or a related tribe

Like this account of their Yggdrasil, the Kafirs themselves have now been swept away. Shortly after Sir George's visit, Abdur Rahman converted them at sword-point, destroyed their idols and forbade the making of wine. Their land was triumphantly re-named Nuristan, meaning "land of light".

Louis Duprès, in 1974, noted that nearly sixty thousand Kafiri speakers remained in eastern Afghanistan, adding: "In villages I have visited, I have found between 10 and 40 per cent of the males (few females were examined or questioned) to have blond or red hair, blue or mixed eye color combinations".

One Kafir tribe, the Kalash, fled in the 1890s to what was then the British-dominated principality of Chitral. Three or four thousand survive there today and they were visited in the 1980s by *National Geographic* correspondent Debra Denker. From the photos accompanying her article, some Kalash show clear Indo-European origin. Denker referred in passing to some of the women as "pretty" and some of the men as "handsome" – and since she singled out one blond and blue-eyed child for praise, we can assume that her idea of beauty is based on Nordic aesthetic standards.

The Kalash have almost forgotten their religion, retaining only a few relatively meaningless ceremonies. Their beliefs are shallower and more fragmented than those of their ancestors only a century ago. Their principal god today is called Dezao. Others include Sajigor, in charge of flocks and shepherds; Mahendeo, associated with honeybees; and Jestak, a goddess of family and home. The original Thor-god of the Kafirs, great Gish, seems to have shrunk to a being called Balomain, a "demigod who once lived among the Kalash and did heroic deeds".

Of course, such a proud people didn't voluntarily forget their gods. They were ferociously persecuted when Chitral became Muslim. All were subject to forced labor (slavery). Many were forcibly converted. If they wished to visit the town of Chitral they had to wear humiliating and bizarre hats. By the time that this oppression was partially ameliorated with the creation of Pakistan in 1947 the damage had been done.

One Kalash boy told Denker of the abuse he suffered in the nearest school, ten miles from his village. His Muslim religious teacher used to call on him: "Stand up and read the lesson, dirty Kalash". Another said: "We have been told so many times that we are low that it is carved on our brains, like the carpenter carves on wood".

It is tragic to think of those Kafirs who were killed or forcibly converted and enslaved by Abdur Rahman Khan. Or to compare the still recognizable religion of the Kafirs with the piecemeal fragments of heathen faith that is all the Kalash have left. Or to think of the Kalash children trudging miles to school, only to suffer daily racial and religious abuse. Yet even theirs may not have been the worst of all possible fates.

The Visigoths

The Visigoths, or Western Goths, made a great name for themselves in Roman times. By about 230 CE they had a vast kingdom to the north of the Black Sea. By 376, still Odinists at that stage, they were pressing against the Roman Empire. In 410, by now partly Christianized, they sacked Rome. Then they wandered over to Gaul and established the kingdom of Toulouse. Under pressure from the Franks, who had adopted a different version of Christianity, they regrouped in Castile and after 554 they created the kingdom of Toledo.

The glory days of the Visigoths came to a sad end in 714, when they were conquered by the Muslims. But all was not yet completely lost. The widow of the defeated Visigothic king married a Muslim warlord and accepted Islam. Presumably that was better than being beheaded. No doubt many Visigothic lesser-lights followed her royal example. In this way a few of their genes trickled on after their historical luster had faded.

Caliph Abd al-Rahman (889-961), son of a Berber slave-woman, had blue eyes and red-gold hair. He wasn't alone in this respect. Six of the first ten Caliphs were light-eyed blonds. [24] Presumably their coloration was an outward sign of Visigothic – or related – ancestry.

Sadly, the most outcast people in Spanish history are probably descended from the once fearsome Visigoths. These are the Agostes, a name thought to mean "dogs of Goths". The French name for the same people is Cagots. The Agostes were reviled throughout the middle ages. Forced to live in ghettoes, accused of spreading leprosy and the plague, they could only enter churches on their knees through a separate door, after which they were passed the holy wafer on long sticks so as not to contaminate the priests. They were treated far worse than the Jews.

The Victorian novelist Elizabeth Gaskell described the persecution of the Cagots in France. Her article, *An Accursed Race*, is too dispiriting to summarize here. These outcasts seem to have endured their lot like thrashed animals. Only once does Mrs Gaskell mention a Cagot uprising, after which: "… henceforward and for ever no Cagot was to be permitted to enter the town of Lourdes by any gate but that called Capdet-pourtet: they were only to be allowed to walk under the rain-gutters, and neither to sit, eat, nor drink in the town. If they failed in observing any of these rules, the parliament decreed, in the spirit of Shylock, that the disobedient Cagots should have two strips of flesh, weighing never more than two ounces a-piece, cut out from each side of their spines."

A few of them still survive here and there in the Pyrenees, still largely despised. Mrs Gaskell said the Cagots of her time were "tall, largely made, and powerful in frame; fair and ruddy in complexion, with gray-blue eyes". Some of them are still fair-skinned and blond. None of them seem likely to revive the glories of their Visigothic ancestors.

The lessons of history are clear. If we wish to honor our ancestors, we must remain Odinists – unlike the Tocharians and the Visigoths. If we wish to be allowed to remain Odinists, we must strive not to become a minority in our own lands – unlike the Kafirs. If we fail to retain our religious and ethnic identity, we will become extinct like the Tocharians; or, as with the Kalash and the Cagots, perhaps worse than extinct.

7

DIVINE BLOOD: THE NATION OF ODIN

We touched on the matter of divine descent in Chapter 3, but now we will cover some new aspects. First, though, the mathematics. The sums are not hard, so don't be intimidated by the appearance of a few figures on the page.

You have two parents, four grandparents, eight great-grandparents, sixteen great-great grandparents, and so on. The number doubles in each generation.

Let's look back to the year 400 CE. That was about sixteen hundred years ago. If each generation covers about 25 years, that comes to a total of 64 generations (25 × 64 = 1600).

Now, if all those ancestors of yours back in the year 400 CE were separate people, there would be eighteen and a half quintillion of them. One quintillion is one with eighteen zeroes after it, or 1,000,000,000,000,000,000. To make it easier on the eyes, the mathematical notation for a quintillion is 10^{18}.

Clearly, you didn't have 18½ quintillion ancestors in the year 400. That would be vastly more than the number of people who have ever been born, and vastly more than the earth could sustain. Instead, a relatively small number of ancestors are related to you many times over. If it were possible to draw a complete family tree, you would find that the lines of your descent cross over, again and again and again.

Let's suppose your ancestors lived on some remote island in the year 400, and let's suppose no-one had visited that island in the last 1600 years. Our imaginary island is fertile enough to have had a population of perhaps 2 million in the year 400. So almost all those original 2 million and their descendants simply *must* have bred together a huge number of times to account for the missing 18½ quintillion in your family tree.

Before we continue, one point that is often but wrongly raised needs to be addressed. Your imaginary ancestors on that imaginary island must have been doing a lot of breeding between close relatives. "Inbreeding" is usually frowned upon because in the early generations of an inbred population deleterious recessive genes are more likely to be expressed, leading to severe health problems. However, in nature, all island species are inbred, yet they are healthy. This is because, over time and generations, the bad genes are slowly culled out of the isolated gene-pool, leaving it healthier than ever.

As it happens, in the year 400 there was a fairly isolated group of islands with an estimated population of about 2 million. These islands had no very substantial population influx of unrelated people until about fifty years ago. We are speaking here of the British Isles (Irish: *Na hOileáin Bhriotanacha*; Scottish Gaelic: *Eileanan Breatannach*; Welsh: *Ynysoedd Prydain*).

If, like most of our readers, you are descended from British Isles stock, you are probably related over and over again to just about every one of those 2 million ancestors. A few direct lines will have died out, which only means the indirect lines of inbreeding must be increased to accommodate those 18½ quintillion *theoretical* ancestors.

So what was happening in Britain in the year 400? For the purpose of this chapter we can only go on the written sources, which in fact tell us some remarkable things.

If we look at the kingdom of Wessex, the earliest king for whom we have a reasonably firm date is Cerdic, who died in about 534. Assuming that one generation is, on average, 25 years, it would take five generations to go from Cerdic back to about 400. Cerdic's predecessors are recorded in the royal genealogy of Wessex. His father was Elesa, then there was Gewis, then Brond, then Bældæg – whose father was Wóden.

If we turn to Mercia, the earliest king with a firm date is that mighty Odinist warrior, Penda, whose rule began in about 626. If we trace his predecessors back through nine generations, we reach King Uermund. The great-grandfather of Uermund was Wóden.

In Northumbria, we need to start with Ida, who came to the throne in about 547. Six generations before Ida, therefore some time around 400, his ancestor was Ingibrand. The great-grandfather of Ingibrand was Bældæg – and once again, the Northumbrian royal genealogy tells us that Bældæg's father was Wóden.

And so it goes with the lesser Anglo-Saxon kingdoms ... In short, all the great early Anglo-Saxon monarchs were descended from Wóden – or so they said. Kings usually had more children than their subjects, which means they spread their genes around more than most. So did their children. Therefore if, as the mathematics imply, you are related to almost every one of the 2 million or so people in Britain in the year 400, and related to them repeatedly through multiple descent-paths, then you are almost certainly even more closely related to kings like Cerdic, Penda and Ida. It follows that the blood of Bældæg (Balder) and Wóden (Odin) is flowing in your veins.

We would not wish our Celtic readers to feel left out of this analysis. From the earliest days of which records exist, many of the Anglo-Saxon kings married Celtic women. The best-known example is Ida, who married the Celtic princess known as Bun or Bebban. Her name was given to Bibban-burh, modern Bamborough, the mightiest castle in that part of Britain.

Similar crossings have occurred time after time, throughout the British Isles population. Thus, the semi-legendary history of Ireland tells us that about the year 370 the Irish High King married a Saxon woman, Cairenn, who gave birth to Niall of the Nine Hostages and therefore became the ancestress of nearly all the later High Kings. Furthermore, Niall may have been one of the most fecund men in history. On 17 January 2006 the *New York Times* reported some genetic research suggesting that 8.3% of all living Irish males are descended from Niall – and thus from his mother, the Saxon Cairenn. The Irish later settled extensively in Wales and the west of Scotland, many of them no doubt bringing with them the genes of Cairenn. The Scottish MacNeils claim descent from Niall, so their earliest known ancestress was a Saxon lady.

Meanwhile, the vast majority of the British Isles people, those whose names have not been recorded, were also intermarrying despite their differences in language. Celts and Anglo-Saxons, always essentially the same physical stock, with related languages and cognate religions, bred together from the moment that the first Saxons set foot in the British Isles. It could not have been otherwise, bearing in mind the impossibility of a person of British Isles descent having 18½ quintillion *actual* ancestors. Therefore almost everyone alive today who identifies as "Celtic" will have had ancestors who traced their descent from Wóden. There is no room for chauvinistic point-scoring here: the Celtic and the Germanic nations of Britain (and hence most English-speaking countries) were never very different and are now totally intertwined.

Our ancestors were proud of their divine origins long after their official conversion to Christianity. In Liège University there is a manuscript catalogued as 369C. It is of English origin, and is clearly dateable to the 13th century, 600 years or so after the last English kingdom declared itself Christian. It contains an illustration of Wóden. He is wearing a crown that is surmounted by three *eolh* runes – the rune of divine protection, known as the "life-rune". From Wóden's mouth the divine breath streams out to the kings of Kent, Wessex, Mercia, Northumbria, Essex and Sussex, just as the same god gave the breath of life to Askr and Embla. (See Chapter 11.) The text surrounding this small portrait lists the kings of these six nations in their order of descent from the god.

The majority of modern, white, English-speakers around the world are descended from a population that claimed descent from Wóden. According to our ancestral records we are truly the sons and daughters of gods, a race of divine descent, and because of our numbers worldwide we form the core part of the Nation of Odin.

8

WHAT IS RELIGION?
WHAT IS MYTHOLOGY?
WHAT ARE GODS?

> From this the religion of the gods is variously changed among individual nations and provinces, inasmuch as no one god is worshipped by all, but by each one the worship of its own ancestors is kept peculiar.
>
> - Cyprian, Bishop of Carthage

> I believe that the reality exposed by modern physics is fundamentally alien to the human mind, and defies all power of direct visualization. The mental images conjured up by words such as 'curved space' and 'singularity' are at best grossly inadequate models that merely serve to fix a topic in our minds, rather than informing us of how the physical world really is.
>
> - Paul Davies, *The Matter Myth*

In Chapter 2 we noted that religion is notoriously difficult to define, and added: 'For the purpose of this introduction we will take *religion* to mean a set of beliefs concerned with the nature and purpose of the universe and life itself, with the spiritual nature of humans and with the role in life of "supernatural" powers such as the gods.'

One way around the problem of *defining* religion is to concentrate on how it *functions* as a phenomenon in people's lives. This approach was largely the creation of the English scholar Ninian Smart, who founded the first UK university department of Religious Studies. Smart believed that, regardless of their actual doctrines or beliefs, all religions contain the following "dimensions", or essential elements: Doctrinal, Mythological, Ethical, Ritual, Experiential, Institutional and Material. To put some flesh on the bones of Smart's "religious dimensions", we will look briefly at all seven, giving examples from both Christianity and Odinism:

Doctrinal: The systematic formulation of religious teachings in an intellectually coherent form. Christian example: any theology book; Odinist example: this book.

Mythological: Stories that work on several levels, and shed some light on the universe and our place in it. Christian example: the *Bible*; Odinist example: *Beowulf*.
Ethical: Rules about human behavior. Christian example: the Ten Commandments; Odinist example: the Nine Noble Virtues.
Ritual: Ceremonies, which may be public or private. Christian example: *The Book of Common Prayer*; Odinist example: *The Book of Blots*.
Experiential: The emotions which the religion inspires in its adherents. Christian examples: dread, guilt, devotion; Odinist examples: liberation, mystery, bliss.
Institutional: Attitudes shared by the religion's adherents. Christian example: universalism; Odinist example: folkish ancestor-worship.
Material: Ordinary objects or places that symbolize the sacred. Christian example: Jerusalem; Odinist example: "the North".

The first three of these dimensions (doctrinal, mythological, ethical) Smart regarded as "historical". The last four (ritual, experiential, institutional and material) he called "para-historical". The "historical" dimensions can be studied from texts, but the "para-historical" dimensions require participation, "for one has to enter into men's intentions, beliefs, myths, desires, in order to understand why they act as they do – it is fatal if cultures including our own are described merely externally, without entering into dialogue with them." [25] This explains why academics employed in university departments of Germanic Studies and the like may be great linguists, or even experts in comparative religion, but are usually unable to engage with the essence of our ancestral faith.

Broadly speaking, a *myth* is a narrative, or story, that deals in some way with the Other World. The characters in a myth may be beings such as gods and goddesses that are not part of the normal human world. They may be humans who react in some way with the world beyond our normal senses. An example of the latter is the Christian myth of Adam and Eve, well known through its depiction by many artists and its re-telling in poems such as John Milton's *Paradise Lost*.

When used in this special sense, the word "myth" has no negative connotations. A myth is something quite different to a work of fiction or a fairy tale. The crucial distinction is that myths contain messages that are intended to influence the ways in which people both view themselves and interact with the world – whereas a work of fiction that attempts to do this is merely propaganda. People may believe in a myth quite literally, or they may believe that it is somehow "true" at a deeper level. An example of the latter is the frontier mythology of Hollywood Westerns. Some of the characters in some of those films really did exist, while others, such as Clint Eastwood's "man with no name", are a distillation of the self-sufficient Western "hero" – yet viewers accept that the West may have been "something like that", at least occasionally, and that Western movies can and do teach us something about how our lives should (or should not) be lived. [26]

"God" is another word that is almost impossible to define. After nearly two thousand years the finest minds among Christian theologians have failed to agree on what they mean when they write about their own god. We are unlikely to do better, but a little background may help.

The modern English word *god* was spelled the same way in Old English. It was *guþ* in Gothic, *guð* in Old Norse, is *gud* in modern Scandinavian, *god* in Dutch, and g*ott* in modern German. It derives from a Proto-Germanic word which may have been *ǥuđán. No-one today knows precisely what the term meant to our Indo-European forebears. Several linguists have linked this word with the names of three tribes of our Germanic ancestors: the Geats (mainly known from the Old English epic *Beowulf*), the Goths, and the Gutar (a descendant of people born on the island of Gotland). These tribal names are thought to derive from "Gautr", which is one of Odin's many names in the surviving literature. If so, the word "Goth" and its equivalents would be an ethnonym (the name of an ethnic group) – and it would essentially mean "the Nation of Odin".

We can seek to clarify the concept further by following Ninian Smart's lead and looking at some of the meanings that various people, believers and otherwise, have attributed to the word "god".

Euhemerus was a 4th century BCE Greek philosopher who believed that the Greek gods had originally been great human leaders, who were falsely regarded as gods after their deaths by their grateful followers. Snorri Sturluson, the Christian Icelandic scholar, made the same claim about the Norse gods. When this argument is used about Christianity, it is referred to as "adoptionism", which has repeatedly been condemned as a heresy. It should go without saying that no serious modern Odinists believe, with Snorri, that Odin was once a king in what is now Turkey.

Apotheosis refers to people known to be human beings but worshipped as divinities in their own lifetime or shortly afterwards. For instance, Julius Caesar was formally recognized as a god in Rome, as were some of his successors. Some Shintoists believe the Japanese emperor is divine. Some Tibetan Buddhists believe the Dalai Lama to be a god. Many Rastafarians see Haile Selassie (1892-1975) as having been divine.

Avatars. Adherents of many religions believe that gods and goddesses exist in another realm but can take human form, even animal form, at will. This belief was common in the pagan Greek religion, and may explain why early Christians, who lived in a Greek cultural region, claimed that Jesus was their god in human form. In Hinduism the term for a human incarnation of a god is "avatar": Buddha is often seen as an avatar of the god Vishnu.

Archetypes, according to followers of Carl Jung, are something like epitomes – for instance, the archetype of "the Great Mother" is an epitome of motherhood, although also considerably more than that. Archetypes can be seen as moral examples, or as ways of expressing in universal terms the internal psychological world that is the product of our human evolution. It is impossible to do justice to Jung's concept in the space available here, but it may be said that most religions could be reduced to their component archetypes by a determined Jungian.

James Frazer (1854-1941), author of the extremely influential book *The Golden Bough*, believed that all mythologies, including the Christian one, are ways of telling the universal story of the cycle of life, death and rebirth. Frazer would have us believe that the "death and resurrection" of a god like Balder somehow represents the changing seasons. Frazer's work is much criticized today as not being confirmed by field studies. Yet in very general terms it can hardly be denied that most religions are largely concerned with life, death and rebirth.

All the above interpretations of the word "god" have been applied, at one stage or other, to the gods and goddesses of our own ancestors. Other interpretations, such as pantheism, appear to be irrelevant to a religion with many deities unless we distort both the faith and the word beyond recognition.

Another possibility, however, is that our deities really do exist, in a physical sense, "out there". The great evolutionary biologist, Richard Dawkins, has argued repeatedly that the existence of "God" is an empirical question, since a universe with a god would be a completely different kind of universe to one without a god. The rest of this chapter suggests one way in which the gods and goddesses of our people may be as physically "real" as the author and readers of this book.

Clifford Pickover's *Surfing Through Hyperspace* [27] was a scientific work concerning realms of existence beyond our direct comprehension. Its ideas may eventually change the way we conceive of our religion and the universe.

Pickover, a molecular biophysicist, was interested in the notion of higher dimensions. We are all familiar with the first three dimensions: the sideways and forwards movements traceable on a map, plus up and down. Even babies have some idea of these three directions long before they can walk. But are there, perhaps, other dimensions? More than just the three we can all sense? Modern physicists think so. According to one well-known theory there are perhaps eleven dimensions – ten (give or take) of space and one of time. Although the extra spatial dimensions are invisible to us, scientists believe they can measure them as forces. Furthermore, certain phenomena only make sense to modern physics if these extra dimensions really exist.

Pickover's originality lay in asking what implications these modern scientific theories have for our everyday human lives. For instance, chess is almost a two dimensional game. Almost but not quite, because the knight can "jump". Pickover asks whether chess would be simpler or harder if it were really two-dimensional. But the big question he raised is this: what if living beings actually exist in the higher dimensions?

To try to imagine what such beings could do in our 3D world, we only have to pretend for a moment that there is a race of beings that exist in only two dimensions. They would have length and breadth but no height or thickness. Clearly they would have no "bodies" in the sense with which we are familiar, somewhat resembling moving shadows. We could see all their world at a glance. We could make them seem to "disappear" just by lifting them up into our third dimension.

If these two dimensional beings had any inkling of our existence they would probably feel us to be all-seeing, all-knowing beings, able to perform miracles. Similarly, if other beings existed in more dimensions than we can experience, they could do all sorts of things that would seem to us like miracles.

Pickover was really asking whether humankind's gods may be real beings living in further dimensions to which we have no sensual access.

As most readers will recall, our own Germanic ancestors said that our god Odin sits on a high throne from which he can see everything that happens in "all the worlds". That sounds very like a 3D explanation of the (to us) "magical" powers of a being who inhabits the higher dimensions.

Our ancestors were astute observers of the natural world. For instance, as H. R. Ellis Davidson famously pointed out: "Long before astronomy revealed to men the terrifying extent of the great starry spaces, the idea of vastness and of distances to tantalize the mind was already present in heathen thought". [28]

Did our ancestors also have some insight into "worlds" – or in modern terms, dimensions – beyond our senses? It would seem so. The seeress in *Völuspá* stated quite plainly that there are precisely *nine* worlds. If "worlds" here refers to dimensions (and *Völuspá* is, after all, poetry) then our ancestors' conceptions eerily approximate the superstring theory of modern physics.

Pickover points out that according to our current state of knowledge there are theoretical constraints on the existence of beings in higher dimensions. For instance, the inverse-square law of electromagnetism would be altered in higher dimensional worlds, threatening the stability of atoms. Our current theories, however, are largely based on our experience of our own three-dimensional world. They are also curtailed by the imaginative restrictions of modern secularized Christianity, as we shall see in later chapters. There is no guarantee that they will hold up as our scientific knowledge advances.

On the other hand, beings who really inhabit more dimensions than we can comprehend with our limited human senses – the "gods" that Pickover is seeking – would have a much more profound scientific understanding of both their own nature and ours.

It is even possible that our own gods and goddesses bestowed some of their higher knowledge to our ancestors, who recorded it in poetic fashion. Unless this idea is countenanced, it is scarcely possible to imagine how our ancestors could have had such a clear premonition of modern evolutionary theory, or modern theoretical physics, or even how they mastered forms of technology thousands of years ago that have not been matched until the last few decades. (These issues will be examined further in Chapters 11 and 12.)

One way by which this process has been expressed in our inadequate words – one way among many – is this: "The second possibility is that our observable universe is a created entity within a larger one, subject to intervention by higher beings. If we can conceive of the possibility of creating artificial intelligence, then we must admit the possibility that we are so created. In that case, we could easily concede as possible that the evolution "program" was not only started off by the design of a specific replicator – DNA or its precursors – but that there has been intervention from time to time to kick the process along, much in the manner that we can tweak a stuck computer program" [29]

We will see in due course how our own ancestors believed this actually happened. Meanwhile, let's keep an open mind about our gods and goddesses, and how they might relate to our own lives.

9

ODIN

God the Nordics regarded as being too great for any man to wholly understand or wholly comprehend. But something of God they could in some measure understand, and that something they called Odin...

- Alexander Rud Mills

But every hour is saved
From that eternal silence, something more,
A bringer of new things; and vile it were
For some three suns to store and hoard myself,
And this gray spirit yearning in desire
To follow knowledge like a sinking star,
Beyond the utmost bounds of human thought.

- Tennyson, *Ulysses*

We have seen above (Chapter 2) that our modern word "Odin" probably originally meant something similar to "excitement, inspiration". That is not its primary meaning today, although there is no reason why that meaning should not be restored.

Most readers probably first encountered the word as a component of the third week-day, Wednesday. That name comes from the Old English *Wódnesdæg*, meaning "Wóden's day". In Old Norse the day was called *Oðinsdagr* (Oðinn's day). In modern Swedish and Danish it is *Onsdag*, meaning the same thing. In Dutch it is *Woensdag*; and so on.

In non-Germanic languages this day is often named after Mercury, whom we have seen to be in some ways a counterpart of Odin. Thus in Latin it was *dies Mercurii* (Mercury's day), and the languages derived from Latin retain this link.

It is clear, then, that Odin was regarded by our ancestors as a god significant enough to be celebrated in the name of a week-day. However, at least three other days in modern English are also named after Germanic deities – Tuesday, from Tiw, Thursday, from Thunor, and Friday, from Frige. (Monday may be named for the god known in Old

Norse as Máni, or may be simply a translation from the Latin name *Dies Lunae*.) So although our forebears regarded Odin as a very important deity, they did not see him as existing on a plane significantly higher than that of the other gods and goddesses.

Yet most modern histories of the heathen north state that Odin was regarded by our ancestors as the chief, or most eminent, god. This may not have been the belief of all our ancestors, even in Viking times. As Gabriel Turville-Petre pointed out: "In Iceland there are neither place-names nor personal names associated with Óðinn, but Óðinn is mentioned in Icelandic literature more often than any other god." [30] He added: "While there are no place-names containing the element Óðin- in Iceland, there are a number in Norway, more in Sweden and proportionately more in Denmark. Some of these appear to be of great age, e.g. those compounded with *-akr* (cornfield), *-vin* (meadow). These last two suggest that for some people, at one time, Óðinn was god of fertility ..."

Odin, as Wóden, was paid greater honor in Anglo-Saxon England, where, as we have seen (Chapter 7), the great royal families claimed descent from him. Several place-names incorporate the god's name, including various Wansdykes (in Wiltshire, Hampshire and Somerset), the former *Wodens beorh* and *Wodnes denu* (both in Wiltshire, now re-named by Christians), Wednesbury and Wednesfield (both West Midlands), Woodnesborough and Wormshill (both in Kent), and possibly Wanborough (Wiltshire). Other places are named after the god's by-names, including those with a *Grim-* component. For instance, *The Concise Oxford Dictionary of English Place-Names* [31] says of Grim's Ditch in Wiltshire: "The name is synonymous with WANSDYKE. In Old Norse *Grímr* is used as a byname of *Óðinn*. The name is identical with ON *grímr*, 'a person who conceals his name', lit. 'a masked person', and related to OE *grīma* 'a mask'. It refers, like *Grímnir*, to Oðinn's well-known habit of appearing in disguise. No doubt the Saxons used *Grīm* in the same way."

It should be noted that the names of at least three other gods are honored in English place-names: Tyw (Icelandic *Týr*) Thunor (*Þórr*), and Frige (*Frigga*). These names are also enshrined in the names of our weekdays Tuesday, Thursday and Friday. So if Odin was in some sense a "chief god" to the Anglo-Saxons, other deities were given similar respect. Yet only Odin is commemorated in place-names in the territories of all of the three main "English" nations: the Angles, Saxons and Jutes. [32]

The surviving *literature* contains only vague hints of the worship of Odin in the British Isles. After the official conversion, Christian writers such as Bede went out of their way to avoid any references to heathen beliefs (although we shall see later that these beliefs were far from superseded). For detailed information about Odin we must rely on Icelandic literature.

According to Snorri Sturluson, a Christian who flourished two centuries after the official conversion of Iceland, Óðinn was the *Alfǫðr*, the All-Father. Snorri tells us the heathens believed: "He will live throughout all ages governing all his dominions and ruling all things great and small". This is emphatically *not* what the surviving heathen poems tell us! It is clear that Snorri, like many eminent Christian scholars since, could not comprehend what the heathen poems actually *meant* to practicing heathens. He has distorted their meaning to accord with the Christian assumption of a supreme, all-powerful divinity like the god of the Old Testament. The Icelandic poems actually stress that Óðinn was not seen as all-powerful, or destined to live beyond the present cosmic age, or was even particularly interested in "ruling" anything.

What the poems do stress is that Óðinn's overwhelming function is to preserve the stability of our high-level cosmic order against the forces of chaos. On this cosmic level, he can be seen as opposed to the second law of thermodynamics, which essentially states that an isolated system that is not in equilibrium will tend to break down over time, ultimately approaching total disorder. Óðinn's calling, according to the surviving poems, is to strive against this collapse of order into chaos.

To some extent all the gods and goddesses are involved in this function, and they each perform their own roles, rather like players in a team-sport. To the degree that this analogy can be sustained, Odin is similar to a team captain, or perhaps a quarterback in American football. Other gods and goddesses have their own special abilities, but all are striving for order, stability, and perhaps above all for the cosmic beauty that cannot survive any collapse into universal chaos.

Odin's special role in the preservation of higher order and beauty is his quest for knowledge. One of the few academic scholars who understood this fully is Jens Peter Schjødt. Rather than make the same case ourselves, we will honor Schjødt by relying on his perceptive words:

> Óðinn seeks knowledge across the whole mythology, and gets it. To wonder that he does not know everything is to put a contemporary, and therefore an anachronistic, rationality over the myths. Óðinn's main role in the mythology is to seek knowledge and become wise. Obviously, it has never been imagined that he was omniscient: he knows a lot, but there is always more knowledge to be had. It is the very process of acquiring knowledge rather than its result that is Óðinn's *raison d'être*.[33]

In the same work, Schjødt added:

> In recent years, there has been a tendency on the part of some scholars to see Óðinn in the context of shamanistic concepts – as the divine shaman (e.g. Hedeager 1997 and 1999; 1999, 2003 includes references to older discussions of Óðinn and shamanism; see also Solli 2002 and Price 2002). In another

context, I have demonstrated (Schjødt 2001) that, although there are several features about Óðinn which we can also find in the complex of ideas relating to shamanism, he is in addition characterized in a way that makes it meaningless to reduce him to a 'shaman'. In the same article, there is also a brief analysis of all of Óðinn's functions in which knowledge and sovereignty are pointed out as the central semantic part from which the rest is to be understood.

The Icelandic poems stress that Óðinn is mainly interested in superhuman knowledge and wisdom, especially in order to use this acquisition to combat the forces of entropy and chaos. The poems also depict Óðinn sometimes *sharing* his wisdom with humans, who are his allies in the quest for knowledge, stability and beauty.

If that were true, Odinists in the pre-Christian period should have left us evidence of knowledge that was in advance of what could reasonably have been expected for the times in which they lived. We will see that they did. Future chapters will discuss some astonishing scientific advances in the pre-Christian, European world that have been opposed, denigrated, or simply ignored by Christian historians. Chapter 11 will look at our ancestral concept of evolution, which is still opposed by some Christians today. Chapter 12 will compare our hereditary cosmological theories to the modern conceptions of physics. But before we do, this is an appropriate place to pause in order to clear up potential misunderstandings about some words that will be used increasingly in this book.

10

"PAGAN", "HEATHEN" AND "CRETIN"

Barking Anubis, a whole progeny of grotesque deities, are embattled against Neptune and Minerva and Venus.

- Virgil, *Aeneid*, VIII, 698

Some people don't like the terms "pagan" and "heathen", feeling that they are derogatory. That is because these words have indeed been used in a negative way by Christians. Yet there is no reason why we should attach Christian values to these words. Instead, we can look at how they came to be applied to our ancestors, and in doing so we will see that, far from their being innately offensive, we can actually take pride in them.

The word "pagan" comes from the Latin term *pagus*, meaning a country district. It was applied to our ancestors at the stage in Roman history when believers in the indigenous religion of Rome were more often to be encountered in the country than in the city. *Pagenses* meant "people of the rural districts", and the former Welsh kingdom of Powys is said to have taken its name from a Celtic spelling of this word.

We have seen that during the reign of Augustus (27 BCE-14 CE) up to 85% of the "Roman" menial workers were slaves, or the descendants of slaves, of non-Roman descent. Amongst the unemployable underclass the percentage of non-Romans must have been even higher. Rome had become mostly a city of non-Romans, although it was still ruled by the descendants of its founders. Since the city was subject to foreign plagues, and crime was rife, most of the dwindling minority of aristocrats were happy to continue the old Roman custom of devoting themselves to their charming country estates. This was officially encouraged by Octavian himself, the future Caesar Augustus, in his "back to the land" policy after the Civil War. The greatest of Roman poets, Virgil, devoted an entire book, the *Georgics*, to the robust and traditionally Roman virtues of farming and agriculture.

Meanwhile, the "Roman" mob, the non-Romans who were becoming an increasing majority in the city of Rome, had no such access to idyllic country estates – or to luxury resort towns like Pompeii. The lives of this underclass were not enviable, which is why the cry arose among them for *Panem et Circenses*, for free food and entertainment. Many of them naturally turned for spiritual refuge to strange cults imported from the East. These cults were usually tolerated by the aristocratic authorities, although real Romans were sometimes forbidden to participate in cults such as that of the goddess Cybele. Even the participation of the urban underclass in these cults was regulated. For instance, excess of emotion (called *superstitio)* was forbidden.

One of these new and "superstitious" cults was Christianity. Initially the Christians were a despised group, meeting furtively in the back rooms of high-rise apartment slums (called *insulae*). As they grew in numbers, they were increasingly blamed for the plagues that racked the empire. Given that they often imported their religious leaders from the East, there may well have been some truth to this accusation.

The stage was thus set for a showdown between the last real Romans and the predominantly alien, uneducated, urban underclass, who turned more and more to Christianity. On the one hand were the traditionally pious Romans with their lofty moral code, who were able to escape the escalating chaos of the city of Rome to the countryside and their equivalent of our modern, luxurious "gated estates". On the other hand there was the mostly illiterate, superstitious, undernourished, violent and often diseased alien proletariat and underclass, penned up in the city and asserting their "rights" – to free food and entertainment in this life, and domination in the life to come.

Naturally, the urban underclass identified its opponents as country-dwellers, "pagans". It is a term that we can accept with pride.

"Heathen" is merely a translation of the Latin word "pagan", as used by Christians in Imperial Rome, into the Germanic languages. It has no independent meaning. It does *not* imply any form of rural backwardness or lack of sophistication. Nor does it suggest that our non-Christian ancestors lived on some sort of "blasted heath" like Macbeth's witches. In fact, the cities of countries such as Ireland were established by Scandinavian Odinists. Meanwhile the Celtic Christians, who had been established in Ireland for hundreds of years prior to the Odinist founding of cities like Dublin and Cork, continued to eke out a sometimes worthy but necessarily frugal existence among the peat bogs.

Just in case any Odinist reader is still offended by the terms "pagan" and heathen", we should note that the word "Cretin" is defined in the *Concise Oxford Dictionary* as: "Deformed idiot of a kind found esp in Alpine valleys ... [f. F *crétin* f. Swiss F *creitin, crestin* f. L *Christianus* CHRISTIAN ...]" So if Christians are happy to accept the etymological connection between "Christian" and "Cretin", it would be rather precious of Odinists to worry about being labeled (by Christians) with a term that originally described our ancestors' preference to live on Arcadian country estates where learning and the arts were fostered, rather than in decaying urban slums.

11

THE GERMANIC CONCEPT OF EVOLUTION

> We don't need ideology, much; we've got genetics instead. Our social order is hard-coded into our nervous systems.
>
> - Gwendolyn Ingolfsson in S. M. Stirling's novel, *Drakon*

> A scientific view of man offers exciting possibilities. We have not yet seen what man can make of man.
>
> - B. F. Skinner, *Beyond Freedom and Dignity*

Wherever pre-Christian Odinist beliefs (which in northern Europe survive mainly in poetry) can be compared with those of modern science, the two seem to be almost fully in tune. Indeed, the overlap is as perfect as it could be between a poetic and a prosaic exposition. Modern Odinists believe, in fact, that if our ancestors had never been forcibly half-converted to the crude Biblical conception of nature, the state of our contemporary scientific knowledge would be centuries ahead of where it is currently. This can certainly be said for the theory of evolution.

Christian creationist theory insisted that their god, Yahweh, created the first couple, Adam and Eve; and that these first people were every bit as human as we are. It wasn't until the nineteenth century, which witnessed the towering intellects of Charles Darwin and Alfred Russel Wallace, that this belief began to be seriously questioned.

Today, of course, most of us accept that modern humans have evolved – physically, intellectually and culturally – from earlier and more primitive versions of our species. But few, even among enlightened Odinists or the scientific community, are aware that this was what our ancestors believed before they were led astray by Christian ideas.

The poem *Völuspá* mentions three "powerful and loving" (*ölfgir oc ástgir*) gods who found two primitive beings, Ask and Embla, who were "feeble", "weak" and "fateless". Each god gave this couple life-enhancing blessings. These were: the breath of spirit; mind and feeling; the warmth of life; and a desirable appearance. It should be noted that this proto-human pair, Ask and Embla, was placed on the path to human status by an act of pure favor by the "powerful and loving" gods.

Snorri Sturluson's Christianized prose version of this event states that Ask and Embla were mere lumps of wood before our gods animated them with qualities that could only be bestowed by divine beings. We needn't take this reference to timber too seriously. Old Norse poetical traditions frequently compared humans to trees. For instance, in Egil Skallagrimson's masterpiece, *Sonatorrek*, the poet describes his son as a warrior by using a phrase that means "shield-tree", and his own wife by a phrase that translates as "kin-timber". One of the by-names for Odin is *svinnr sigrunnr*, "wise victory-tree". Snorri himself notes that "poets have called man 'ash' or 'maple', 'grove' or other masculine tree-names" – and that the same applies to kennings for women. These comparisons would have been as transparent to our ancestors as any modern reference to young women as "chicks".

Western science has long since accepted our ancestral understanding that modern humans have evolved from vastly more primitive predecessors. But to understand how far we have evolved since the first modern humans with whom we could physically interbreed, it helps to look at another Old Norse poem, *Rígsþula*.

According to *Rígsþula,* a god who goes by the name of Ríg visits three human-like couples and impregnates in turn each of the three females. His children are, respectively, thralls, farmers, and aristocrats. The thralls are unattractive, swarthy-skinned, dark-haired, dull-eyed. The farmers are ruddy-faced with sparkling eyes. The aristocrats are fair-haired and attractive – in appearance and in accomplishment everything that you might expect of the descendants of a god.

Some scholars, basically following Georges Dumézil, have insisted that this myth is intended to account for the tripartite class system that existed in most early Indo-European societies. To some extent their views have merit. But myths function on many different levels, just like poetic or artistic imagery. A much more striking way in which *Rígsþula* functions is as a poetic account of human evolution.

We have seen how the gods elevated the primitive Ask and Embla to something approaching human status. Snorri tells us that this happened by the sea-shore. *Rígsþula* starts in the same fashion, with Ríg travelling along the shore until he comes to a "house". The descendants of Ask and Embla have clearly progressed somewhat by this time. At least they can construct shelters for themselves. But the fire is set directly on the floor, suggesting that the floor was little more than rammed earth, and all they can offer their divine visitor is the most coarse and simple food. Given the ugliness of the child who was later born to the woman and to Ríg, the mother must have been downright hideous – just like some of the species that preceded *Homo sapiens*. Still, that child's own children (with names such as Howler, Stumpy, Swarthy and Stinker) were able to put dung on fields, herd goats and pigs, and grub for peat. A step up.

Some time later Ríg again intervenes in human evolution. The emblematic couple that he visits this time is well-dressed. The man is whittling some wood and the woman is spinning yarn. Ríg again impregnates the female, and the boy that is born is a pretty baby with sparkling eyes. He becomes a proper farmer, plowing the land, erecting tall buildings, taming oxen, crafting carts. His own children in turn have names like Man, Yeoman, Master, Franklin ... and Woman, Wife, Maiden and Lady. By this stage the species is truly human, yet Ríg's tasks are still not complete.

He visits a third couple, known as Father and Mother. They are a loving couple, and well-off, with silver platters, fine clothes, and delightful food. Significantly, Ríg sits drinking and chatting with them all day long. The son that is born of this union is the handsome boy "Jarl", who becomes a horseman, a hunter and a warrior. Ríg returns to visit him, teaches him runes, and acknowledges him as his son and heir.

Now if *Rígsþula* were primarily intended to justify class divisions, it obviously does a very poor job of it. All the children are Ríg's own, and if they are meant to be representative of different classes or castes *coexisting at the same time* each one of them could claim divine origin. As an exercise in politics the poem would therefore be inept.

On the other hand, as a poetic and religious account of evolution, *Rígsþula,* especially taken as a sequel to story of the gifts of the gods to humanity in *Völuspá*, makes perfect sense.

Ask and Embla can be viewed as a very early form of human ancestor, perhaps somewhat like the sloping-browed Australopithecus with his primitive brain volume of about 500 cc. Their descendants progressed culturally as far as they could, but were still living at a very primitive level, and by modern standards they were hideous to behold. They needed an evolutionary boost, and Ríg provided it.

This next stage in the human species as depicted in the poem represents a level of development somewhere between that of the Acheulian stage, said to be about three hundred thousand years ago, and early historical times.

The third visit by Ríg ushers in a thoroughly modern type of person, participating in all the aristocratic sports of the Viking period – like swimming for pleasure, and playing the board game known as "tables".

Unfortunately, *Rígsþula* is incomplete. The ending is missing. If we had the lost lines today they would perhaps shed more light on the moral and spiritual aspects of the poem – such as the symbolism of the doors of the three dwellings, the first of which is shut, the second half-shut and the third open. We can speculate on these and other issues, but the purpose so far is to show that our heathen ancestors had at least a general and workable concept of human evolution.

Of course, this ancestral account differs in some ways from modern neo-Darwinism. In particular, it posits the existence of a god who "breeds up" our ancestors with his own divine genes, just as modern farmers and stock-breeders have improved their sheep and cattle by crossing them with superior animals. But Ríg is definitely not a creator in the way that Christians claim their god to be. He is more like those Nobel Prize-winners who have donated their genes to sperm banks in order, they hope, that the next generation of humanity will be more intelligent than it would be without their generosity.

Yet the poem is only claiming for Ríg a supervisory role in the direction that evolution has taken in one single species – humans. And as one of the most prominent neo-Darwinians of our era has written: "If there are versions of the evolutionary theory that deny slow gradualism, and deny the central role of natural selection [through random mutation], they may be true in particular cases". [34] *Rígsþula* requires only one such "particular case" – divine intervention in the evolution of the Northern branch of our species.

What is truly marvelous about this ancestral concept of evolution is that it existed at all. As far as we are aware there was no understanding of the fossil record at that time. So how might our ancestors have known that humanity had undergone a very lengthy period of physical development before it could reach its then-present level of culture? There seem to be only three possibilities: perhaps they made a series of incredibly lucky guesses; perhaps they were informed by the gods; or perhaps they were heirs to an earlier and extremely technological and scientifically advanced culture.

The implications of these possibilities are awe-inspiring. If our ancestors arrived at something extremely similar to the views of Darwin and Wallace by brilliant guesswork, we would do well to trust their other "guesses" – such as the existence of the gods and goddesses and the "nine worlds" (dimensions?). On the other hand, if the gods revealed the truth to our ancestors in this particular matter, then we would equally do well to accept that their other beliefs may have been divinely inspired. Yet again, if our ancestors were heirs to a scientifically superior culture, it ought to be possible to see whether they knew other ideas that "should" not have been available to them in those times.

One way or another, *Rígsþula* ought to be taken seriously. And that leads to the vital question of what Ríg's purpose may have been. Why would he, and earlier the other three gods, have intervened to give our somewhat sorry species such a series of massive boosts?

Ultimately, we cannot answer that question. All that we can observe is that the consistent purpose of the gods has been to improve us as a species. Furthermore, we have now reached the point where we can take our destiny into our own hands. We have enough understanding of genetics to transform ourselves within a few generations to the extent that our descendants may look back on us the way we ourselves look back on Australopithecus.

Whether we choose the upward evolutionary path depends on the moral values we hold dear, and these in turn depend on our religious or spiritual outlook. What is certain is that we cannot stand still as a species. Far more people like Howler, Stumpy, Swarthy and Stinker are being born today than people like Jarl. We can go forward, or we can continue to regress. Those are our only choices. The implications for Odinism, and the world at large, are huge. Can we examine them, in Professor Oliver's words, "without vertigo"? Let's try.

The gods and goddesses of our people are engaged in an epoch-long struggle against the forces of chaos. For some reason known only to them, they chose one unprepossessing species among many, a "feeble", "weak" and "fateless" species, and raised them to a proto-human level somewhat like Australopithecus. The same "powerful and loving" deities clearly had a policy concerning us, and as a result Ríg intervened repeatedly in our evolution – until these repeated infusions of divine matter raised us to the highest level that the Viking age could imagine. If the ending of *Rígsþula* had survived, we might know where this process was supposed to lead. We don't have that ending, but we do have another surviving poem, *Völuspá*, which many Icelandic speakers say is the greatest literary creation of the Viking age.

In a sense, *Völuspá* takes over where *Rígsþula* was truncated. It tells of the final battle between the gods (and their human allies) and the forces of chaos, at the end of the present dispensation. Many of the gods will die in the process of defeating chaos, and nearly all humans will also perish. Yet although the victory of the gods is costly, it is total. The divine progeny of the gods survive. The most gracious of all the gods, Balder, is at last restored to the earth. The planet itself is reborn and pure; new life is restored to it. What might be called "evil" is abolished.

Völuspá again does not survive in its original form. Various attempts have been made to restore it to its correct stanza-order. Perhaps some parts may be missing. The aspect of the final battle that most concerns us here is the fate of humanity.

Another poem, *Vafðruðnismál*, completes the picture. During the last battle two human beings take shelter in a forest. Their names are Líf and Lífþrasir. (They mean something like "Life" and "Abounding with life".) These two, and these alone, survive to repopulate the earth.

But are the children of Líf and Lífþrasir entirely our kind? Throughout the history of the gods' interaction with humans they have been intervening directly to raise our evolutionary standard. Once chaos has been defeated in the triumphant final battle, is it logical to assume that the gods and goddesses presiding over a vastly improved earth would be satisfied with the level we have reached so far? The poetry suggests not. There is a direct and presumably deliberate parallel between Ask and Embla, our proto-human ancestors, and Líf and Lífþrasir. Furthermore, there are the other named couples along the way, each of which has been helped up by an infusion of divine matter. So why should Líf and

Lífþrasir be any different? The whole world is to be renewed in transcendent beauty, the surviving gods will be young and fresh, and it seems unlikely that they would be satisfied with people like us who are, in Nietzsche's terms, "Human, all too human". In short, it seems to be the will of the gods that humanity will be surpassed by a higher species, based on the best that already exists – as happened every time Ríg improved our species in the past.

This, in effect, was also what the renowned physicist Stephen Hawking was predicting when he told the White House in 1997 that the new millennium would see the development of superhumans. While our ancestral religious myths make this prophecy in symbolic terms, Hawking was speaking as a rational scientist with a deep understanding of modern technological power. Although not an Odinist himself, he was echoing age-old Odinist concepts.

Predictably, his address raised howls of outrage. His notion of superhumans was savaged by critics from a Christian ethical heritage, who reject the idea of further evolution just as firmly and blindly as the American judge who thought Darwinism was a "monkey mythology". Their fear led many of them to trivialize Hawking's vision, to reduce it to the idea that we would – for unspecified reasons – choose to create people who could run faster, jump higher, or whatever.

The truth is, of course, that we are already influencing future human evolution, and not always in positive ways. Our social and political structures encourage the less intelligent to breed, for instance, thus lowering the average human IQ. On the positive side, the prevalence of certain diseases is already lessening as a result of pre-natal screening.

But Hawking was referring to far more than this. He believed that we are on the verge of being able to re-engineer ourselves as a species.

This will come about as a result of the human genome project, which by 2003 had mapped all of the 3 billion or so bits of information that make up human DNA. According to the driving force behind this project, Nobel Laureate James Watson: "It is the most important scientific project ever attempted ... [It will identify] those normal genes whose mutant forms are the cause of the countless genetic diseases that diminish the lives of so many human beings and their families." In short, future gene therapy will be able to manipulate genes that have gone wrong.

Hawking himself suffers from a degenerative illness called Lou Gehrig's disease. He can only move his eyes, mouth, and right thumb. Yet "Hawking is marvelous," said one of his audience in the White House, geneticist Craig Venter, adding: "I wish the project could help him now." Any of us with a loved one who is suffering from a terrible genetic illness would agree with Venter. The sooner the technology is available, the better – although many fundamentalist Christians disagree, vehemently, with this statement. To take our destiny into our own hands, they say, would be to "play god". Therefore there were critics of

Hawking. One such was Dr Christopher Newell, an ethicist at the University of Tasmania and an Anglican priest. Newell asked: "In the brave new world that Hawking suggests is inevitable, will there be a place for people with disability to make the contribution that he has?" To which the obvious answer is that, if we'd had the technology sooner, Hawking may have been spared his disability.

Newell also said that the "notion of superhumans will be inherently racist". It is hard to see why this should necessarily be so. Of course it will be pioneered in wealthy, Western-style societies, but there is no inherent reason why it should not spread. After all, penicillin was pioneered in the West, but it didn't stay confined to the rich nations.

Another Newell argument was this: "It seems likely that despite the promise of genetics, future superhumans would still need to deal with the basic human struggle of frailty, disability and death." Here Newell was putting on his priest's collar, albeit unconvincingly. It is doubtful that, with hindsight, he would have banned the development of penicillin just because it didn't improve human morals. In fact, a world with far less misery and illness is likely to be far more productive and therefore also less competitive. Perhaps that would assist our moral development. At any rate, human beings would, by definition, live longer. It is possible that greater age combined with better health might lead to greater wisdom. Should that happen, a wiser world would, logically, be a better one.

The shallowness of the arguments used by people like Father Newell indicates that their true motivation is fear. But what are they afraid of? Obviously they aren't worried that the Christian god will punish us for daring to improve on the rather feeble human model that was supposedly made "in his own image". Yet it seems they feel that taking charge of our evolution is somehow "just not right", and they are desperately casting around for pseudo-logical excuses.

Is there really anything to fear about the human future sketched by Hawking? Of course there is. The most obvious problem is the risk of unintended consequences. As soon as the technology becomes available it will be used. That is the way things happen. And despite any regulations that may be placed upon it, those who are both rich and desperate will find ways around those regulations. Once again, that is the way things are. If individuals rush into using the technology before its effects are fully known, they may harm their own offspring. They will probably not, however, do serious harm to humanity as a whole. We will not rush, lemming-like, into becoming a race of clones, for the simple reason that we already know how a major loss of genetic diversity can damage the future health of any species.

A far greater cause for concern would be the consequence of attempting to prohibit the new technology. This would not prevent illicit use. Prohibition never does. And while the use of a technology as significant as this by occasional "rogue scientists" would probably not be devastating, it would have the potential to cause terrible fear and hostility in the community at large.

One thing, though, is certain. If the Odinist view of evolution had prevailed, this debate would have occurred centuries ago. Meanwhile the technology is all but on our doorstep already – begging the question: "how are we going to use it?"

Before addressing that question, one further aspect of the relationship between our ancestral religious concept of evolution and modern science needs to be addressed.

The second law of thermodynamics is often summarized as stating that any closed system tends to "run down" toward a state of chaos – meaning total disorder. Order decays into disorder, or to express it in another way "information" decays into "noise". If left untended for a few decades, the glorious gardens at Versailles would become a weed-choked wilderness. If left without maintenance for a few centuries, the most superb cathedrals would crumble into rubble. Even the mighty Egyptian pyramids are slowly reverting to the desert. The measure of this decay is known as entropy. The higher the level of entropy, the greater the decay from order to disorder.

The second law of thermodynamics states that in a closed system the total entropy can never decrease. In simple terms, all observable systems are collapsing toward total disorder, toward maximum degeneration. Even the cosmos itself is burning up its finite supply of fuel and perhaps heading toward a state of thermodynamic equilibrium, a state in which there is no discernable order whatsoever and in which the temperature of the universe is an unvarying -273° Celsius. Some scientists of the Victorian era referred to this as the "heat death" of the universe, in which, one by one, the stars burn out, ceasing to heat planets like our Earth, until there is not only no life but not even any subatomic activity.

In this somewhat depressing scenario of general and eventually total decay, one would perhaps not expect to find nature also showing the opposite tendency – to increasing order, to increasing "information", to increasing complexity. Yet that is what has apparently happened in human evolution. From extremely primitive living creatures we can trace the gradual ascent of humankind to its present state of extreme complexity – and perhaps, one day, to a level of even less entropy than we have currently attained.

Admittedly, the "fuel" for this evolutionary ascent is sunlight, so human life on this planet is an "open" system, dependent on energy inputs from elsewhere. Yet the "ascent of man" from microbes to Mozart, from sandworms to Shakespeare, has its unique features. Specifically, it has been a process of increasing organizational complexity.

If you drop your coffee cup on a hard surface, it shatters into many shards. They never reassemble into their previous state of higher complexity. Nor do lumps of clay spontaneously arrange themselves into beautiful sculptures. By contrast, human evolution has created increasing order out of earlier states that were more chaotic – in the sense of being more primitive, less ordered or "evolved".

Human evolution is therefore a natural anomaly. The fact that it is fuelled by solar energy is almost irrelevant, in the sense that a modern car might be fuelled by oil, or hydrogen cells, or steam power. Even so, cars can only become more efficient as a result of human designers and engineers. Spontaneous improvement does not normally happen in cars or in nature. Sea-squirts have hardly changed in 500-600 million years. They are perfectly adapted to their niche in the web of life. Sea-squirts have also never created a symphony, a sculpture or a sonnet.

The fact that our ancestors singled out human evolution as the subject of three of the major surviving Scandinavian religious poems is significant. Once again, we need to ask whether they addressed this issue as a result of a series of incredibly lucky guesses; or whether they were informed by the gods; or whether they were perhaps heirs to an earlier and technologically and scientifically advanced culture.

12

ODINIST COSMOLOGY

Everything goeth; everything returneth; eternally rolleth the wheel of existence. Everything dieth, everything blossometh forth again; eternally runneth the wheel of existence. Everything breaketh, everything is integrated anew; eternally buildeth itself the same house of existence. All things separate, all things again greet one another; eternally true to itself remaineth the ring of existence. Every moment beginneth existence, around every *Here* rolleth the ball *There*. The middle is everywhere. Crooked is the path of eternity.

- Friedrich Nietzsche, *Thus Spake Zarathustra*

Two conflicting concepts of the nature of time and space have competed for thousands of years. Modern science is at last on the verge of resolving the conflict one way or the other, and the ethical consequences may change the course of human development.

The Judeo-Christian myth of history is simple. In the beginning there was a god. He created "the heavens and the earth" out of nothing. In the end he will destroy everything and create a new, eternal, unchanging cosmological order that will be more to his liking. This picture of time is linear, with creation and "original sin" at one end, and the "last judgment" at the other.

Our Indo-European heathen ancestors, by contrast, believed in a universe of endlessly repeated cycles. Vedic tradition, for instance, conceives of "great cycles of Brahma" made up of 2,560,000 "mahayugas" of 12,000 years each. [35] Every cycle fits within another, larger one, and so the universe continues, endlessly renewing itself. The Classical pagan philosophers inherited this Indo-European cosmology of eternal recurrence, which is most familiar to us today from Empedocles, Heraclitus, Plato, Eudemos, Aristotle, and the Stoics. It is an idea that is central to all intellectually developed forms of paganism.

In every known ancient tradition there is also a *purpose* within the sequences of cycles. That purpose is embodied in the gods, who are seen as beings within nature, rather than its creators. Often, they strive against the forces of chaos to ensure that the initial Golden Age of each cycle will be higher than the one preceding it. The gods then try to ensure that the endlessly recurring cycles spiral constantly toward a future that happens to be more meaningful to us as humans.

This is the view of the earliest, least corrupted, written account of our native cosmology, the Sanskrit *Vedas*. It is also the view of the last, somewhat corrupted, written account, the Norse *Eddas*. In basic outline, the poetic or symbolic cosmological myths are often astonishingly similar. Thus, in the Vedic *Hymn of Man*, the Gods assemble our present world by dismembering the cosmic being Parusa. In the *Eddas* they assemble our world from parts of the cosmic being Ymir. In the *Vedas* the image of a great cow is often used as "a symbol of the inspiration implicit in the thought of the gods". [36] Snorri must have been familiar with some poem in which this image survived, judging by his confused introduction of the cow named Auðumla in *Gylfaginning*.

In neither tradition can the poets conceive any meaningful order before the gods emerged to structure our role in the universe. The Vedic *Creation Hymn*, for instance, reads in part: "There was neither non-existence nor existence then; there was neither the realm of space nor the sky which is beyond. What stirred? Where? In whose protection? Was there water, bottomlessly deep? ... There was neither death nor immortality then. There was no distinguishing sign of night nor of day... There was impulse beneath; there was giving-forth above. Who really knows? Who will here proclaim it? Whence was it produced? Whence is this creation? The gods came afterwards, with the creation of this universe. Who then knows whence it has arisen?"

The corresponding section of *Vǫluspá*, discussing the time before the Gods, is only three terse lines [37]:

[There] was no sand or sea, no surging waves,
Nowhere was there earth nor heaven above,
But a formless void and grass nowhere.

Although the most distant past is inconceivable, *Vǫluspá* presents the new beginning after Ragnarok as facilitating a higher stage of evolution, both of the Gods and of humanity:

I see Earth rising a second time
Out of the foam, fair and green ...
... Unsown acres shall harvests bear,
Evil be abolished, Baldur return
And Hropt's Hall with Hödur rebuild,
Wise gods.

In similar vein, the pagan Roman poet Virgil wrote:

Ours is the crowning era foretold in prophecy
Born of Time, a great new cycle of centuries
Begins, Justice returns to earth, the Golden Age ...

This heathen understanding of a guided unfolding of the universe toward a greater purpose was interrupted by the Judeo-Christian myth of time, in which god creates; god destroys; god re-creates; and his "new heaven and earth" constitute the end of history. The Judeo-Christian universe is static. Its laws are inflexible and unchanging, precisely because its god made them that way.

Scientific discovery was immensely hampered by the Christian authorities, but nevertheless it happened, accruing many martyrs along the way. By the 19th century, scientific circles saw the universe as something like an enormous clockwork mechanism. It didn't really need a Christian god to start it off, it was without obvious purpose, and it would probably eventually run down.

This mechanistic view was an essentially Christian concept, stressing linear rather than circular time, but with the supernatural Christian beliefs left out. Yet to some degree it was also a partial step back toward our ancestral beliefs. At least the notion of a capricious creator-god who stood outside nature was abolished. The path had been cleared for scientific investigation free of Judeo-Christian theology. Scientific thinkers, from Spencer and Haeckel to Rey [38], began to provide new evidence for the doctrine of eternal recurrence. Nietzsche considered it to be the fundamental issue of his philosophy, seeing it as "the way out of two thousand years of falsehood".

Our modern cosmological thinking may have developed much further by now were it not for the theory of the Big Bang. According to recent science, the universe began with an explosion about 15 billion years ago. Before that there was no space, no time, no matter, no energy – there was absolutely nothing. Then, suddenly, everything was created *ex nihilo*. Once established at the moment of the Big Bang, the laws of physics became immutable. This concept is a return to something like the Biblical creation story, with the Universe itself taking the place of the Judeo-Christian god.

The Big Bang theory could have had little respectability until some of St Augustine's ideas were revived in Einstein's theory of relativity, re-affirming the idea of a universe that came into being with time rather than in time. Einstein's ideas were in this sense the culmination of the Judeo-Christian cosmology. They reigned supreme, with a lot of over-promotion for the sake of ethno-politics, for much of the 20th century.

Quantum theory, with its discovery of over 200 types of subatomic particles which behave in surprising ways, has shattered the rigid determinism of the Einsteinian or Judeo-Christian universe. Desperate attempts to reconcile the conflicting relativity and quantum theories are now being made, without noticeable success.

Another sign of progress is the articulation of the *Strong Anthropic Principle*, which states that: "The Universe must have those properties which allow life to develop within it at some stage in its history." This implies that the universe has a grand purpose. As one author [39] explains:

"Suppose that for some reason the Strong Anthropic Principle is true and that intelligent life must come into existence at some stage in the Universe's history. But if it dies out at our stage of development, long before it has had any measurable non-quantum influence on the Universe in the large, it is hard to see why it *must* have come into existence in the first place." With acceptance of the Anthropic Principle, no barriers remain to either (a) a universe embodying purpose, similar to the pre-Christian European concept of Wyrd or Fate, or (b) a universe given purpose by the gods.

Despite all this progress, the Big Bang theory still remains the dominant cosmological model. Only a few scientists dare to question it. One was Fred Hoyle, the great English cosmologist. "The Universe didn't start," he said. "It's infinite." [40] According to Hoyle, the universe is eternal, with matter being continuously created at the centers of galaxies.

In 1996 a prominent Australian scientist challenged the Big Bang theory head-on, claiming that it is fundamentally flawed because it violates the first law of thermodynamics. The laser physicist Dr Len Hughes said: "You can bet that law is correct. Matter isn't being created or destroyed. Every particle is unstable, changing constantly and cyclically in obedience to that law". In his book, *Laser Cosmology* [41], Dr Hughes created a complete update of the cyclic universe of eternal recurrence – one that is infinite, without a creation point, constantly renewing itself through the birth and death of galaxies. To simplify, Dr Hughes believed that giant clouds of gas condense into galaxies. After about 10 billion years the new galaxies themselves begin to contract by gravity until the black holes at their core erupt into quasars. The quasars recycle matter back into huge gas clouds which will once again, in time, congeal to form new galaxies. Essentially, the universe is an eternal, self-perpetuating and self-sustaining system.

This theory is a return to the doctrine of eternal recurrence, by way of late 20th century physics. If Hughes was right, our ancestral heathen cosmology was also correct. The Judeo-Christian and Einsteinian cosmologies were therefore wrong. Hughes claimed that the evidence already available favors his theory, as against the Big Bang. He pointed out, for instance, that Big Bang cosmology cannot explain why there seems to be so little antimatter in the universe, despite Einsteinian theories that it should make up the bulk of the universe. According to Hughes, each galaxy must eventually contract to the point where the black hole at its core, where the theoretically "missing" antimatter has to exist, goes critical.

Hughes' work suggests that the old pagan doctrine of eternal recurrence may be proven when lasers can be built that are sufficiently powerful to study photons. According to the Big Bang theory, photons must be stable, while in Dr Hughes' theory they are as unstable as anything else in the universe. "I believe if we could isolate a photon from the surrounding universe, it would decay – into mass and other particles.

It would show that a cyclical universe is possible." He added: "They can call me crazy for the next 20 years, but when there are big enough lasers they'll change their tune." [42]

As Friedrich Nietzsche pointed out, if eternal recurrence is ever proven to be an objective fact, the ethical consequences are enormous. The fullness of life will again be recognized as both creation *and* destruction, joy *and* suffering, order *and* chaos – and as being beyond good and evil. Humankind will once again be seen to have absolute freedom, in contrast to the existentially meaningless automata to which we were reduced by the Judeo-Christian cosmology. Eternity will become the "Eternal Yea" – the ecstasy and rapture implied by Odin's name – rather than the endless and sterile subservience to a domineering god that Christianity envisages. And humankind will at last become a stage of evolution that exists *in order* to be surpassed, as prophesied in *Völuspá*.

13

THE ODINIST SOUL

Is it so terrible a thing to die?

- Virgil

As we have seen, modern science is only beginning to catch up with our ancestral understanding of human evolution (Chapter 11) and heathen cosmology (Chapter 12). Given the astonishing percipience of our ancestors, it is no longer acceptable to apply to their surviving beliefs the analytical language of some modern, supposed "expert". We are beyond the stage of "needing" the ideology of a Frazer, a Marx, an Eliade, a Derrida, a Freud, a Clunies-Ross, or anyone else, to illuminate our ancestral spirituality and religion. All that, say, a Dumézilian approach can achieve now is to submit one set of beliefs to the criteria of a wholly different set of assumptions – assumptions which have been formed, in large part, under Christian influence.

Instead, it is time to meet our ancestors face-to-face as it were, to try to understand their beliefs as they themselves would have understood them. To a large degree this task requires us to "unlearn" many of the assumptions of our recent cultural past. Those assumptions are influenced by our people's experience of Christianity. To try to understand Odinism in such terms would be as futile as trying to analyze the *Mona Lisa* according to Marxist ideas about the revolutionary potential of the proletariat, or to analyze the melody of *Auld Lang Syne* according to Julia Kristeva's ideas about feminism.

To remove the distortion, to try to see things as our ancestors saw them, is not easy. The "distorting lens" that hampers us is the lens of Christianity. While most Western societies are now post-Christian, secularized Christian concepts are still common. Perhaps this is nowhere as evident as in the concept of the human "soul" – sometimes described as a "ghost" in the "machine" of the body. For that reason the rest of this brief chapter will examine the very different Odinist view of the soul, mainly (at this stage) as expressed in late Germanic literature.

Most religions hold that individual life survives the death of the body. (Perhaps ancient Judaism is unique in identifying *sheol* merely as the grave, and discounting any after-life.) Yet modern Christian theology is increasingly shying away from the concept of the soul, largely due to increasing recognition that the idea owes more to Greek thinking than to Biblical revelation. It is appropriate that Christianity should begin to drop the very concept of a human soul. After all, Christians have always been very conflicted about the idea of continuity from one life to the next. For instance, souls in the Christian heaven have usually been depicted as incorporeal spirits, while those in the Christian hell have been described as undergoing bodily torments.

The Indo-European religious tradition, on the other hand, has highly developed concepts of life after death. The trouble is that, in the later periods, we cannot be certain of *exactly* what our ancestors believed. Only a few of our sacred texts have survived from that time, and that small proportion was sifted by Christians. Not a single one of the Norse texts has come down to us without Christians having played a role in its survival. Much has been lost, and much has been mutilated and confused. Unfortunately archaeology and folklore can only take us to a certain point – and not beyond it – in understanding our original ancestral beliefs.

This ignorance led an otherwise interesting scholar [43] M. I. Steblin-Kamenskij, to claim, comically, that in Germanic heathen belief: "After death, a man continued to exist either as a disembodied soul (named and imagined in various ways), or – and this is found most often – as a completely corporeal 'living corpse'; and his abode was Óðinn's palace Valhöll, or Hel, the kingdom of the dead (it is not clear where it was situated) or inside a mountain in which all his dead ancestors lived, or, if he had drowned, in the abode of Rán the sea goddess, or simply in his grave, or finally in one of his descendants in whom he continued to live." Likewise Johannes Brøndsted: "The various burial rites of the Vikings reveal just how vague and complex were their religious beliefs". [44]

It is possible to clear up much, although certainly not all, of this confusion. The first step is to acknowledge that our ancestors believed in life after death. There may be some apparent contradiction in surviving accounts of how this takes place, but within this tradition there is no evidence of a belief that personal identity ceases with bodily death.

Second, if we examine the sagas, we find not a single instance of fear of death. The warrior's last words are usually matter-of-fact and often laconic or grimly humorous. The people of the sagas had no concept of spiritual extinction, or of an afterworld of sadistic maltreatment similar to the Christian hell. (Nor had other branches of our family tree, which will become apparent in Chapter 14.)

Several words have survived that allow us to consider different aspects of how the soul was perceived.

One of these terms is the Old English *Æðm*, usually glossed as "vapor, breath", but which is related to the Sanskrit word *ātman* – "breath of life", used in roughly the way we say that a cat has nine lives.

Then there is Old English *Fæcce*, modern "fetch", meaning an apparition or double of a living person. People were and still are said to meet their fetch at momentous stages of their lives, or just before death. The fetch is clearly a semi-independent part of the soul, and has been viewed as the embodiment of all that we have ever been.

Closely related to the soul are two words from Old Norse, *Fylgja* and *Hamingja*. Both refer nowadays (in modern Icelandic) to aspects of human afterbirth, but both used to have separate spiritual meanings.

Even in modern Icelandic *fylgja* means "attendant spirit, guardian spirit". This is an aspect of the soul that accompanies people throughout their lives. It can take the form of a personal reserve of spiritual power, and can be used to attack one's enemies – as happened to Gunnar of Hlíðarendi. Before the fight at Knafahólar he was attacked in his dreams by a pack of wolves, the form taken by the *fylgjur* of his opponents.

Hamingja, which is also used in modern Icelandic, means "destiny, fortune, mana". We have trouble with this word in modern English because we have largely forgotten its original meaning. It can be seen as that aspect of the soul which commits us to the great task in this life for which every individual is incarnated.

Then there is the *Kynfylgja*, a part of the soul that has been conferred by one's family or ancestry. This word usually refers to family traits, but we get a sense of its earlier power in the Morris/Magnússon translation of *Volsunga Saga*: "I wot, by my fore-knowledge, and from the fetch of our kin [*kynfylgju*], that from this counsel will great evil fall on us ..." We can infer from this that there was an implicit belief in a racial component to the soul as well.

The Odinist soul, then, was seen in late Germanic heathen times as having many parts, or aspects, or dimensions. In life, as we have seen, different aspects of the soul did not have to be present in the same space. In some cases they couldn't be. There is no reason to assume this to be otherwise in the after-life, either.

Now, having glanced at some dimensions of the soul, it is time to return to the list of possible after-lives given by Steblin-Kamenskij and quoted above.

Much evidence survives of the belief that devotees of Óðinn who die heroic deaths will be his guests in Valhalla. The death-song of Ragnar Loðbrók exults in this certainty. So, too, does the poet of *Eiríksmál*.

In *Ynglinga Saga* it is further said that all those who are cremated with their possessions after death will also go to Óðinn. This need not be a contradiction. Óðinn is the god of warriors, but also of poets and intellectuals.

Is there room in Valhalla for women? The literary accounts hint at this idea, and archaeology seems to confirm it. Many Viking-age women had splendid burials of the sort associated with devotion to Óðinn, accompanied by rich grave goods. Several were also admired poets.

Other honorable women who die become guests of the radiant goddess Freya. Even suicides can expect to join her. For instance, when threatening to kill herself, Egil's daughter said: "I shall take no food until I sup with Freya".

It is also claimed in *Grímnismál* that half of the heroic slain go to the goddess Freya. This confuses academic scholars. For instance, Jens Peter Schødt tried to explain it by arguing that physical death is linked with fertility under Freya's care, while Odin links death and intellectual fruitfulness. This is only partly correct. After all, "intellectual fruitfulness" has little bearing on the after-life of the *einherjar* warriors.

Another destination for some souls is *hel*, a place, or state, which is similar to the heathen Greek Hades. The word *hel* is linked to the verb *hylja*, "to cover", and applies both to the place and to its female guardian. According to *Gylfaginning* the goddess Hel was given "authority over nine worlds, such that she has to administer board and lodging to those sent to her, and that is those who die of sickness or old age". Elsewhere we are told that wrong-doers are also looked after by Hel.

There are many points of comparison between Hel and the Greek goddess of the underworld, Persephone. Most significantly the story of the attempts to save Persephone from her fate echoes the doomed quest to release from Hel her most illustrious guest, Balder. Óðinn's son, the Shining God, Balder, will remain a guest of Hel until Ragnarok, after which he will return to rule a rejuvenated world. Since Balder did not "die" of sickness or old age, and was and is not a wrong-doer, we may have to assume that much information about the northern Hades has either become garbled or has not survived.

After-life within a burial mound is particularly associated with followers of the god Frey. Frey is said to live in *Alfheim*, and the burial mounds on which some saga characters confer with the dead are presumably portals to that world.

Living on in mountains, to which Steblin-Kamenskij referred, is often linked to followers of Thor. This is said to have been the case with Thorolf of Most. In *Eyrbyggja Saga* a shepherd sees the sacred mountain Holyfell, behind Thor's Ness, gaping open. Within, Thorolf was welcoming Thorstein and his crew with great rejoicing. We shouldn't be too literal here. Mountains are associated with Jotunheim, where Thor does so much of his work, and a local mountain might in certain circumstances be a portal allowing us to glimpse those who have found haven with their patron, Thor.

There is no uncontaminated evidence about what an after-life with Rán might involve. The whole concept is suspiciously poetic. Only an unlikely archaeological discovery could assist us here.

Nevertheless, even in the case of Rán, a clear pattern has emerged. The Odinist concept of the after-life involves people either going to their patron god or else following a course dictated by the *hamingja* part of their souls. There are two exceptions to this pattern.

First, those who have not been committed to the after-life appropriately, or whose *hamingja* has been thwarted, can return to haunt the living as harmful, powerful *draugar*. There are many examples of these in the surviving literature, together with tips on how to deal with them. Sometimes *draugar* can even be endearing. In *Eyrbyggja saga* the Hebridean woman Þórgunna comes back from the dead because a farming family refused to prepare a meal for the people carrying her corpse to its resting place. She shamed them by making the meal herself – in the nude, to spite those who hadn't stitched up her shroud properly.

The second exception is the idea of reincarnation. This is a constant across the Indo-European religious spectrum, and the fact that it is only lightly reflected in the surviving Germanic literature no doubt conveys the priorities of those Christians who chose to transmit it. Even so, two out of the three Helgi poems of the *Elder Edda* refer to the reincarnation of both the valkyries and their male lovers. Helgi and Sigrun, for example, are specifically said to have lived on this earth more than once.

The Christian king "Olaf the Holy" was descended from an earlier King Olaf. *Flateyjarbók* gives us a revealing impression of the thoughtful, enquiring Odinist belief in reincarnation, and its contrast in Christian fear of the concept. According to the source, Olaf's troop of bodyguards once rode past the burial mound of the elder Olaf, the ancestor of their king. One of the bodyguards asked, "Tell me, lord ... were you buried here?" Olaf replied that his soul "has never had two bodies, it cannot have them, either now or on the Resurrection Day". The Odinist persisted, saying that when Olaf had ridden by here in his previous life he was meant to have said such-and-such a thing. The narrative resumes: "And the king was much moved, and clapped spurs to his horse immediately, and fled from the place as swiftly as he might."

Other examples of belief in reincarnation can be teased out of the surviving Germanic literature, but there's little point. What has survived dovetails well enough with the surviving Classical and eastern versions of our original Indo-European religion, and in this broader context it is obvious that the fate of some soul-complexes is to be re-born.

Significantly, the aim of reincarnation in the eastern forms of our once-common faith was to acquire enough wisdom to avoid the need to be re-born. Perhaps the most touching reference to this concept in the surviving Germanic literature is found in the *Poetic Edda*, when Brynhild determines to be buried along with the dead Sigurd, and it is said:

Delay her not longer from dying,
That born again she never may be.

Some gaps still remain in our knowledge of the Odinist after-life, but the apparent confusion highlighted by academic scholars of late-Germanic texts has been largely dispelled. Generally speaking, the self-aware parts of the souls of our illustrious dead go to spend time with their patron gods and goddesses, or else with those gods and goddesses to whom they are destined. A very few are thwarted in this aim and become, at least for a while, *draugar*. Some go to *hel*, whose guardian goddess perhaps releases them with Balder after Ragnarok. Some are doomed to be reborn in this world, where lover will again find lover, and again suffer the tribulations of mortal existence. Of these, some can hope, like Brynhild, "that born again they never may be".

In this chapter we have looked at the Indo-European concept of the soul as it was recorded in the last extensive literature on the subject, that of the northern Germanic peoples. In the next chapter we will see that this account is consistent with the views of Classical pagan authors from the pre-Christian Mediterranean world. But first we need to mention another possible source of evidence, one which may be even more valuable than the poems Christians have permitted to survive.

In his book, *A New Science of Life*, [45] Rupert Sheldrake suggested that there may be "fields" in nature that science has not yet discovered. We are all familiar with the idea of a gravitational field. We make use of electro-magnetic fields every time we use our eyes, or operate electrical equipment, or turn on our radio and TV receivers. Quantum fields may be obscure to the average person, but equipment such as the electron microscope works because of their existence.

Sheldrake argued that everything in the universe is also affected by what he called "morphic" fields. These fields cause atoms, crystals, animals, insects, even planets and galaxies, to have their characteristic structure and behavior. The influence of morphic fields on current behavior he termed "morphic resonance". This involves tuning in to morphic fields, in much the same way as TV sets tune in to other fields that are equally invisible to us. Because of morphic resonance, a rat in a maze should learn a new task more rapidly if other rats elsewhere had previously learned the same task.

The publication of Sheldrake's *A New Science of Life* created a storm. The prestigious magazine *Nature* called it "a book fit for burning". Heavy language, bearing in mind that Dr Sheldrake was merely proposing theories that were scientifically testable. To its credit, *New Scientist* countered by offering a prize for experimental designs to test Sheldrake's ideas, as did various U.S. and European foundations.

The Presence of the Past [46], Sheldrake's next major work, described some of these experiments. One involved pairs of genuine and scrambled words in Persian script. After looking at these unfamiliar squiggles for ten seconds each, volunteers were asked to draw them. "In 75% of the pairs the real words were judged to be better reproduced than the false." The odds against this being a chance result were over 10,000 to 1. This suggests that, because of our ability to "tune in" to past habits, real words that have been read by millions of people are easier to perceive than non-words. Many other examples were given, for which conventional science has no explanation.

If Sheldrake's theories are correct, they affect Odinism in several ways. To start with, despite the destruction of most of our sacred texts, the morphic fields – or in more traditional terms, the cultural and spiritual resonances – of our ancestors' religion remain undiminished in our midst today. We should be just as able to enter them now as our ancestors ever were, and the religious behavior and spiritual development of a modern Odinist returning to the faith will therefore be stabilized and maintained by morphic resonance from previous members. If Sheldrake is right, this is true in the way that gravity and electro-magnetism are true.

Second, Sheldrake agrees with Jung that we can "tune in" to past members of our own race and culture more readily than to members of other races and cultures. The strength of morphic resonance depends on the degree of similarity. We can enter the religious fields of our own ancestors much more easily than we can, say, the beliefs of the ancient Chinese. But even more: our very ability to form religious concepts is a physical bequest from the beliefs and practices of our ancestors. For this we owe them more than mere respect. In our native religious traditions, the ancestors have always been honored in the same way as the gods. Thus, in the Icelandic *Harkonar saga goða,* we read of a ritual banquet. A sacred toast was drunk to Odin (for power and victory), then to Njorth and Frey (for good harvest and peace). "Then many men were accustomed to drink a solemn toast. Men drank also a toast to their kinsmen who were buried, and that was called a memorial toast (*minni*)."

If Sheldrake is correct, there are scientific grounds for believing that a religion that doesn't regard the ancestors with a reverence approaching worship can scarcely be true to itself. Reverence for our own ancestors is an integral part of Odinism (see Chapter 3). Sheldrake sees nature itself as organic, evolving, truly vital and alive, perhaps having its own evolutionary purpose. Odinists have always believed that nature is more like Sheldrake's conception than the static, created machine envisaged by the monotheists. The theory of morphic resonance is a contemporary scientific model of a world very similar to the one portrayed in the mythology of our ancestral faith. Both models imply that we can "tune in" to the thoughts of people from the past, and to our own ancestors more than to the ancestors of other peoples.

14

THE PAGAN AFTERLIFE

> It may be we shall reach the Happy Isles
> And see the great Achilles, whom we knew.
>
> — Alfred Lord Tennyson, *Ulysses*

To understand our ancestors' beliefs as well as we can, we must seek them out at a time before there was any possibility of contamination by later religions such as Christianity.

Most readers will be familiar with the name "Hades", which refers both to the Greek god of the underworld and to his realm, the land of the dead. The name means something like "the unseen". Hades' equivalent in Rome was Pluto, and in the Germanic North, the goddess Hel.

Perhaps the best known account of a visit to the realm beyond the grave occurs in Homer's *Odyssey* (probably written in the 8th century BCE). After the Trojan War, the Greek hero Odysseus visits the underworld and encounters the ghost of the mighty warrior Achilles. The dead hero is incorporeal and despondent, and he says:

> O shining Odysseus, never try to console me for dying. I would rather follow the plough as thrall to another man, one with no land allotted to him and not much to live on, than be a king over all the perished dead.

On this evidence alone, Hades would seem to be a dour and gloomy realm. Yet we must remember that Homer had no high regard for Achilles, great warrior though he was. The very opening of Homer's other masterpiece, *The Iliad*, is a curse:

> Wrath – sing, goddess, the accursed wrath of Achilles, son of Peleus, which placed countless sufferings on the Achaeans and hurled so many strong souls of heroes to Hades, but made their bodies the spoil of dogs …

In fact, and no doubt in keeping with Homer's sense of justice, Achilles is in a part of Hades known as the "Fields of Asphodel". There are other parts of the underworld. One is the "Elysian Fields", where the souls of the virtuous live in bliss. The poet Pindar (5th century BCE) gives us a glimpse of this world:

> And those that have three times kept to their oaths,
> Keeping their souls clean and pure,
> Never letting their hearts be defiled by the taint
> Of evil and injustice,
> And barbaric veniality,
> They are led by Zeus to the end:
> To the palace of Kronos,
> Where soothing breezes off the Ocean
> Breathe over the Isle of the Blessed:
> All around flowers are blazing with a
> Dazzling light:
> Some springing from the shining trees,
> Others nourished by the water from the sea:
> With circlets and garlands of flowers they
> Crown their heads …

Pindar adds that Achilles' mother, the goddess Thetis, eventually persuaded Zeus to allow the hero to pass on to Elysium. Perhaps Achilles had atoned for his fatal wrath.

A related concept, or maybe just a different version of the Elysian Fields, is the Garden of the Hesperides, a blissful island somewhere in the West, where three nymphs tend the apples of immortality. It is depicted as lush and beautiful by both Pliny and Plutarch, and is probably another name for the Happy Isles to which Tennyson's poem refers.

The surviving Greek accounts of the underworld are sketchy, but we are fortunate in that the greatest of Roman poets, Virgil, described it at some length in the sixth book of his masterpiece, the *Aeneid*, which was written in the reign of Augustus – and was read to the emperor by the poet. Since it is the most complete description of a visit to the underworld the rest of this chapter will follow the journey of Aeneas, a hero of the Trojan War, and his guide, a priestess of Apollo.

First, they pass through the "domiciles of Dis (i.e. Persephone), the bodiless regions". Here are the vile shapes of diseases, old age, death, agony, war, guilty joys and squalid indulgence.

From here they reach the dismal river Acheron, on the near bank of which a multitude of souls are pleading for the ferryman, Charon, to take them across. Aeneas learns that only those who have received proper funeral rites are given immediate transport; the rest must wait.

Charon is persuaded by the priestess to take the two of them across, in his ramshackle boat, to a dreary mud flat. They enter a cave, where they hear the wailing of children who died in infancy, of people who had been executed on false charges, of suicides, and of those who died of a broken heart. They are waiting for their cases to be heard by a jury of the dead.

One of these is Queen Dido, Aeneas' former lover, whose ghost turns away from him in hatred.

Weeping tears of compassion for Dido, Aeneas and his companion move on to a place inhabited by the shades of dead warriors, some of whom had fought against him at Troy. He talks with an old comrade, Deiphobous, the son of Troy's King Priam.

They arrive below the battlements of Dis. From a track they do not take they hear groaning and the sounds of torture. The priestess explains that here the guilty who escaped detection in life are forced to confess.

Next they encounter the torture of Titans who had opposed the rule of the gods, also of traitors, adulterers, children who had struck their own parents, parents who had defrauded their children, child molesters and other abominable souls. Most numerous of all are misers who gave none of their wealth to their own kindred. These souls are learning justice.

The travelers pass through the gate of Proserpine's castle and enter a blessed and beautiful land. The souls of the good, the kind, the pure, the truly brave are here. Some are exercising on the grassy fields, some dancing, some playing music, some reciting poetry, some tending their chariots and horses. Here also is the ghost of Aeneas's father, Anchises, who asks about the life of his heroic son.

Aeneas spies a multitude of souls in a beautiful river valley. Anchises tells him that this is the river Lethe, where souls destined for reincarnation must drink to forget their past lives. Aeneas is amazed that anyone would wish to live on earth again, rather than remain in such a beautiful realm. Anchises explains that they *must* return, for their souls are not yet pure enough to dwell in the Elysian Fields. He shows Aeneas the spirit of a young man who is destined to be reborn as Aeneas' own son, Silvius. Anchises shows Aeneas other glorious shades who will play heroic roles in Rome's future greatness, then he escorts his son and the priestess back toward the land of the living.

This brief summary cannot even hint at the beauty of Virgil's poetry, nor suggest the compassion it evokes for the souls who must face other destinies before they may reach, or return to, the Fields of Elysium. Readers should at least be aware that these are the views of the afterlife held by the greatest of Roman writers. Essentially, after death each soul experiences whatever is required in order for it to proceed to a higher level. Even from this brief account, it should be obvious that the Classical pagan view of the afterlife differed greatly from the Christian view that was soon to prevail. The earlier vision stresses atonement, expiation, eventual redemption and renewal, and growth. The later one emphasizes eternal punishment and agony.

In the next chapter we will look at some of the significant ways in which pagan and Christian views were so diametrically opposed that no reconciliation was possible.

15

THE CLASH OF VALUES

The Greek, as well as the Roman, was self-controlled. This with the Greek meant a self-proportionment akin to his artistic love of beauty in the visible world and in the world of the spirit. His life should be fair and good, beautifully proportioned, each element cherished at its due worth. He would seek nothing excessively, nor anything excessive (μηδεν άγαν), he would observe the glorious and beauty-giving principles of άίδώς, shamed at all things shameful, reverence for all things to be revered; thus rightly distinguishing between what to fear and what not to fear. So might his life and his life's close be beautified by fame.

- Henry O. Taylor, *The Classical Heritage of the Middle Ages*

[The Christian] dependence of reason upon the dictates of faith is central to the whole of medieval thinking. It meant that there was an ultimate yardstick by which to judge the validity of an argument. However impeccable its reasoning might be, it had to conform to the tenets of revelation. Thus to deny God's existence, or the creation of the world, or the necessity of grace, was to fly in the face of Christian authority; it was to make philosophical error into heresy.

- Gordon Leff, *Medieval Thought: St Augustine to Ockham*

Both Classical pagans and Germanic heathens believed that the standard for right conduct could be found within, aided by contemplation of the virtues of great men and women who have gone before. The Christian, though, was not at all self-reliant. To him, the ultimate pattern for human life was laid down in the Bible. The rules imposed on mankind by the Christian god, as stated in the Bible, were to be followed without question. Even Jesus himself taught that he was the messianic fulfillment of "Scripture" (here meaning the Old Testament).

It followed that Christian conduct had to be "scriptural", which the *Oxford Dictionary* defines as: "Founded on, reconcilable with, laying stress on, appealing to, doctrines contained in the Bible." Therefore the individual human must accept the Bible as the ultimate source of knowledge and wisdom. Truth is that which has been "revealed" as truth, and the final "authority" is the Bible in which that "truth" was revealed. The purpose of Christian philosophy was therefore not to understand the world around us, but to explain the supposed truths of revelation. As St Anselm was to write, addressing himself to his god: "I desire in some measure to understand thy truth, which my heart already believes and loves. And indeed I do believe it, for unless I believe, I shall not understand". St Anselm summed up his own method of enquiry in the motto: *Fides quaerens intellectum*: "faith seeking to understand". He was not alone: St Augustine had quoted from the Septuagint version of *Isaiah* 8:9: "unless ye believe, ye shall not understand". It follows that any attempt to explain or measure the natural world that did not begin with the Christian revelation was on shaky ground, and any such attempt which reached a different conclusion to the self-proclaimed "truths" of the Bible must be false.

By contrast, the pagans had always been particularly interested in science and technology. Unlike the later Christians they were aware that the earth was spherical, and in about 240 BCE the head of the great library at Alexandria, Eratosthenes, calculated the earth's circumference to be the equivalent of 39,690 kilometers. 2,250 years after Eratosthenes, modern science tells us that earth's average circumference is 40,008 km. With similar accuracy, Eratosthenes also seems to have calculated the tilt of the earth's axis.

In pre-Christian times scientific knowledge of this kind was so common in the Classical world that analog computers were built to make astronomical computations easier. Cicero described one that that had supposedly been made by Archimedes and brought to Rome. A highly sophisticated example was found in 1901, salvaged from an ancient (perhaps 70 BCE) shipwreck off the island of Antikythera. [47] This is a geared device which a non-specialist might find comparable to the intricate mechanism of a 19th century clock. Nothing as advanced in workmanship was produced for at least a thousand years after the introduction of Christianity.

Since Christianity emphasized above all other things obedience to the will of an arbitrary and ultimately incomprehensible god, the Christian self required utter humbling. Human ingenuity became, at best, a source of unrighteous pride; at worst, a sinful rebellion against Scripture. The doctrine of Original Sin pandered to this Christian sense of worthlessness: humankind itself was born in sin, and could only be redeemed by a divine scapegoat, Jesus. All humans were miserable sinners. Nothing less than the sacrifice of Jesus could "redeem" us.

It is hard to imagine anything more different from the pagan conception of human nature. To illustrate this in the briefest way, consider the biography of the Roman legislator Poplicola by Plutarch, himself a priest of Apollo. Plutarch says that Poplicola's death: "did not only draw tears from his friends and acquaintance, but was the object of universal regret and sorrow through the whole city; the women deplored his loss as that of a son, brother, or common father." Poplicola, in short, seems to have been mourned almost as much as the god Balder, for whom all nature wept. What were the qualities that made him so revered? Here are some of the terms Plutarch uses approvingly in his account of Poplicola: "merit", "noble", "eloquence", "charitably", "liberal", "integrity", "freedom", "justice" – and these are only in Plutarch's first paragraph! In his conclusion he adds: "the greatness of his virtue", "The fountain of ... honor", "justly", "nobly", "doing good to the distressed", "happiest", "aversion to tyranny", "victorious", "courage and resolution", "peaceable language", "reconciliation", "friendship", "wise". These are some of the pagan virtues that made Poplicola the "most eminent amongst the Romans". Readers of this book could profitably study Plutarch's entire essay and compare it with the Christian view of miserable human nature.

The Christian doctrine of Original Sin insists that all humans have inherited sin through our descent, by way of sexual propagation, from the first sinner, a woman called Eve. That is why, in Christian mythology, Mary the mother of Jesus had to be a virgin. (As St Augustine explained, if Mary had conceived in the human way, she would not have been sinless.) This doctrine led to two direct consequences. First, sexuality itself was pathologized as sinful. Second, women, as the objects of men's sexual desire, were regarded as inferior, a means of arousing sin.

Throughout the New Testament sexuality is condemned, but it is hard to imagine how low the sexual act stood in the eyes of the later Church. We will allow Joachim Kahl, a former Protestant priest, to summarize:

> Sexual intercourse was forbidden on Sundays, Wednesdays and Fridays, which amounted to almost half the year. In addition to this, it was prohibited during the forty days of Lent and forty days before Christmas. In case this was not enough, it was also forbidden for three days before receiving communion. What's more, even the position of love-making was prescribed and the Church laid down punishments for anyone who wished to vary this official position. The sexual act had to be performed as quickly and as uninterestingly as possible. Long, heavy night clothes with an opening at the requisite place were worn, so that the husband could fertilize his wife without it being necessary or even possible to touch her too closely. If a man had an involuntary nocturnal emission, he knew that he had committed a sin and had to get up at once and recite seven penitential psalms. The next morning he had to recite another thirty. [48]

It is obvious that any man with a healthy body who believed in these views would have been tormented by recurring feelings of guilt and sinfulness, and fear of eternal damnation. His very identity as a member of the species *homo sapiens*, a mammal that reproduces by sexual means, was rendered a cause for despair. There was, however, one creature even lower than man in the Christian view: woman.

The Germanic heathen attitude to women is summed up by the Roman historian Tacitus in his book *Germania*:

> It stands on record that armies already wavering and on the point of collapse have been rallied by the women, pleading heroically with their men, thrusting forward their bared bosoms, and making them realize the imminent prospect of enslavement – a fate which the Germans fear more desperately for their women than for themselves. Indeed, you can secure a surer hold on these nations if you compel them to include among a consignment of hostages some girls of noble family. More than this, they believe that there resides in women an element of holiness and a gift of prophecy; and so they do not scorn to ask their advice, or lightly disregard their replies. In the reign of the emperor Vespasian we saw Veleda long honored by many Germans as a divinity; and even earlier they showed a similar reverence for Aurinia and a number of others – a reverence untainted by servile flattery or any pretence of turning women into goddesses. [49]

Women in most Indo-European traditions could also be revered priestesses. Even in the war-filled Viking period, the people buried with honor in the most beautiful of all known Viking ships, Oseberg, are thought to have been Odinist priestesses. (See Chapter 26.) In the most martial state of Ancient Greece, Sparta, women were so powerful that critics referred to Sparta as a "gynocracy", a state ruled by women.

Christianity took the opposite view of women. Jesus himself did not have even one token woman among his disciples. He was so hostile to women that he was full of praise for the sexlessness of eunuchs, whether they had been born that way, or had been castrated (Matthew 19, 11-12). St Paul followed his leader. In his first letter to Timothy (2, 11), Paul wrote: "Let a woman learn in silence with all submissiveness. I permit no woman to teach or to have authority over men; she is to keep silent. For Adam was formed first, then Eve; and Adam was not deceived, but the woman was deceived and became a transgressor." Tertullion, the Bishop of Carthage, called woman "the gate through which the devil enters". St Chrysostom called her "a necessary evil, a natural temptation, a desirable calamity, a domestic peril, a deadly fascination, and a painted ill!" Yet again, here is St Jerome, author/translator of the Vulgate Bible, echoing Tertullion: "Woman is the gate of the devil, the way of evil, the sting of the scorpion, in a word, a dangerous thing." St Gregory, Bishop of Tours, wrote of a church synod that debated whether women were human. St Thomas Aquinas settled that by defaming woman as a "failed man" –

femina est mas occasionatus – which, despite recent attempts to rehabilitate Aquinas, summed up the Christian attitude for centuries.

Throughout the different versions of the Indo-European religion, one thing is common: they all honor a goddess embodying, signifying, representing, or concerned with the enduring health of the earth itself. This goddess is usually associated with other related functions, such as eternal energy, renewal, life and rebirth. She is fundamental to most of our ancestral pagan traditions. The *Rig Veda* calls her Mahimata, which means "Mother Earth". To the Hittites she was Hebat. In the ancient Greek world she was Gaia ("Earth"), and Rhea ("Ground"). In Rome she was Magna Dea ("Great Goddess"), Venus Genetrix ("Mother Venus"), Magna Mater ("Great Mother"). Two of her manifestations were Juno and Minerva. In the Celtic tradition she was Dana or Danu, and this Celtic form of the goddess may have bestowed her name on the Russian rivers Don, Dniester and Dnieper.

In the Germanic North, according to Tacitus, she was Nerthus. In describing the Germanic tribes of his day Tacitus wrote: "After the Langobardi come the Reudigni, Auiones, Angli [= Angles], Varni, Eudoses, Suarines and Nuithones, all well guarded by rivers and forests. There is nothing remarkable about any of these tribes unless it be the common worship of Nerthus, that is Earth Mother." According to Grimm [50] other names for Nerthus include Erda, Erce, Fra Gaue, Fjörgynn, Frau Holda and Hulodana. Another name for her is Hertha, under which title we will encounter her again in Chapter 31. Three of her northern manifestations may have been Jörð and the two goddesses best rendered into modern English as Frige and Freya.

In all of these forms and manifestations, it is clear that the Earth Mother required respect and reverence for the planet on which we live. Christianity had no such reverence for the earth, or for the earth goddess. After creating the original couple, Adam and Eve, the first thing the Christian god said to them (Genesis, 1, 28-30) was this:

> Be fruitful, and multiply, and replenish the earth, and subdue it: and have dominion over the fish of the sea, and over the fowl of the air, and over every living thing that moveth upon the earth.
>
> And God said, Behold, I have given you every herb bearing seed, which is upon the face of all the earth, and every tree, in which is the fruit of a tree yielding seed; to you it shall be for meat.

Therefore the Christian attitude is that humanity is ordained by its god to be the dominant species, and to subdue the earth, and to have dominion over it. There is no concept of an Earth Mother in Christianity, nor any notion that the earth itself is sacred or deserves reverence.

We have seen (Chapter 3) that ancestor worship is common to all forms of the Indo-European religious tradition. To use a 19th century term, this tradition is "folkish", in the sense that it is confined to our own people, our own "folk" or in a broad sense, race. We do not worship the ancestors of other races, and we would not ask them to worship ours.

Christianity, by contrast, has always been universalist. It seeks the conversion of all peoples to its beliefs. When St Paul wrote to the Colossians that Jesus was the fulfillment of creation, he added that Christians "have put on the new man, which is renewed in knowledge after the image of him that created him: Where there is neither Greek nor Jew, circumcision nor uncircumcision, Barbarian, Scythian, bond nor free: but Christ is all, and in all." (Colossians, 3, 10-11)

For this reason, Christians have always sought to convert non-believers. That is why "missionaries" have, since very early Christian times, travelled to distant countries to try to bring them to what they regard as the only possible "salvation", belief in Jesus. (We shall learn more about some of these missionaries in Chapter 19.) Since heathens do not believe in Original Sin, we do not believe that anyone needs to be saved from it. Hence, there are no historical examples of heathens sending "missionaries" to convert Christians – or anyone else.

As long as Christian missionaries behaved themselves, their proselytizing was tolerated in heathen lands. For just one instance, in 849 CE Archbishop Ansgar of Hamburg was allowed to build a church at Hedeby, a major trading city in Odinist Denmark. The general heathen attitude was that people are free to choose their own religion, or to favor their own gods, as long as no-one else is harmed in the process.

Polytheistic tolerance contrasted strongly with Christian intolerance, and Christian intolerance was firmly rooted in the sayings attributed to Jesus. For instance, in his parable of the "sheep and the goats" (Matthew 25, 31-46), Jesus threatens that soon he (Jesus) "shall come in his glory, and all the holy angels with him". Then those who had been favorable to Jesus will be "blessed of my Father", while those who had not done so will be told: "Depart from me, ye cursed, into everlasting fire, prepared for the devil and his angels." "And these [non-Christians] shall go away into everlasting punishment: but the righteous [Christians] into life eternal." In 1 Timothy 16, 22, St Paul wrote: "If anyone love not the Lord Jesus Christ, let him be Anathema Maranatha [i.e. accursed]."

Essentially, Christians regarded all non-Christians as sub-humans, and the very virtues that pagan Romans most admired were denied to them in Christian propaganda. Thus, St Paul's hate-filled letter to "all that be in Rome" curses the pagans in these terms (Romans 1, 28-32):

> And even as they did not like to retain God in their knowledge, God gave them over to a reprobate mind, to do those things which are not convenient; Being filled with all unrighteousness, fornication, wickedness, maliciousness; full of envy, murder, debate, deceit, malignity; whisperers, backbiters, haters of God,

despiteful, proud, boasters, inventors of evil things, disobedient to parents, without understanding, covenantbreakers, without natural affection, implacable, unmerciful: Who knowing the judgment of God, that they which commit such things are worthy of death, not only do the same, but have pleasure in them that do them.

Pagans were thus accused of all the crimes or sins that litter the Old Testament, a gory text which was supposed to be "fulfilled" by the incarnation of Jesus. Their own pagan virtues were systematically and specifically denied them, and they were declared to be "worthy of death".

Summing up, we can see a series of diametrical oppositions between the Christian and the pagan viewpoints. The most fundamental of these are, in no particular order:

* Biblical rules, *as opposed to* moral self-reliance
* Revelation/authority *as opposed to* science/technology
* Slavish adoration of "God" *as opposed to* human dignity and morality
* Denigration of sex and women *as opposed to* acceptance of natural sex and the moral equality of women
* Dominion over nature *as opposed to* respect for nature
* Universalism *as opposed to* ancestor-worship/folkish values
* Intolerance *as opposed to* heathen tolerance
* A fixed afterlife *as opposed to* spiritual progression through reincarnation
* Damnation/salvation *as opposed to* the Indo-European ideas of destiny, wyrd, *amor fati* or *karma*

It should be noted that all of the Christian positions above imply a dualistic mentality, whereas the pagan viewpoints do not. From a pagan perspective, the Christian positions usually involve a form of false dichotomy – an either/or fallacy, when in fact there may be more than two possibilities. To take some of these in turn, a Christian either follows Biblical rules or she sinfully breaks them. She believes that the Bible is "true" in an absolute sense, whereas pagans believe the quest for truth is ongoing and subject to revision. The Christian mentality must adore the Semitic god or else his opposite, Satan; while heathens, who believe in neither Yahweh nor Lucifer, believe that humans can achieve their potential with or without the active help of the gods. To the Christian, men and women are opposed, with women being the cause of sin, while to a pagan men and women are complementary. To a Christian, humanity is opposed to nature, whereas a pagan sees humans and indeed the gods as part of nature. The Christian believes that people of other religious paths are ignorant, deceived, or actively sinful, while the pagan does not condemn other paths as long as they reciprocate tolerance and respect.

And so on. In a very important sense, then, Christian dualism is fundamentally opposed to pagan openness.

The reader who has reached this page is invited to consider the contrasting pairs above. Do you respect the qualities that Plutarch attributed to Poplicola? Do you accept the science and geometry behind what the Greek branch of our ancestors knew about the earth? Do you believe that human ingenuity can improve our lives? Do you believe that women are equal in value to men? Do you believe we should respect nature, of which we are a part? Do you revere your ancestors? Do you believe in tolerating the deities and followers of other religions as long as they extend the same respect to us? Do you believe in reincarnation? Do you think that we can improve our spiritual progress by good deeds and acts? If so, you are well on the way to becoming an Odinist.

On the other hand, perhaps you believe that humans thrive best if they follow the "Ten Commandments" of the Bible. Or that the earth is flat, despite the arguments of Eratosthenes and modern scientists. (Or equally, that it was created in the morning of October 3rd, 4004 BCE, as determined by Bishop Ussher, rather than billions of years ago.) Or that the highest destiny of humanity is to worship a god who was first heard of in the deserts of the Middle East. Or that women are inferior to men. Or that we humans as a species have every God-given right to destroy our planet. Or that the ancestors of unrelated people are just as important to us as our own. Or that everyone who doesn't believe in your own god should be converted, on pain of death. Or that once we're dead, that's it – until some future once-only resurrection. Or that "sinners" will be and should be tortured for all eternity, while the "righteous" can take pleasure in looking down from "heaven" and gloating over their torments. If so, you are not yet ready to be an Odinist.

Whichever way the reader may lean regarding these views, it is obvious that they are incompatible. That is so today, and so it was in the days of the Roman Empire. A clash could not be avoided.

16

THE RISE OF INTOLERANCE

The traditional Roman attitude to foreign cults was essentially tolerant, as any polytheistic belief should be, but it required a degree of reciprocity, and this it could naturally not gain from any people holding a monotheistic faith.

- H. H. Scullard, *From the Gracchi to Nero: a history of Rome from 133 BC to AD 68*

Given the fundamental differences between the two religions, it was inevitable that Christianity and our own ancestral faith would come into conflict. Since Christianity could brook no criticism, it was also inevitable that the conflict would be violent, brutal, and one-sided.

We have seen that Christianity's initial appeal was to Rome's enormous numbers of slaves of alien origin and their descendants (Chapters 6 & 10). It gave them a surrogate sense of spiritual self-worth, which compensated to some degree for the contempt in which they were held by Rome's educated aristocracy.

After many generations, a few real Romans began to pay attention to this new creed of the slaves. The first Christian known to have access to the imperial family was Victor, a bishop of Rome (189-199 CE), later known as Saint Victor. He had the ear of Marcia, a mistress of the Emperor Commodus. The latter was the utterly unworthy son of a pagan philosopher-king, Marcus Aurelius. The degenerate Commodus was unsuccessfully poisoned by his Christian Marcia, then successfully strangled by a wrestler friend of hers, on the last day of 192 CE.

As the slave-descended population of Rome grew, so did Christianity – and so did Christian demands upon the state of Rome. The emperors Maximin, Decius and especially Diocletian (who abdicated in 305 CE as a result of ill health) resorted to persecuting the Christians. Persecution did not dissuade them. In the year 324 an obscure provincial now known as Saint Constantine ascended the throne after a series of civil wars. He had originally claimed the throne in 306, but it took him 18 years to gain sole possession. He presumably needed as much support as he could get, particularly from the numerically dominant "Roman" mob. By the year 313 all penal edicts against Christians had been rescinded. By 333, the remaining Roman officers were ordered to enforce the wishes of Christian bishops. Rome was being surrendered to its majority of non-Roman Christians, and even the imperial property of the Lateran was donated by Constantine to the Pope.

Constantine moved the capital of the Roman Empire to Constantinople (also known as Byzantium, today's Istanbul). In 361 his nephew Julian ("Julian the Philosopher") became sole emperor of what remained of Rome. Julian had been brought up as a Christian, but rejected this upbringing and sought to restore the faith of his Roman ancestors. Unfortunately for his and their cause, he fell in battle against the Persians in 363. According to his friend and fellow-philosopher, Libanius, he was assassinated by a Christian soldier. Julian was the last pagan emperor of Rome. In 390, under Theodosius, pagan worship became a civil crime.

That is the background to the rest of this chapter, in which we look at the fate of one of our best-loved heathen martyrs. In the next chapter we give a brief history of the Christian conquest of Europe. Then we look at the methods used by the Christians to force our ancestors to "convert".

Hypatia was the leading mathematician, scientist and philosopher of 5th century Alexandria, which was in those days the greatest centre of learning and scholarship in the world. She was also a leading heathen who was murdered by a Christian mob driven to madness because they could not tolerate her pre-eminence.

Hypatia was born shortly before 380 CE, the date when Christianity became the official religion of Rome. Christianity may have been the state code, but it was still vying with the heathen tradition for dominance. The heathens assumed that their intellectual superiority would prevail. They saw Christianity as an absurd and vulgar faith, little more than a subversive ideology for the descendants of slaves – Christians were *hostes humani generis*, "the enemy of all [noble] mankind". The Christians, for their part, were intent on the destruction of everything that was outside their religion.

After studying under her father Theon, Hypatia attended the university at Athens, where she was awarded a laurel wreath – similar to those that were bestowed on elite athletes. On her return to Alexandria, Hypatia wore this wreath whenever she lectured in public, much as a modern military hero might wear medals on formal occasions. She was soon elected president of the university at Alexandria, a brave honor to bestow on a woman in those darkening days.

Among the educated people of the best-educated city in the Classical world, Hypatia was regarded as their foremost citizen. It has been said that: "When she appeared in her chariot on the streets people threw flowers at her, applauded her gifts, and cried, 'Long live the daughter of Theon.' Poets called her the 'Virgin of Heaven,' 'the spotless star,' 'of highest speech the flower'." [51]

She was also regarded as the most beautiful woman of her era; but even sex-obsessed Christians recognized that she was also chaste and moral. A heathen female philosopher of renowned genius was too much for the leader of the Christians in Alexandria, an archbishop named Cyril (who has since been canonized by the Church). He decided that Hypatia would have to be destroyed, just as the Christian followers of his uncle Theophilus had already torn down the magnificent temple of Serapis, which also housed the great Library of Alexandria.

On a spring morning in 415 Cyril goaded a ragged mob including 500 half-starved Christian monks to deal with the beautiful heathen philosopher. The fanatics dragged her from her chariot, then hauled her by the hair into a Christian church. There they insisted that she should kiss a cross. Hypatia refused. The Christians ripped off her clothes, then killed her by scraping off her flesh, probably with sharp oyster-shells.

> The marble floor of the church was sprinkled with her warm blood. The altar, the cross, too, were bespattered, owing to the violence with which her limbs were torn, while the hands of the monks presented a sight too revolting to describe. The mutilated body, upon which the murderers feasted their fanatic hate, was then flung into the flames.

The Classical heathen world can be thought of as symbolically collapsing with the hideous death of one of our most brilliant jewels, Hypatia the Martyr. In the coming centuries Christian views derived from the Bible were to prevail, and that period is known today as the Dark Ages.

Yet the Christians were not the only ones to blame. Perhaps the last stage of the descent into barbarism came in 642, when the Muslim Caliph Omar conquered Alexandria. The great Library had been partially restored since the Christians destroyed nearly all its original books in 389. Omar decreed that any books contradicting the Koran must be false and should therefore be burned. Furthermore, any books that agreed with the Koran were unnecessary and should also be burned. "The manuscripts were used to stoke the furnaces which heated the public baths and Greek mathematics went up in smoke." [52]

17

HEATHEN VICTIMS OF CHRISTIANITY

Whatever is sacred to us is profane to them; again, they allow what we think impure
— Tacitus, *Histories* v.4

Christian apologists have complained a lot about the persecutions they sometimes suffered in ancient Rome. Given that the Christians were trying to destroy the heathen spiritual values that had made Rome great in the first place, it is not surprising that the pagans eventually defended themselves. What those same Christian apologists seldom remember is the very real persecution Christians inflicted, as soon as they could, on pagans and heathens who chose to retain the faith of their forebears.

The purpose of this chapter is not to criticize Christianity, or to condemn the atrocities committed by Christians. It is rather to provide a general overview, and for reference purposes a brief timescale showing how Christianity acquired its dominance, particularly in the north of Europe. This is essential if we are to understand the tensions that gripped Europe during the Period of Dual Faith (see Chapter 25 ff).

Christianity became legal in the Roman Empire in 313 CE, during the reign of Constantine. Paganism was not made illegal in this year, nor was Christianity made the official religion of Rome. Nevertheless, from 313 on, Pagan temples were increasingly destroyed by Christian mobs. Some famous temples that were ruined in this way include the Sanctuary of Æsculapius, the Temple of Aphrodite in Lebanon, the Heliopolis, and the Temple of Serapis in Egypt. There were many others. Christian priests such as Cyril of Heliopolis and Mark of Arethusa became renowned as "temple destroyers", which was regarded as a term of praise. Pagan priests were increasingly murdered, together with their congregations.

In 384 pagan services became punishable by death. In 391 the Christian Emperor Theodosius decreed that "no-one is to go to the sanctuaries, walk through the temples, or raise his eyes to statues created by the labor of man". Since pagans could not legally visit their temples, the temples were declared to be "abandoned" and under this pretext their sites were seized for Christian churches. Theodosius even murdered children caught playing with the remains of heathen statues.

In about 550 Germanic heathen beliefs were outlawed in the Frankish kingdom. All heathen temples and symbols were ordered to be destroyed. Heathen songs, dances and holidays were forbidden.

In 719, Frankish Christian missionaries ravaged heathen Frisia with fire and sword.

In 774 the Frankish emperor Charlemagne vowed to convert the continental Saxons, or, failing that, to wipe them out. In 780 Charlemagne decreed the death penalty for all who failed to be baptized, who failed to keep Christian festivals, who cremated their dead, who were hostile toward Christians, etc. In 782, on Charlemagne's orders, 4,500 Saxon nobles were beheaded in one day at Verden on the Aller. Their "crime" was that they had refused to convert to Christianity. In 804 the last heathen resistance in Saxony was put down. In thirty years of genocide, from 774 to 804, probably two thirds of the Saxons had been killed. (We will look closer at this in Chapter 19.)

In 597 CE the Augustinian mission arrived in Kent, England. Its aim was to convert heathen kings, who would then force the new religion on their followers. What followed was often confusing, since kings seldom lived to a great age at that time, and their successors often repudiated the alien faith. However, some significant dates can be recorded here.

In 616, Æthelfrith, king of heathen Northumbria, defeated a huge multinational Christian crusade against the Northumbrians at Chester. In 617 Æthelfrith was slain at battle of River Idle. His neurotic rival Edwin became king and was subsequently converted to Christianity, forcing his subjects to give up their old faith. (See Chapter 18.)

In 653, King Sigibert foisted Christianity on heathen Essex.

In 654, King Penda of Mercia, the last great heathen Anglo-Saxon monarch, was slain by Christians at the battle of Winwæd. Only Sussex and the Isle of Wight held out (until perhaps 686) against Christianity.

From the late 8th century onwards, heathen Scandinavians settled in all parts of the British Isles. They were particularly prominent in eastern and north-eastern England, in northern and western Scotland, and in the cities they founded in Ireland.

From 1066 onwards, William the Conqueror was still passing laws against Odinism. Its last redoubt, in practice if not in theory, was the Border counties which formed a buffer between England and Scotland. (See Chapter 23.) In 1603 King James VI of Scotland became also James I of England. He crushed the Borderers and destroyed their culture.

In 994, Olaf Tryggvason of Norway adopted Christianity after taking a vast bribe from the English. Through a brutal campaign that tolerated no opposition he "converted" Norway to Christianity. With Norway fell Shetland, the Orkneys and the Faeroes. (See Chapter 21.)

In c.1000 Olaf held prominent Icelandic Odinists hostage in Norway, demanding that Iceland accept the new religion. Iceland had no choice but to capitulate. (See Chapter 22.) On the death of Olaf Tryggvason, Norway returned gladly to paganism. However, in 1016 another Olaf,

Olaf the Stout, later called Saint Olaf, seized the throne of Norway. He murdered, blinded and maimed heathens who upheld the faith of their ancestors. Heathen temples were ruthlessly robbed and destroyed.

In 829 Bishop Ansgar obtained permission from the heathen King Björn of Sweden to build a church at Birka. This ultimately led to three hundred years of religious warfare. Some time in the twelfth century the great Odinist temple at Uppsala was destroyed by Christians.

It is impossible to estimate the numbers of Eastern Europeans killed by crusading Christians. The Teutonic Knights, for instance, conquered heathen Prussia in 1226. All Prussians who refused to convert to Christianity were murdered. The Lithuanians were another heathen nation attacked by the Teutonic Knights throughout the 13th century. They held out successfully, with the help of religious refugees from Prussia and Lettonia, until a monarchy emerged. King Mindaugas betrayed the ancestral religion of his subjects in 1251, after which Lithuania was forcibly converted to Christianity.

It is equally impossible to estimate the numbers of pagans murdered in the New World. Columbus planted a cross wherever he went, vowing to "do all the mischief that we can" to natives who refused to convert. The Christians brought with them skills of torture that had been refined on their own people in Europe for hundreds of years. One Indian chief, Hatuey, was burned alive. "(As) they were tying him to the stake a Franciscan friar urged him to take Jesus to his heart so that his soul might go to heaven, rather than descend into hell. Hatuey replied that if heaven was where the Christians went, he would rather go to hell." [53]

Hatuey's attitude is mentioned here simply because it must have been expressed time after time in Europe in the period when Odinists were forced to convert to Christianity or else be tortured, maimed and killed. The 4,500 Saxon nobles callously slaughtered by Charlemagne on one day in 782 must have had similar thoughts. The Old Norse sources record occasions when Christians tortured entire Odinist families in the hope of forcing parents to convert, thereby sparing their children further pain. Sometimes the children were stronger than their parents, urging the adults not to yield and thereby bring disgrace on their ancestors.

It is clear that Christianity prevailed over European heathenism mainly because Christians resorted to torture and murder. Meanwhile the Odinists upheld the old "rules of engagement" that they considered honorable, not realizing – or not accepting – that northern Europe had now entered an era of "total war".

Overwhelming violence explains how Christianity won these campaigns, but does not explain how the Christians finally subjugated the Odinists. That was achieved through the systematic theft of heathen property, which will be examined in Chapter 24. Meanwhile, though, we must look more closely at a few of the main turning points in the Christian war against the Odinist culture of northern Europe.

18

ÆTHELFRITH

...the continuous history of Northumbria, and indeed of England, begins with the reign of Æthelfrith

- Frank Stenton, *Anglo-Saxon England*

The people who became known as the English were made up of the four most powerful North Germanic nations of the fifth century. The **Frisians** lived in what is now northern Holland, including the offshore islands. To their east, in what is now Lower Saxony, lived the **Saxons**. To their north-east lived the **Angles**, in two provinces that have since been contested between Denmark and Germany: Schleswig and Holstein. To the north of the Angles lived the **Jutes**, occupying what is now Denmark.

Under the pressure of a growing population living on poor soil, large groups of these people emigrated, seeking a better life elsewhere. Some sought their fortunes further south, in Europe. Possibly as early as 360 CE, and certainly by 397, people from the region between Holland and northern Denmark were raiding the British Isles. The Roman rulers in Britain responded by building a series of forts around the south-east coast of what is now England. By the late 4th century the commander of these defenses had the title *Comes Litoris Saxonici per Britannium*: "Lord of the Saxon Shore in Britain".

These "Saxons" were not the only people causing trouble for the native Britons. Probably the Picts of what is now Scotland, and also the Irish, were a greater problem. The power of Rome was disintegrating. The imperial city itself was seized by the Goths in 410. Rome could no longer defend its remote province of Britannia, and the legions that had not already been withdrawn faded away through attrition. The only surviving source tells us that: "Honorius dealt with the states of Britain by letter, telling them to look to their own defense ... ".

In response to the increasing violence of the times, a British leader named Vortigern invited three shiploads of "Saxon" mercenaries to come and help him maintain his rule. Their leaders were Hengest and Horsa, and they arrived some time around the year 428. Soon many other "Saxon" warriors joined this initial small band, and by about 441 they rebelled against their British overlords, claiming that they hadn't been paid what their contract stipulated. They were soon masters of fertile Kent and Sussex, and more of their countrymen came across the North Sea to enjoy the richness of this new homeland.

The newcomers and the established Britons fought many battles with varying results, and although the surviving sources are confusing, it seems that the Christian Britons found a successful military leader in Arthur. He probably flourished between about 475 and 515 CE. After the death of Arthur the heathen newcomers, no doubt reinforced by many more of their own people, prevailed – to the extent that theirs is the language spoken today in all of England and nearly all of Scotland.

The Romans called these people "Saxons", and the name stuck among the dispossessed Celtic-speaking tribes of Britain. The newcomers, however, called themselves "English" and their new home "England", "Angle-land", the land of the Angles – the *Angli* of Tacitus. The Frisians are still remembered in the name of the Scottish town, Dumfries, "fort of the Frisians". Other Germanic tribes were also involved, with the Suebians having given their name to Swaffham in Norfolk.

Since many of the original Saxons had stayed behind in the far north of Germany, it became necessary to distinguish between the two branches of the Saxon nation. Those in Britain were soon called "Anglo-Saxons", meaning English Saxons, as distinct from the Continental Saxons.

The Anglo-Saxons were heathens. From their names for the days of the week we know that they worshipped the gods Tiw, Wóden, Thunor and the goddess Frige. From other sources we know that they also worshipped Balder, Freya and Eostre – as well as other deities who are today better known from later Scandinavian sources.

Most of the Celtic Britons were at least nominally Christian. Saint Gildas, writing in the 6th century, describes how the Anglo-Saxon onslaught may have been seen by some of these Britons:

> Some of the wretched survivors were caught in the hills and slaughtered in heaps; others surrendered themselves to perpetual slavery in enemy hands ...; others emigrated overseas, loudly wailing and singing beneath their swelling sails no shanty but the Psalm: 'Thou has given us like sheep appointed for the eating, and among the Gentiles thou hast scattered us.' Others entrusted their lives ... to the rugged hills, the thick forests and the cliffs of the sea, staying in their homeland afraid ...

In 597 Pope Gregory sent a missionary named Augustine, together with forty supporters, to convert the English. Augustine landed in Kent and was received hospitably by the heathen king, Ethelbert, whose wife was a Christian Frankish princess named Bertha. In this way Christianity gained a foothold among the English of the south-east.

The men of Wessex were not so accommodating. According to legend they attacked Augustine and his monks, sending them packing with the tails of skates pinned to their cassocks. God then punished the English, according to medieval legend, by ensuring they were all born with tails – hence the medieval continental insult for an Englishman: "tailard."

No-one knows when the first Anglo-Saxons settled in the north-east of England. By the sixth century they had two small kingdoms: Deira, approximately the modern East Riding of Yorkshire, and Bernicia, the coastal lands further north. They were Odinists, and no doubt were greatly outnumbered by the surrounding Christian Celts. For a while the two nations may have lived together in relative peace.

At some date near the middle of the sixth century (one suggestion is 547) a Bernician king, Ida, fortified the natural stronghold at Bamburgh. We can only guess at his reasons for doing so, but the result was that Bernicia effectively became independent. In about 580 two Celtic kings from what is now York marched against Bernicia. They were defeated by King Adda, the power of Celtic York vanishing after one crushing defeat. From then on there were many battles between various alliances of Christians and the Odinists. According to the historian known as Nennius: "During that time, sometimes the enemy [the English], sometimes our countrymen were victorious."

In about 590 the Bernicians were attacked by a joint force led by Urien, king of Rheged (roughly, modern Cumberland and Westmoreland). His many Christian allies included the kings of Ireland and of the Dal Riada Scots, so the assault had the nature of a crusade. The Odinist leader was known to the Celts by a nick-name, "Fflamddwyn", or "Firebrand", and was probably King Æthelric. He was so hard-pressed that he had to fall back on the small tidal island of Lindisfarne, where the Odinists were besieged for three days. At this crucial moment Urien was assassinated by one of his own Christian allies. That saved the English Odinists. They fought their way back to the mainland, but were soon at war with Urien's son Owain. In about 593 Æthelric and Owain fought at an unknown place. Æthelric was slain. It was to be the last victory of Celtic Christians over Odinist "Saxons".

The successor to Æthelric was his son, Æthelfrith, as far as we know the most brilliant of the heathen kings of the English. Little is recorded of his personal or family life, but it is plain from the known facts that he was a magnificent general and a staunch, unyielding defender of the Odinist faith of his people. Even Bede, the most Christian of historians but an English patriot for all that, was forced to admire Æthelfrith.

The king's earliest male ancestor was said to be Wóden. After that god, the king's line ran as follows (with the names rendered in modern English spelling): Baldag, Bernic, Wegbrand, Ingibrand, Alusa, Angegeot, Athelbert, Oesa, Eoppa, Ida and Æthelric. At the time of Æthelfrith's succession there were still two separate Anglo-Saxon kingdoms in the north-east of England, Bernicia and Deira. Æthelfrith's first wife was Bebba; the second was a princess of Deira named Acha.

We cannot be certain of the date of the battle of Cattraeth (fought near Catterick in Yorkshire), but 598 seems reasonable. A British invasion force comprising allies from several Christian states, but led by an army from the Firth of Forth, attacked the Bernicians. The Odinists had a massive victory over the invading Christians, who were annihilated. Their fate is mourned in the Welsh poem, *Gododdin*. Anglo-Saxon power was then consolidated as far north as Edinburgh, and the crusaders who escaped the general slaughter at Cattraeth were largely enslaved or else managed to flee to Wales and other Celtic Christian redoubts. Bede probably had Cattraeth in mind when he wrote:

> At this time Æthelfrith, a most mighty king and one very anxious for glory, ruled the kingdom of the Northumbrians and harried the British people more than all the other rulers of the English. In this he might seem comparable to Saul, once king of the Israelites, excepting only that he was ignorant of the religion of God. No-one among the commanders, no-one among the kings made more of the lands of the Britons either tributary to the English people or available for their occupation by wiping out or subjugating the inhabitants.

King Aedan of Dal Riada rallied another great army to try to crush the Odinists of Bernicia. The scope of the expedition is indicated by the fact that one of its leaders was Mael Uma, brother of the High King of Ireland. In 603 Æthelfrith utterly crushed the Celtic Christians at "Degsastan" (possibly either Dalston near Carlisle or Dawstone Rigg in Liddesdale). Bede had this to say:

> Aedan, king of the Irish who live in Britain, was disturbed by his advance and came against him with a vast and mighty army, but fled away with a handful of men, defeated. For at the famous field of Degsastan ... almost all his army was slain. Theobald, brother of Æthelfrith, was also killed in that battle with all the forces he commanded. Æthelfrith brought this war to an end in the year of our Lord 603, the eleventh year of his own reign ...

Æthelfrith was now without question the most powerful king in the north of England. In 604 he took York and joined the two kingdoms of Bernicia and Deira, forming the greater kingdom of Northumbria.

Still, the Christians wouldn't leave heathen Northumbria alone. By about 615 they had regrouped, and now led by a king of Powys named Selyf map Cynan they attacked again, only to be smashed once more at the battle of Chester. It was in this battle that the religious aspect of the wars came to a head. Here is how Bede describes what happened:

> When Æthelfrith was about to give battle, he observed the enemy's priests (who had gathered to pray to God for the soldiers as they fought) standing by themselves in a safer place. He asked who they were and what they had gathered there to do. Most of them were from the monastery of Bangor .... Many of

these, having observed a fast of three days, had come, with others, to this battle to pray. They had as their protector one Brocmail, who was to defend them from the swords of the barbarians while they were intent upon their prayers. When King Æthelfrith was informed of the reason for their coming, he said, 'If they cry out to their God against us, then indeed they are fighting against us, even though they do not bear arms; for they pursue us with curses.' He therefore ordered them to be attacked first, and then defied the rest of the impious army, not without great loss to his own forces. It is said that about twelve hundred of those who came to pray were killed, and that only fifty escaped by flight.

Throughout all these invasions, Æthelfrith – and Northumbria – stood alone, bearing the full brunt of the Christian onslaught. Heathen Mercia, adjoining Northumbria to the south, didn't raise a finger to help. Even more significantly, neither did heathen East Anglia. Its king was Rædwald, who had at one stage professed to be Christian but whose death was nevertheless celebrated with full heathen ceremony. Rædwald is believed to be the king who was honored in the Sutton Hoo ship burial. If so, he must have been wealthy and powerful. If Bede can be trusted, he was also one of the most disgraceful heathens ever to sit on a throne.

After 604 a prince of the former Deira, Edwin, fled to the Christian British kingdom of Elmet, near Leeds. He then found his way to East Anglia. Æthelfrith paid Rædwald to have Edwin either extradited or executed. The East Anglian king seemed to accept this deal. Then he had a sudden change of heart. Bede attributes this to a prophetic dream, but the dates make it clear what happened.

In 615 at Chester, Æthelfrith had suffered "a great loss to his own forces". In 617 the treacherous Rædwald proclaimed Edwin the true king of Northumbria, marched north, and defeated the sorely undermanned Northumbrians at the Battle of the River Idle. The pious and noble Æthelfrith was slain, and the supposed East Anglian puppet, Edwin, was installed on the northern throne.

A form of poetic justice ensued. Edwin went on to reduce the Mercians and East Anglians to vassalage. In 627 he converted to Christianity. In 633 he was defeated by an unholy alliance of Catwallaun, the Christian king of Gwynedd, and Penda, the heathen king of Mercia.

Æthelfrith's sons had meanwhile fled from Edwin to find shelter among the Irish and the Picts, pretending to have converted to Christianity. In 633 the eldest son, Eanfrith, was crowned king of Bernicia. At the same time Osric, the baptized son of Edwin's uncle, assumed the throne of Deira. Both immediately renounced the religion that they had been forced to adopt to save their lives. Odinism was once again the official faith of Northumbria.

Unlike the slippery Rædwald and the inscrutable Penda, Æthelfrith had been a staunch defender of his faith and his people. Not once could he be accused of sacrificing his religious principles for worldly gain. He was a true Odinist sacral king: brave, indefatigable, a servant of his folk, and a warrior who died with his face to the foe.

By chance or fate, Æthelfrith's legacy was not entirely lost. His royal capital, Yeavering, near The Cheviot in Northumberland, seems to have been burned down in the war of 633. It has since been excavated, revealing the only heathen English temple discovered so far. The temple was a double-walled timber building of just under 12 meters long by 6 meters wide. Also on the site were free-standing pillars of presumably ritual significance (see Chapter 25), and a sort of "grandstand", like a slice of a Roman amphitheatre, able to hold about 320 people, facing a raised platform. Bede could no doubt have told us how these various features were used. He maintained a strict Christian silence on the matter, but modern archaeology has disclosed at least some of what he tried to conceal. [54]

19

DESTRUCTION OF THE CONTINENTAL SAXONS

> And David and his men went up, and invaded the Geshurites, and the Gezrites, and the Amalekites: for those nations were of old the inhabitants of the land, as thou goest to Shur, even unto the land of Egypt. And David smote the land, and left neither man nor woman alive, and took away the sheep, and the oxen, and the asses, and the camels, and the apparel, and returned, and came to Achish.
>
> - 1 Samuel 27, 8-9

The Emperor Constantine I was the son of Constantius I, ruler of the Western Roman Empire from 303-306. His mother was a woman named Helena.

Constantius' ancestry has long been debated and is still uncertain. Eusebius' *Life of Constantine*, unfinished at the author's death in about 339, said that Constantius was a Christian who pretended to be a pagan. Saint Ambrose said that Helena was a *stabularia*, which can mean either a stable-maid or an inn-keeper. It may be that she was a prostitute. She was supposedly a native of the northern, coastal part of what is now Turkey. Helena was a Christian, and she was eventually made a saint.

The son of this couple, Constantine, became an emperor on the death of his father in 306, but the position was contested and it was not until 324 that he was secure on the throne.

During the reigns of these two emperors, one of them probably a Christian and the other definitely so, the Franks made their first major appearance in Roman history. They were a heathen Germanic tribe from what is now Holland who were evidently causing trouble for the Romans.

According to the Latin Panegyrics (*Panegyrici Latini*), in 296 Constantius invaded the Franks in a marshy and forested area around the Scheldt river. Given the low carrying capacity of their homeland the Franks were probably hopelessly outnumbered. They were certainly crushed, probably mainly being captured from undefended villages in the forests. The Panegyric gloats that:

> In all the porticoes of our cities sit captive bands of barbarians, the men quaking, their savagery utterly confounded, old men and

wives contemplating the listlessness of their sons and husbands, youths and girls fettered together whispering soothing endearments, and all these parceled out to the inhabitants of your province for service, until they might be led out to the desolate lands assigned to be cultivated by them. And so it is for me now that the Chamavian and Frisian plows, and that vagabond, the pillager, toils at the cultivation of the neglected countryside and frequents my markets with beasts for sale, and the barbarian farmer lowers the price of food. Furthermore, if he is summoned to the levy, he comes running and is crushed by the discipline; he submits to the lash and congratulates himself upon his servitude by calling it soldiering ...

By 310, the Franks must have re-grouped. This time it was Constantine who invaded them. He killed their two kings, who are known today as Ascaric and Merogaisus. The Dutch historian F. J. Los [55] wrote:

The unwary were waylaid in their own hamlets, their kings Askarik and Gaiso gruesomely martyred, their womenfolk killed and their children sold as thralls. For weeks on end the Roman rabble cheered in the circus at Treves where dozens of Frankish noblemen were torn to bits 'until their weight of numbers had wearied the savage beasts'.

As part of the vast movement of tribes and small nations that was occurring at this time, the Franks and their Germanic allies eventually fought their way into France, the country to which they gave their name. This is not a history book, and the full saga of the Franks can be read elsewhere. What we are concerned with here is the relationship of their general history to the course of Odinism, down through the centuries.

Chlodwig, known to history as Clovis, began his reign as king over one part of the Frankish nation. Through a series of wars he became king of all the Franks, and between 486 and 511 he took control of nearly all the Roman province of Gaul – more or less modern France. He thus became perhaps the most powerful military man of his era.

The conquest of France left the Germanic Franks as a thinly spread dominant class ruling over a defeated majority. Most of their new subjects were "Romans" in a legal sense, although of very mixed backgrounds, and most of these were Christians.

Clovis' wife was a Burgundian princess named Clotilda, a Christian who was later made a saint. Pious Christian writers claimed that she converted Clovis to the Catholic form of Christianity in the year 496. The truth seems to be that the Church recognized Clovis' rising star and determined to use him against its opponents, the Germanic Burgundians and the Visigoths. The leaders of these two kingdoms had, for reasons that remain obscure, converted to a "heretical" form of Christianity known as Arianism. Clovis was just the man the Church needed to lead its crusade against these heretics. The deal was that he should adopt the Roman form of Christianity. This done, he received every help the Church could offer him, from general espionage to the opening of the gates of besieged towns by Catholic priests and their followers.

Clovis died without success in converting many of his Frankish nobles, but his sons were less half-hearted. In 535 the Christians of the Frankish kingdom were banned from having any contact at all with their Odinist kinsfolk. In 558, Odinist beliefs were banned, and Christianity was then enforced by the power of the state. Heathens who had found the arguments of priests unconvincing were forced at least to pretend to accept Christianity.

For the next two centuries the so-called "Merovingian" kings, Clovis' Christian descendants, fought each other in seemingly endless wars, assassinated each other, and often even murdered the children of each other's families – when they were not themselves busy fathering children to servants and prostitutes, or in the case of the queens and princesses, prostituting themselves to servants and poisoning each other.

> Thus, during the 6th and 7th centuries, the old nobility of the pre-conquest and conquest period disappeared, together with a great many members of the dynasty ... The dynasty, weakened by feuding, became dependant on a new aristocracy, which issued from the servants of the royal palaces and the bodyguards of the *antrustiones*, who served the king and were rewarded by grants of lands from the royal demesne. [56]

The kingdom might still be called "Frankish", but within little more than two centuries after Clovis accepted Christianity his own people were effectively extinct. With very few exceptions, the people living in the kingdom he had created had little of the old Frankish blood.

In 732 a new dynasty came to power in the form of Charles Martel, the illegitimate son of an obscure palace "mayor" (Latin: *majordomo*). Charles was the undisputed overlord of the Frankish kingdom, but he did not achieve formal kingship. That role fell to his son, Pepin the Short, who with the help of the Pope deposed the last of the wretched Merovingians. They had served their Roman master and were now discarded, never to be heard of again. From this point we will speak of "the French", reserving the term "Franks" for the Germanic people of earlier times.

Charles was the victor at the Battle of Poitiers, thus saving northern Europe from the Muslim invasion, but rather than pushing south and expelling the Muslims from all of Europe his focus was on the Germanic heathens to his north and east. His main targets were Frisia, the north-western part of the German lands, and Swabia in the south-west. Despite the numerical supremacy of the French, the Frisian king Radbod was able to fight back against French might with the help of Saxon allies. In 714 he drove out St Willibrord and his monks, then in 716 defeated Charles

Martel at Cologne. His death in 719 deprived the Frisians of a mighty war-leader, although they fought on as best they could. More and more of Frisia was annexed to the French empire, with the heathen Frisians being given the option of conversion or martyrdom. Their temples were destroyed, their holy places desecrated, their priests murdered. Whenever the Frisians temporarily regained the upper hand they fought back, which the French described as "insurrection", but it was a grim and merciless struggle that was to be determined by the weight of numbers.

The heathen Swabians were similarly sometimes successful, sometimes unsuccessful, in fighting back against French Christian invasion. In 746, all else having failed, the Swabian leaders were invited to a "peace conference" at what is now Stuttgart. Trusting to the honor of their Christian opponents, they seem to have arrived unarmed. They were treacherously set upon, and in the ensuing massacre "many thousands" were killed, according to Christian sources. Like their co-religionists in Frisia, the Swabians fought on, but by 757 they were forced to submit to French Christian rule.

The probably illegitimate son of Pepin the Short was another Charles, subsequently known as "Charles the Great" or "Charlemagne". His mother was Bertrada of Laon, who was known as "Bertha Broadfoot". Los suggested that she may have been a Hun, mentioning one document that claims she was Hungarian, and alternatively pointing out that after the Battle of Châlons in 451 "... a group of Huns had been given a dwelling-place in the present-day Vendée". We will probably never know the truth, since even Charles' first biographer, Einhard, wrote: "It would be folly, I think, to write a word concerning Charles' birth and infancy, or even his boyhood, for nothing has ever been written on the subject, and there is no one alive now who can give information on it."

Charles ascended the throne in 768, and ruled until his death in 814. He made one main foray against the Muslims to the south, which resulted in the massacre of his rearguard under Roland (although not by Muslims), which is celebrated in the famous *Song of Roland*.

One of the titles Charles inherited from his father was that of *Patricius Romanus*. When he visited Rome in 773 he was hailed as *imperator*. In 778 the Pope referred to him as a new Emperor Constantine. It will be recalled how Constantine had treated the Franks, some of whom may have been ancestors of Charles himself. The comparison was ominous.

Charles' life-task was to be his war against the heathen Saxons. After the defeat of their Frisian co-religionists and their Swabian brethren, the continental Saxons were caught between two foes. Against them were poised Charles and his French armies, which by the end of his reign controlled an empire stretching from Brittany to the Spanish border, from Lombardy to Croatia, from Moravia and Bohemia to the Baltic Sea. The "soft power" of the allied papacy was arguably even more powerful than the new "Frankish" empire.

Many missionaries had tried in vain to convert the Saxons. The usual pattern was that the Christians were permitted to preach, but in frustration at their lack of success the priests and their followers took to desecrating Odinist sacred sites, and were then expelled. In 772 Charles decided that if the Saxons could not be converted by words, swords would suffice. He invaded their homeland, killing, plundering, storming their redoubt at Eresburg (modern Marburg), destroying their sacred sites, and laying waste to their land with fire.

In 773 Charles was called away to another war against the Germanic Lombard kings of northern Italy. Naturally, the Saxons took the opportunity to "rebel", as it was termed by the Christians, and burned down some churches that had been built on free German soil under the protection of French troops. Charles found his imperial duties less important than dealing with this relatively minor assertion of self-determination. In 774 he said that the Saxons must choose between baptism and death. He then began the grim task of enforcing his decree, which even the *Catholic Encyclopedia* calls "the Saxon crusade".

The ensuing years are a tragic sequence of French invasion and Saxon resistance. By 776 the Saxons had re-taken Eresburg, but in 777 at Paderborn most of the Saxon leaders were compelled to "accept" Christianity, their alternative being death. One leader who managed to avoid this dishonor by fleeing to Denmark was Widukind, a nobleman of Westphalia. He was to become the leader of the Saxon freedom-fighters.

In 782 Charles was again temporarily the ruler of Saxony, and it was probably in this year that he issued a decree called the *capitulatio de partibus saxoniæ*. This ordered the celebration of Christian rites and forbade the celebration of Odinist rites, both on pain of death. Even worse, Charles also divided up Saxony into a series of counties, to be run by local Saxon collaborators who had accepted French rule through either fear or bribery. Charles' actions were therefore a savage assault on both the Saxon religion and Saxon property, which could be stolen by Charles' satraps as long as much of it eventually filtered back to the Church.

The *capitulatio* inevitably welded together the Saxon resistance, and led to another uprising. The free Saxons came close to annihilating the French army near Minden. Charles retaliated with brutal force, and this time was successful. Yet Widukind had again escaped Charles' clutches, so the Saxons were forced to surrender their noblemen. All 4,500 of these hostages were beheaded in one day at the massacre of Verden in 782.

This was no way for Charles to win the peace, and therefore the crusade against the Saxons ground on without mercy. It makes painful reading, with Charles' troops slaughtering Saxons indiscriminately, plundering and burning their hamlets, crushing every least sign of resistance from this free people. In 785 Widukind himself somehow fell into Charles' hands, and was forced to "accept" baptism, yet by 792 the

Saxon resistance movement flared up again, now with the active help of the Danes. In 794 Charles tried the experiment of deporting every third Saxon male still alive, but even that measure failed to crush the spirit of freedom. In 798 the Saxon "rebellion" against foreign and spiritually alien invasion ignited yet again. In one year, 799, Charles was forced to drag 10,000 Saxon men from their families and settle them elsewhere.

The Saxons, then, fought for as long as they could against a blood-thirsty Christian aggressor. In the end, their land was so ravaged by fire and plundering, and so depopulated, that no further resistance was possible. The crusade against Saxony lasted for about thirty years, during which the victims fought almost to the last man against the greatest military power then in existence – which is a measure of how much they cherished their Odinist religious freedom. The Saxons lost about two thirds of their population during this crusade, and no doubt these were in general the bravest and most intelligent of the Saxon nation. Tacitus wrote of the degenerate Romans of his own day: "They make a desert and they call it peace". Charles – "Charlemagne" – who was seen by the Pope as some sort of successor to Constantine, ravaged the free Saxons at least as mercilessly as Constantine had ravaged the original free Franks.

Charles had obviously learned little from history. The revenge of Odinist Scandinavians for their slaughtered Saxon allies was not long in coming. It began during the reign of Charles himself, as we shall see in the next chapter, and it shook the Christian imperium to its roots.

20

ODINIST VENGEANCE

A furore Normannorum libera nos, Domine: "From the fury of the men of the North deliver us, O Lord."

- Prayer chanted by Christians during the Viking period.

O Lord God, to whom vengeance belongeth; O God, to whom vengeance belongeth, shew thyself.

- Psalm 94:1

We have seen that the Christians who came to the fore in Rome's final period of degeneracy gruesomely murdered pagan philosophers like Hypatia. We have seen how Constantius and Constantine went out of their way to abduct harmless Franks from their villages in the forests, then to enslave them or feed them to wild beasts in sporting stadiums in front of baying Christian hordes. We have seen how the Christian kingdoms of Britain allied in a crusade against the Odinist Northumbrians, until sheer weight of Christian numbers prevailed. We have seen how, as late as 794, after three decades of devastation, Charles of France still could not convince the continental Saxons to give up their native Odinism and had to slaughter or deport most of the Saxons.

Widukind, the Saxon freedom-fighter, had several times been forced to seek shelter among the Odinist Danes. By that stage the continental Saxons had almost been destroyed as a people, but the Danes had already allied themselves with what remained of their Odinist kindred to the south. In 793, these new allies struck back.

The Christian missionaries in Germany had prided themselves on destroying heathen temples, with those who were most successful in this trade being rewarded by the Church through being anointed as saints, such as Saint Willehad (who was chased out of Frisia for destroying temples) and Saint Boniface (who was not as lucky as Willehad.)

The Christians liked to build their lavishly endowed monasteries (see Chapter 24) in remote places such as off-shore islands, where they were out of reach of the anger of the ordinary people from whom this wealth had been plundered. Unfortunately for the priests, the ship-technology of the Scandinavian peoples was now far superior to the defensive technology of monasteries in isolated, but usually maritime, places.

The two monasteries that had played the leading roles in the Christianizing of northern European heathenry were on Iona, a small island in the Inner Hebrides of Scotland, and Lindisfarne, an even smaller island off the coast of Northumbria. The entry in the *Anglo-Saxon Chronicle* for 793 states:

> In this year terrible portents appeared over Northumbria and sadly affrighted the inhabitants: these were exceptional flashes of lightning, and fiery dragons were seen flying in the air. A great famine followed soon upon these signs, and a little after that on the ides of January the harrying of the heathen miserably destroyed God's church in Lindisfarne by rapine and slaughter.

This raid was so unexpected that it sent shock-waves throughout Christian Europe. Alcuin, an English Christian at Charles' court in France lamented: "It is some 350 years that we and our forefathers have inhabited this lovely land, and never before in Britain has such a terror appeared as this we have now suffered at the hands of the heathen. Nor was it thought possible that such an inroad from the sea could be made."

The raiders who slaughtered the monks on Lindisfarne are known today as Vikings. It would be as easy now to glamorize these warriors as it was for a 12th-century Irish writer to demonize them – as a "ruthless, wrathful, foreign, purely pagan people". In reality, the Viking raids had many aims, followed many courses, are susceptible to a class-analysis, and fall into two general phases. In Britain, these are from about 793 to about 950, and from 950 to the late eleventh century.

One of the obvious aims in the first period was religious revenge. In 794 the monastery at Monkwearmouth, not far south of Lindisfarne, was successfully attacked. In 795 the raiders sacked Iona itself, the supposedly "sacred" island whose monastery had been founded by St Columba. In the same year they sacked Lambay, an island near Dublin where a monastery had been founded by St Columba before he departed on his mission to Scotland. In 797 they laid waste St Patrick's Isle off the Isle of Man. This causewayed island was said to be the place from which Patrick launched his mission from Ireland to convert the mainland of the British Isles. In 802 and 806 they again ravaged Iona. (It should be remembered that 806-7 is the generally agreed date for the death of the Saxon resistance leader, Widukind.)

The monasteries and churches of other northern countries suffered too, probably as much as those of Britain. It would be pointless to list the Christian centers that are known to have been sacked: in just three decades, the *Annals of Ulster* record eight Irish churches attacked in the 820s, twenty-five in the 830s and ten in the 840s.

Over and over again, the Vikings hammered the Christian sites that had played a role in the chain of events leading to the destruction of the continental Saxons. Some of their early raids may have been partly motivated by the plunder stored in Christian monasteries thought to be immune from attack. Yet the Christians were not altogether stupid, and before long they must have realized that it was a good idea to hide their treasures away from their monasteries – or at least to establish early warning systems, such as that which allowed the monks of Tours to remove their treasure to Orleans just before a Viking raid in 853. The fact that the raids on the centers of Christian evangelism kept coming indicates beyond reasonable doubt the religious aspect of Viking aggression. [57] Without ready treasure, the only financial gain available from monasteries and churches would have been cattle and slaves. Most of the time these would have been hardly worth the bother: at one stage Maredudd ab Owain was buying back Welsh slaves for a penny a head. Even in the later period, from about 950 onwards, Christianity's most visible sites in Wales were repeatedly gutted. From 961 to the end of the century the Vikings ravaged Holyhead, Anglesey, Towyn, Clynnog Fawr, and – significantly – St David's in 999 and again in several other raids.

That the Christians themselves recognized this aspect of the conflict is shown by their later emphasis on the sacrilegious nature of the damage done. The *Anglo-Saxon Chronicle*'s entry on the sack of Lindisfarne mentioned only "rapine and slaughter". Three centuries later, Simeon of Durham invented some lurid religious details. The Vikings, he said on no authority: "Laid everything waste with grievous plundering, trampled the holy places with polluted steps, dug up the altars, seized all the treasures, killed some of the brothers, some taken away in fetters, many driven out naked and loaded with insults, and some they drowned in the sea." Similarly, later Christian sources state that Turgeis, a Norwegian raider of about 840, captured the abbey of Armagh or Clonmacnois. There, in one of the most sacred Christian sites in Ireland, Turgeis and his wife Aud or Ota are said to have celebrated Odinist rites.

While some Viking raids may have had other motivations, nothing less than heathen revenge can explain these repeated assaults on Christian sites, which continued for about two hundred years. Christian missionaries to the Odinist nations had repeatedly achieved their fame as violent destroyers of heathen temples. Now the heathens were striking back. This religious aspect of the Viking raids only came to an end when the religious situation in Scandinavia itself changed, which will be examined in the next chapter.

From a modern Odinist perspective, the Viking raids had two main consequences. First, they undermined, for quite some time, the Christian cult of saints. The relics of saints were said to have special spiritual power; but it was useless to threaten people with a dead bone, however saintly, when the very centers of the saintly cults were destroyed time and again. (The significance of this will become apparent in Chapter 26.)

Another important result of the raids was that they paved the way for new Scandinavian heathen settlement in Christian areas. This is important to modern Odinism because many contemporary heathens from regions that once spoke non-Germanic languages are unaware of the extent of their Scandinavian and specifically Odinist heritage.

In the 840s Norwegian Vikings established Dublin as a base, and from there they went on to found the main towns of Ireland, including Wexford, Waterford, Cork and Limerick. In 851 a Danish Viking army wintered in England for the first time. By 867 the Danes had taken York, by 876 they had conquered Northumbria, and in 886 a treaty with King Alfred gave them the whole north-east of England, which became known as the "Danelaw" since Danish laws now prevailed there. This area roughly comprised Northumbria, East Anglia, Stamford, Leicester, Derby, Nottingham and Lincoln, plus parts of the south-east Midlands. In the 9th century Norwegian Vikings settled in the Isle of Man, the Hebrides and the adjacent north-west Scottish mainland; and also the north-west of England, from north Wales to the present Scottish border. In 911, after over a hundred years of raids and reprisals, a Scandinavian army was given the province of Normandy.

It is impossible to make a precise estimate as to the percentage of the population of these regions contributed by the recent Scandinavian arrivals. We do know from written records that many of them married locals, which is unsurprising. Many a Danish warrior in Northumbria who wed a local woman would have known that her own Anglian ancestors had probably originated in Denmark. Because the new settlers and the earlier ones were so closely related, even modern genetic studies can throw little light on the question of how many Scandinavians settled in these areas during the Viking period. We are therefore thrown back on the evidence of place-names, which is far from conclusive.

The problem is that new settlers in an area with an established population tend to adopt most of the established place-names. Sometimes they will bestow their own names only on new features, such as new farms or villages. Therefore the percentage of Scandinavian place-names in a given area can give us, at best, only a lower limit to the Scandinavian percentage of the population. If 20% of the place names of a given area are clearly Scandinavian, we can surmise that *at least* 20% of the population was once Scandinavian. Possibly the percentage was much higher, but it can scarcely have been lower. The equation is more complex than can be expressed here, but it's all we have. [58]

Some scholars have provided place-name percentages for particular areas. For example, P. H. Sawyer [59] summarized research telling us that in the Outer Hebridean island of Lewis, 99 of the existing 126 village names are Norse, while another 11 are Norse-Gaelic hybrids. In the north-east of Skye only 66% of such names are purely Norse. All we can infer from these figures is that there were far more Scandinavians than Irish in Lewis during the place-naming period, and that the percentage of

Scandinavians was lower in Skye. Yet we could have inferred this from the dominance of Hebridean surnames like MacLeod, MacAulay, MacAskill, MacRauilt and MacSween, all incorporating common Norwegian names: Ljót, Ólaf, Áskil, Harald and Svein.

It would be particularly helpful to know the proportions of "old" Anglian and "new" Danish settlers in the Danelaw. Unfortunately, the problems of place-name interpretation are far greater in the Danelaw than in the Hebrides. All we can say is that a new layer of Odinist Danish settlers was added to an older layer of the formerly Danish population, and that there were few Celts in that region (see Chapter 18).

Nor do we know when, or how, or to what extent, the new Odinist settlers of the Danelaw became Christianized. Their kings tended not to last long. At least one, Rognvald, is said to have accepted Christianity during his year on the throne at York (approximately 948). Yet his successor, Eric Bloodaxe, was such a heathen until his death in battle (c. 954) that the surviving poem about his entry to Valhalla is one of the great set-pieces of Viking-era heathen literature.

Although the historical records often speak of Vikings receiving baptism, or some euphemism such as "taking the cross", this often involved a rite known as *prima signatio*. According to Gwyn Jones [60]: "The sign of the cross was made over them, to exorcise evil spirits, they could attend mass without committing themselves to Christianity, and live in communion with Christians." Jones then cited *Egils Saga*: "This was a common custom of the time among traders and those who went on war-pay along with Christian men; for those who were prime-signed held full communion with Christians and heathens too, yet kept to the faith which was most agreeable to them." *Prima signatio* was therefore something like a modern travel visa: it no more implied a change of religion than a modern visa implies a change of nationality.

Even the evidence of personal names doesn't help us answer the questions concerning Christianization during the Viking period. For example, [61] Gillian Fellows-Jensen argued that:

> The early use of the mythological name *Freyja* as an ordinary feminine name in Shetland may be compared with the employment of *Thór* as a masculine name in the Danelaw. The adoption of the names of heathen deities in everyday use reflects the swift decline of the pagan religion in the face of the Christian religion of the earlier inhabitants of the British Isles.

Since the use of divine names for personal names is the only evidence she gives, one might as well argue that the use of the name "Jesus" in Spain and Latin America indicates that the people there are not Christians. As we shall see in Chapter 23, there is abundant evidence that Odinism survived for centuries on the borders of England and Scotland.

21

THE FALL OF SCANDINAVIA

"What priest-led hypocrite are thou,
With thy humble look and thy monkish brow,
Like a shaveling who studies to cheat his vow?
Canst thou be Witikind the Waster known,
Royal Eric's fearless son,
Haughty Gunhilda's haughtier lord,
Who won his bride by the axe and sword;
From the shrine of St. Peter the chalice who tore,
And melted to bracelets for Freya and Thor ...
Then ye worship'd with rites that to war-gods belong,
With the deed of the brave, and the blow of the strong;
And now, in thine age to dotage sunk,
Wilt thou patter thy crimes to a shaven monk..."

- Sir Walter Scott, *Harold the Dauntless*

The French empire of Charles began to split up as soon as he died in 814. Two centuries later the dominant military power in Europe was Germany. In 962 the king of Germany, Otto I, was crowned as the first ruler of the Holy Roman Empire, which united Germany and northern Italy. This Empire was set up to defend the Church. In theory, no emperor could be crowned without the assent of the Pope, while no Pope could be elected without the approval of the emperor. The amount of power this gave the emperor was awesome: small nations near the Empire had little chance of surviving for long other than as client states.

This may account for the international revival of Odinism in the mid 10th century, since religion has often been invoked as a socially binding force in the face of military aggression. In about 958 King Gorm of Denmark was buried by his son Harald Bluetooth in heathen splendor in the greatest of the Danish burial mounds. As Else Roesdahl wrote . [62]:

> The burial is on a royal scale and is clearly a dynastic monument. It is probably also an expression of a late pagan religious and cultural revival, feeding on ancient religious concepts and ancient monument-types and – very interestingly – built at the

very same time as the composition of the grand skaldic poems *Eiríksmál* and *Hákonarmál*, c. 955-65.

Back in 823, the German king and the Pope had instructed Archbishop Ebo of Rheims to convert heathen Denmark. The idea was to convert the aristocracy first, assuming that the dominant class could then force its new religion on the lower classes. Ebo achieved very little. In about 826 a French monk named Ansgar converted a pretender to the Danish throne, but both Ansgar and the pretender were soon driven out. The fact that Ansgar was later allowed to build a church at Hedeby testifies to heathen tolerance of alien religions. Nothing much came of Ansgar's efforts.

Somewhere around 965, if we can believe Christian writers, King Harald Bluetooth of Denmark formally accepted the Christian god. The later sources claim that he was captured in a battle against Emperor Otto III and forced to convert. Whether or not that is true, it is likely that he had little choice. The growing German power had menaced Denmark for some time, which was why the Danes built their "Danevirke", a great earthwork defending Jutland from the Empire. Presumably Harald did not want the Danes to suffer the same fate as the Saxons, and by accepting Christianity he wished to deprive the Germans of a pretext for invading. Even so, in 974 the German Christians attacked Denmark and seized the important town of Hedeby. Harald built a series of new forts in northern Denmark in the years around 980, probably as deep defense against further Christian incursions and perhaps also to protect his rear against his own powerful heathen rivals. By 983 the Danes, under Harald's son Svein, successfully fought back against the Empire, recovering south Jutland.

Harald Bluetooth is best remembered today for his runic stone at Jelling which claims that he "won all Denmark for himself and Norway, and made the Danes Christian". Just how Christian Harald himself was remains a mystery. He is recorded as having built two churches, which he might have done only to encourage Christian merchants, or as insurance against the German Christians. His most powerful ally against the Germans was the Norwegian chief, Jarl Hákon, a staunch Odinist. Harald's own son, Svein Forkbeard, does not appear to have been a Christian – or at least, not a devoted one. The events that led to Harald's death are particularly obscure, but it seems likely that the Danish aristocracy objected to Harald's (fairly mild) Christianizing policies and also his (related) centralizing of power. In any event, Svein and Hákon appear to have led an uprising against Harald, who died of his wounds a few days after losing his last battle.

Svein was a military man. Whatever his personal motives may have been, it was obvious that Denmark alone could never stand successfully against the Holy Roman Empire, one of the formal aims of which was to destroy non-Christians. If Svein wished to build up his power base, there was only one country with the natural resources to withstand the assault from the south. This was England, which was largely Odinist again as a result of the Danelaw (Chapter 20). In 1003 Swein (as he appears in Anglo-Saxon records) attacked the West Country, in 1004 he raided East Anglia, in 1006 he made inroads in Wessex. In 1013 he invaded for the last time and was subsequently elected king of England.

Swein died of natural causes in February 1014. His death threw England into disarray, and it was not until 1016 that his son Cnut became king of all England. Cnut was also king of Denmark and Norway, so the three largely Odinist nations were briefly unified in one northern empire, to which might be added Cnut's probable overlordship of Sweden. Cnut lived mainly in England thereafter, until his death in 1035.

Cnut's coronation at London in 1017 was administered by Archbishop Lyfing. It is therefore clear that Cnut had "accepted" Christianity – at least as the price for achieving the dream of his father, Swein. Whether Cnut was really a Christian in any meaningful sense we may never know. The laws written in his name by Archbishop Wulfstan proscribed Odinist practices, yet Cnut openly defied the Christian rules by living openly with a woman who was not his wife, a major "sin" at the time – and the poetry of Cnut's court was openly heathen. [63] Modern historians writing about this period tend to seize on one or another of the few things recorded about Cnut's personal life and infer from them that he was a Christian. For instance, it is often pointed out that in 1027 he visited Rome, with the inference that this was some sort of "pilgrimage". Yet he was in fact attending the coronation of Conrad II as Holy Roman Emperor, an event to which all the power-players of Europe at that time would have been attracted.

Regardless of how we interpret Cnut himself, there were still so many Odinists in Cnut's "north sea empire" that archbishops like Wulfstan felt a need to keep pumping out laws banning Odinist practices among the lower classes, even though they judiciously turned a blind eye to Cnut's own heathen court poetry.

At this point we must leave Cnut, and focus on the Christianization of Scandinavia. The intrusion of Christianity into Denmark had been relatively benign. Further north, it followed the old "Roman" pattern of torturing, maiming and slaughtering those who refused Christian conversion. Before we examine some of the ghastly practices resorted to by the Christianizers, it may be well to quote from P. H. Sawyer [64] :

> Other parts of Scandinavia were less vulnerable to external pressure, but their conversion was not much later than that of Denmark. In all areas the lead was taken by rulers: there is no evidence that conversion was ever the result of popular demand. In later tradition three kings are particularly credited with the conversion of Norway and Sweden – in Norway, Olaf Tryggvason and Olaf Haraldson, later Saint Olaf, and in Sweden, Olaf Skötkonung. The Norwegian Olafs were converted and baptized in western Europe, after careers as Viking leaders, and

then returned to Norway with enhanced reputations and great wealth. They had discovered what great advantages Christianity could confer upon kings, and only that can explain the extraordinary ferocity with which they evangelized.

What Sawyer probably means here is that Christians, who were loyal only to their creed, and not to their ancestors or their kindred, now ruled nearly all of Europe. Christian Europe was the super-power of its time. An ambitious would-be king in a peripheral nation like Norway could in theory try to emulate Odinist heroes like Æthelfrith or Widukind, protecting the ancient spiritual ways of his people to his inevitable death, or alternatively could accommodate himself to the new world order and try to ingratiate himself as an obliging puppet of the Pope and the Holy Roman Emperor. The Olafs of Norway chose the latter course.

Norway has very little fertile land and travel between those fertile parts is not easy. In the early Viking period it therefore had, at any one time, various local "kings" and "jarls" (roughly = earls), and at best an ambitious king could aspire to be an overlord of the local rulers.

All that changed with the rise of wealthier warlords who sought to rule all of Norway. Harald Fairhair managed to control much of Norway as a sole king between c. 872 and 930. He was succeeded by an Eirík, who is better known as Eric Bloodaxe, the last independent king of Northumbria. (*Eiríksmál* is one of the great poems of the Viking era, and it celebrates the king's reception in Valhalla.) Eirík was driven out by Hákon the Good, who had been raised in England as a Christian. Hákon made some half-hearted efforts to Christianize Norway, but faced so much opposition that he seems to have given up and reverted to Odinism. (The poem *Hákonarmál* depicts his glorious entry into Valhalla.) He was followed by Harald Greycloak, a Christian son of the powerful Odinist Jarl Eirík. He was ferocious in his persecution of heathens. Harald was defeated by an Odinist, Jarl Hákon, who became king in all but name.

Our main information about Jarl Hákon comes from the poets of his court. Critics who are familiar with Old Norse poetry seem to agree that Hákon's court poets celebrated his reign in the most sublime heathen religious imagery and also the most muscular verse. In particular, Einarr skálaglamm, in his *Vellekla*, characterizes Hákon as the glorious and just descendant of Óðinn. [65]

The poets tell us that in the days of Hákon's predecessor: "there was a great famine, for the herring-fishing failed and all the sea-catch; the crops were ruined. The people attributed this to the anger of the gods because the kings had had their sanctuaries destroyed." But Hákon, who restored the Odinist sacred places, "was powerful and began to sacrifice with greater zeal than had previously been the case; then the harvest improved rapidly and the corn and the herring came back. The earth flourished with abundant growth."

Hákon was deposed by rival jarls from the Trondelag region in 995. The man who was to be his successor, Olaf Tryggvason, realized that no king of Norway could be secure from insurrections by powerful local jarls unless he had outside support. The way to gain the support of Christian Europe was to convert to Christianity. It seems that Olaf had fought for Emperor Otto III against the heathen Danes under Harald Bluetooth, so he had witnessed the political power Christianity gave to Otto. In 994 he led an unsuccessful Viking assault on London. The English king, Æthelred the Unready, bribed "Anlaf" (Olaf) with 16,000 pounds of silver in a Viking form of "protection racket" known as *Danegeld*. The *Anglo-Saxon Chronicle* reports that: "Then the king sent bishop Ælfeah and ealdorman Æthelweard to fetch king Anlaf, and hostages were sent meanwhile to the ships. They conducted king Anlaf with great ceremony to the king at Andover, and the king stood sponsor for him at coronation, and gave him royal gifts; whereupon Anlaf gave him his word, and kept it to boot, that he would never come to England as an enemy again." We will never know whether Olaf converted for honorable reasons, whether conversion was part of the price for the massive bribe and the royal gifts, whether hostages had been threatened, or whether Olaf was merely a clever warlord who could see the political benefits of accepting Christianity. In any event, he determined to become king of all Norway, and to impose Christianity on his subjects.

Olaf arrived in the Trondheim area with a large fleet of battle-hardened Vikings, a strong reputation as a warrior, a big war-chest, and a cargo of English priests. He put himself at the head of a revolt against Jarl Hákon and was elected king of that region. Then came the task of becoming the one king of a united Norway. The problem was that the more the Norwegians learned of Olaf, the less they liked him. A brave, athletic and handsome man, he was also – if we are to believe the writings of his own admirers – a psychopath. He briefly achieved his goal of ruling by force and terror nearly all of Norway, but by the year 1000 he had lost everything. He was defeated in a naval battle somewhere near modern Øresund or perhaps Rügen. When he saw that the jig was up he supposedly jumped into the sea and drowned. His victors were King Svein of Denmark, Jarl Eirík of Norway (the son of Jarl Hákon), and the heathen king of Sweden, another Olaf who was Svein's stepson.

How had Olaf Tryggvason thrown away all his gains so quickly? The surviving sources are contradictory. The most popular of these is Snorri Sturluson (1178-1240), an Icelandic Christian who adored Olaf. Another is the monk Oddr Snorrason. While these accounts may be pure propaganda, they are interesting in that they portray Olaf as the incarnation of an ideal Christian king. This ideal king in fact behaved much like Constantius, or Constantine, or Charles Martel, or Charlemagne. The attitude of all these sadistic torturers was directly derived from both Jesus and Saint Paul (see Chapter 15).

The methods by which Olaf attempted to Christianize Norway do not make for enjoyable reading, so we will look at only a few examples. The point to be remembered is that the people who wrote these stories were Christians who fully approved of Olaf's dealings with heathens.

"Everywhere they [Olaf's henchmen] went they ordered the people to be baptized, and then they would not rob them. Most of the people, for their salvation, accepted baptism, and those who did not want to accept it were killed." When Sigurð of the Orkneys refused Christianity, the king seized the jarl's son and threatened to cut off his head. The jarl chose baptism. A shipload of Odinists due to leave Norway was invited to a sham feast, at which the king's men burnt down the house. The Christian author states gleefully: "a dreadful wailing and howling of women, and men, arose". A leading man of Hálogaland, Eyvind, refused to convert – and the king had placed on his stomach a basin of burning coals. Pagans in Trondheim were forced to stand by helplessly while Olaf's thugs chopped up both their idols and their leader, Járnskaggi. A heathen who objected to Olaf's preaching had a live snake forced into his mouth. Somehow or other it crawled down the Odinist's gullet, then emerged live from his stomach with his heart in its mouth. "And seeing this, all the pagans were very frightened". Another eloquent heathen, Rauðr from Goðey, who refused to accept Christianity after he and his men had been captured in a surprise attack, had another live snake forced down his throat. Then, according to Snorri, "King Olaf there seized much gold and silver and other property, weapons and various treasures, and all the people who were with Rauðr he ordered to be killed or tortured."

Olaf's reign over Norway was mercifully brief. He was succeeded by three jarls – Svein, Eirík and yet another Hákon. According to *Fagrskinna*: "These jarls had had themselves baptized, and remained Christian, but they forced no man to Christianity, but allowed each to do as he wished, and in their day Christianity was greatly harmed, so that throughout Upplönd and in over Þrándheimr almost everything was heathen, though Christianity was maintained along the coast."

From 1015 to 1028, the king of most of Norway was another Olaf, this one known as "Olaf the Fat" in his own day and "Saint Olaf" afterwards. The new Olaf was determined to force Christianity on Norway, and his techniques for doing so are too sickening to list here. Let us simply quote Gwyn Jones' summary: "Olaf's methods were uncompromising; he executed the recalcitrant, blinded or maimed them, drove them from their homes, cast down their images and marred their sacred places". [66] The important point is that the local Christian bishops made a saint of this sadistic maniac – in fact, in 1031, a year after his death. He then became the patron saint of Norway, which was like making Jack the Ripper the patron saint of London.

There is insufficient surviving information for us to understand how Sweden was Christianized. We know the names of some kings who tolerated Christianity, some who tried to impose it, and some heathen kings who chased out the Christians – no doubt after the Christian priests had desecrated heathen sacred sites, as was their practice.

In the early 12th century a monk named Ælnoth gave an Anglo-Danish Christian view of how his faith was progressing in Sweden. He wrote:

> As long as things go well and everything is fine, the *Svíar* [Swedes] and *Gautar* [Goths] seem willing to acknowledge Christ and honor him, though as a pure formality; but when things go wrong – bad harvests, drought, tempests and bad weather, enemy attacks, or outbreaks of fire – they persecute the religion which they seem nominally to honor, and they do this not only in words but also in deeds; then they revenge themselves on the Christians and seek to chase them completely out of their country.

Ælnoth seems to have been less than honest. Some time near when he wrote this the great heathen temple at Uppsala was destroyed. Odinists did not destroy their own temples, so Christians must have committed this sacrilege at a time when they had the upper hand. At any rate, the temple was so obliterated that no conclusive traces have yet been found by modern archaeologists.

We have followed the progress of Christianity in Scandinavia as well as the surviving sources (and good taste) permit. Eventually Christianity prevailed, at least officially, through its usual means of torture and murder. Now we must turn to two areas of Odinist predominance that were outside continental Europe: Iceland, and the "waist" of the British mainland – the area once ruled by Æthelfrith.

22

ÞORGEIR'S TERRIBLE CHOICE

The "settlement period" in Iceland lasted from 874 to 970, and most of the colonists who founded this new nation were heathens. The chief gods worshipped were Thor and Frey. Freya, Njord and Odin also had their adherents. The Icelanders had a form of priesthood in which the chief men of the different regions performed both sacral and judicial duties. Each priest, known as a *goði*, was responsible for maintaining a cult centre, a *hof*, of which 37 can be identified today.

This heathen society came to an end in about the year 1000, when the Icelanders opted to become Christians. Modern heathens may wonder what made them come to this decision. As it happens, we know more about the Christianization of Iceland than of any of the other northern lands. A man named Ari Þorgilsson, known as the "father of Icelandic history", wrote a history of his country, called *Íslendingabók*, shortly after the year 1120. Carefully citing its sources, Ari's account of the conversion seems entirely dependable. There are also numerous secondary accounts that confirm Ari's history. As with other Christian sources, though, we have to be careful in how we approach Ari. Everything he wrote may have been truthful, but he doesn't necessarily give the full story. This is what seems to have happened:

From about 980 onwards various missionaries visited Iceland. They mostly received short shrift. Two of them, Thorvald and Frithrek, were driven out after committing some murders. Another, who was sent directly by Olaf Tryggvason, the vicious Christian king of Norway, was outlawed for destroying sanctuaries of the gods. Olaf's next missionary was Þangbrand, who roamed the countryside with a Christian gang in 997-9, and left in a hurry after killing three heathens. He had converted very few people, and had even been derided in verse by a poet named Steinunn when his ship was wrecked. Thor, she mocked, had brought on the storm, and "Christ did not protect the ship". Þangbrand returned to his Norwegian boss and reported that there was no hope for Christianity in Iceland. Olaf was furious. His first reaction was to "kill or maim" every Icelander who was in Norway at the time.

Two recently-converted Icelandic chieftains, Gizurr and Hjalti, managed to talk Olaf out of this vile plan. He made them promise to have another go at converting the reluctant Icelanders. Olaf kept four prominent men of leading Icelandic families as hostages.

Gizurr and Hjalti, with a Christian priest, landed on the Vestmann Islands. From there they travelled inland to Þingvellir where the Icelandic parliament, the Althing, was in session. Hjalti had been banished the previous year for blaspheming against Odin and Freya. According to law he was not allowed to set his unholy foot on the hallowed ground at Þingvellir. He turned up anyway. Two considerations probably gave him confidence. First, word had been sent ahead instructing all Christians to attend the Althing and to bring their weapons. Second – and here we have to surmise beyond Ari's account – it is likely that the heathens in Iceland were unaware of Olaf's hostages or of his murderous intentions.

Ari says the two factions, the Christian minority and the heathen majority, nearly came to blows. For some reason not given by Ari, they didn't. It seems probable that at this point Gizurr and Hjalti told the heathens what would happen to Olaf's hostages if they resisted.

The Christians then made speeches claiming that their religion conformed to the laws of Iceland. The heathens made the same claim. If either side had prevailed in this legal skirmish, the other would have lost its legal protection, and civil war might well have broken out.

The most significant man at the Althing was the "lawspeaker", a man called Þorgeir the Priest. The Christians asked him to make a binding decision. They also bribed him to favor Christianity, as Ari makes clear. A later account, *Njal's Saga*, says the bribe was "three marks of silver", adding that: "It was taking a risk, for Þorgeir was a heathen". In fact, the bribe may have been much larger than this. *Óláf Tryggvason's Saga*, which is admittedly not very reliable, says that the king had given Gizurr and Hjalti a large sum of money before they left for Iceland.

Þorgeir thought about the problem overnight. Next morning he decreed that the answer was a compromise. He warned against settling the dispute by violence, saying: "If we tear law asunder, we tear asunder peace". Both parties then formally agreed to abide by Þorgeir's decision. When his verdict was announced the heathens must have been dismayed. All Icelanders, declared Þorgeir, had to be baptized as Christians. Anyone who wished to could go on sacrificing to the gods, but only in secret. People who did so in public would be banished for three years.

As *Njal's Saga* relates: "The heathens felt they had been grossly betrayed". Even so, as honorable men, they abided by Þorgeir's edict. They had given their word, had plighted their sacred troth. The Christians, of course, had behaved abominably. There was nothing new in that. Given their experience with Christian missionaries, the heathen majority in Iceland should have expected the worst.

What is particularly interesting, though, is what Þorgeir may have been thinking. Yes, he had taken a bribe, but he could have passed that off as the fee for his work as a lawspeaker. The bribe was therefore probably not decisive. If he had been totally corrupt he need not have proclaimed the "let-out clause" allowing secret sacrifices, which must have infuriated the Christians. Þorgeir was no doubt worried about the fate of the Icelandic hostages in Norway, whom Olaf could "kill or maim" whenever he chose. Yet this was probably not his main concern.

To understand Þorgeir's thinking, we need to consider the international situation at that time. The deranged Olaf was busy torturing and killing anyone in Norway who wouldn't convert to Christianity. Iceland, originally founded as a Norwegian colony, was dependent on the mother country as a trading partner. Olaf also had a stranglehold on the Hebrides, Orkney, Shetland and the Faeroes. Ireland and England were also largely Christian. Given all these realities, Olaf could have used trading sanctions to reduce the Icelanders to starvation almost at will.

Even worse, if civil war had broken out Olaf would not have hesitated to invade in support of the Christians. Iceland would then have lost its sovereignty (as it did eventually in the 13th century) and then even Þorgeir's careful compromise would have been lost.

Finally, most Icelanders still had family ties with Norway. Every Norwegian relative of an Icelander – not just those currently in Olaf's hands – was a potential victim of the mad king. That thought must have been unbearable to a pious heathen like Þorgeir. All in all, it seems that the lawspeaker played the best hand that he could in the circumstances.

As a consequence of Þorgeir's painful decision, some aspects of the old faith became briefly a part of the new Icelandic Christianity. Others survived as folklore among the common people. Mainly, though, Odinism went underground in Iceland for centuries, as we know from the fact that as late as the 17th century Christians there were still burning people like Jøn Rögnvaldsson for possessing runes.

By 1096 the Church in Iceland was so powerful that it was able to impose tithes, which altered the whole system of land ownership, leading to extreme social inequality. [67] The end of the Icelandic Free State was now at hand. The new changes led to a virtual civil war. In 1262 Iceland became subject to Norway, and in 1380, to Denmark. It was not until 1918 that Iceland was to regain its independence. As Hastrup wrote:

> Apparently the Icelandic literati saw what was happening, but too late. It is significant that they produced their remarkable saga-literature in the last period of the Freestate, when the breakdown was imminent. The sagas were pre-eminently a glorification of the 'free state' and of the times just before or around the period of Christianity. On the verge of a new age, a new character was invented in the shape of the Noble Heathen representing the Icelandic statesman.

Still, Þorgeir may have had the last laugh – when Iceland became the first "Christian" country to restore Odinism as an "official" religion in the early 1970s. Perhaps that makes amends for Iceland having been the only Germanic nation to fall to Christianity without putting up a fight.

23

ODINISM ON THE BORDERS

Thou hast conquered, O pale Galilean; the world has grown grey from thy breath;
We have drunken of things Lethean, and fed on the fullness of death.

- Swinburne, *Hymn to Proserpine*

William of Normandy invaded England in 1066. He defeated the English army and was crowned King of England. He did not, however, immediately control all of that country. Anglo-Danish Northumberland remained unoccupied by the Normans, while Anglo-Norwegian Cumberland was claimed by Scotland.

In 1067, 1068 and 1069 the Northumbrians rose in resistance to William. After defeating them for the third time, he laid to waste all the land from the Humber to the Tees, essentially the modern county of Yorkshire. People were massacred indiscriminately, livestock destroyed, buildings burned down. A pro-Norman writer, Orderic Vitalis wrote: "To his shame he made no effort to control his fury and he punished the innocent with the guilty. He ordered that crops and herds, tools and food should be burned to ashes. More than 100,000 people perished of hunger." A flood of refugees poured into southern Scotland, which was English-speaking as a result of the conquests of Æthelfrith (see Chapter 18) and his successors, seeking the protection of the Scottish king. Malcolm Canmore took up the refugees' cause; William marched north in anger; and in 1072 Malcolm made formal submission to William. Even so, Malcolm continued raiding in the north of William's claimed possessions, carrying off so many captives that "for a long time after, scarce a little house in Scotland was to be found without English slaves".

The Normans built a castle at Durham to try to enforce their rule, but the north was still not properly subdued. In 1080 the men of Gateshead, chanting "slay ye the bishop", set fire to the church in which the Norman Bishop of Durham was hiding and slew him as he tried to escape the flames. In 1086 the Normans completed the Domesday Book to record their possessions in England. It did not cover the area north of the Tees. In 1091 the Normans abandoned all attempts to rule the north directly.

The Bishop of Durham was designated a "Prince Bishop", with the power to raise armies, appoint sheriffs, administer laws, levy taxes and customs, create fairs and markets, issue charters, salvage shipwrecks, collect revenue from mines, administer forests and mint coins. In effect, he was a local king in his own right.

From this period to the late 13th century the lands on either side of the current Scottish border enjoyed some periods of peace, punctuated by raids and counter-raids. Typically, the Scottish kings wasted the lands south of the modern border, while the English kings did the same on the northern side. In this region, where people spoke a common language with a common dialect, where the lifestyle was similar, and where the locals had little reason to feel loyalty to monarchs in London or Edinburgh, a common culture evolved.

In 1290 Edward I invaded Scotland, and for three hundred years the two nations continued to fight it out. The Border counties suffered more than anywhere else, and laws made in distant London or Edinburgh became irrelevant. Furthermore, the constant battles and raids made life itself precarious in this wild and rugged land. It was pointless to grow grain when it was likely to be burned in the next raid before it was ready for harvest. The economy therefore came to be based on cattle and sheep.

The people living on the Borders received no protection from any government, so they relied on their families for support. Great clans sprawled across both sides of what is now the border, with names like Armstrong, Maxwell, Johnstone, Scott, Rutherford, Kerr, Trotter, Dixon, Selby, Gray, Graham, Elliot and Forster. Life was harsh, and physical survival often depended on successful cattle-raiding. It is said that when the larder was bare, the woman of the family would sometimes bring a roasting dish to the table. Removing the lid, she revealed that the dish contained nothing but a horse-riding spur. That was the sign for the men of the clan to go out "reiving" (rustling).

There was some attempt to establish a form of international control, and both Crowns appointed Wardens who were supposed to administer special international laws in what later became the counties of Kirkcudbright, Dumfriesshire, Peeblesshire, Roxburgh, Berwickshire, Northumberland and Cumberland. It was mostly a hopeless task, and several of the Wardens behaved much like any other border reiver.

An indication of the lawlessness and bloodshed on the Borders can be seen in the escalating nature of clan feuds. Two clans, in particular, detested one another: the Maxwells and the Johnstones. After a century of intermittent warfare Lord Maxwell decided to end it by exterminating the Johnstones. On 6 December 1593 he rode into Johnstone territory at the head of a clan army of 2,000 superbly trained light cavalry, only to be ambushed by 400 Johnstone cavalrymen. 700 Maxwells are said to have died at the Battle of Dryfe Sands. (For comparison, there were only 500 dragoons in the Hanoverian army at Culloden in 1745.) If Dryfe Sands had occurred near London or Edinburgh it would have resulted in massive royal retribution. It happened on the Borders, so the English and Scottish kings had no real jurisdiction and took no serious action

In their isolated fastnesses the Borderers kept alive many elements of an earlier Anglo-Scandinavian culture that had been suppressed elsewhere. It is no coincidence that the only Odinist song known from the Anglo-Saxon pre-Christian era, *Teribus*, survived in precisely this region.

Through their ballads, in particular, the Borderers kept alive older beliefs, thoughts, practices and folklore, passing them by word of mouth from generation to generation. The ballads are short stories in verse, swift, impersonal and dramatic, turning the daily lives of the Borderers into poetry that still ranks among the glories of English literature.

Murder, treason, love, and death all feature in the ballads, but so do magic, sorcery, and necromancy. The ballad world is one in which a woman might drown her sister to gain access to the sister's lover. In the ballad that pursues this story, *The Twa Sisters*, a passing musician makes a harp of the dead girl's breast bone and strings it with her golden hair. He takes the instrument to the wedding of the guilty sister and the drowned girl's betrothed. There the harp speaks, accusing the murderess.

The ballads don't just mention magic of this kind in passing. They insist on it. It is clearly an integral part of the life and thought of the people from whom the ballads sprang.

As the folklorist T. F. Henderson commented [68], the Border ballads "bring us into immediate contact with the antique, pagan, savage, superstitious, elemental characteristics of our race." His attitude may be Christian, but at least he makes the point. More valuable than buried coins, the ballads are a treasure hoard of the traditions and usages of our ancestors. Taken collectively, they amount to a slightly corrupted autobiography of a late Anglo-Scandinavian, mostly pagan tribe.

J. A. MacCulloch discussed early forms of literature in his *Childhood of Fiction.* [69] What he said there about folk-stories can be applied to those of the Border ballads into which a degree of Christianity has intruded:

> The ideas of later ages have entered into and colored these primitive stories; comparatively modern social customs and names jostle those of a remote antiquity without any feel of incongruity; the tales have a firm root in a past paganism, but they are full of later Christian conceptions. ... But this is only the veneer of a later age; the material of the stories is old, so old as to be prehistoric.

Despite MacCulloch, the Christian intrusions in the ballads are obvious, and usually so inept that the essential viewpoint of the ballad is not twisted. A supernatural being, for instance, may be given a cloven foot to identify him as "the devil". This sort of contamination is easily set to one side, and it is wise to recall York Powell's comments on the ballads [70]:

The religion of the ... ballads, save for the few poems that deal with the popular Catholic mythology, is absolutely as heathen as that of the Helgi Lays; the sacredness of revenge, remorse, and love, the horror of treason, cruelty, lust and fraud are well given, but of Christianized feelings there are no traces. The very scheme on which the ballads and lays are alike built, the hapless innocent death of a hero or heroine, is as heathen as the plot of any Athenian tragedy can be.

The magic that occurs in the ballads is quite straight-forward. It is not like the metaphors of other genres of poetry. It is portrayed as something that unquestionably happens, that is simply part of the way things are.

The ballad characters inhabit a world that is only precariously stable. In several ballads (such as *Child Rowland and Burd Ellen*) this world is called "middle-eard", which is, of course, cognate with the Norse "Miðgarðr". Dwellers of other worlds, including the dead, can manifest in middle-eard. If a human kisses them, or accepts food from them, he or she will fall under the jurisdiction of the Otherworld to which they properly belong. This is a common Germanic pagan theme, forming a main plot strand in Saxo's account of King Gormo's visit to Guthmund. In the ballads, though, it can appear with beautiful and sudden brevity. *The Unquiet Grave* is a lovely example. A man mourns his dead love for too long. Here is part of one version:

"The wind doth blow today, my love,
And a few small drops of rain;
I never had but one true-love,
In cold grave she was lain.

"I'll do as much for my true-love
As any young man may;
I'll sit and mourn all at her grave
For a twelvemonth and a day."

The twelvemonth and a day being up,
The dead began to speak:
"Oh who sits weeping on my grave,
And will not let me sleep?"

"Tis I, my love, sits on your grave,
And will not let you sleep;
For I crave one kiss of your clay-cold lips,
And that is all I seek."

"You crave one kiss of my clay-cold lips?
But my breath smells earthy strong;
If you have one kiss of my clay-cold lips
Your time will not be long."

Many of the ballads express ideas and themes that are similarly found in the sources on earlier Germanic paganism. Thus in both *Allison Gross* and *The Laily Worm*, the enchantress blows a horn as part of her magic. As the great ballad collector Francis James Child commented: "The horn is appropriate. Witches were supposed to blow horns when they joined the wild hunt". Child's comment here is as terse as any ballad, but it takes us straight back to the Wild Hunt of 1127 CE described in the *Anglo-Saxon Chronicle*:

> ... many people both saw and heard a whole pack of huntsmen in full cry. They straddled black horses and black bucks while their hounds were pitch black with staring hideous eyes. ... All through the night monks heard them sounding and winding their horns.

It is impossible to do justice here to all the aspects of Germanic heathen folklore that the Border ballads accept as being perfectly unremarkable. Readers who wish to explore them fully should obtain a copy of Child's *The English and Scottish Popular Ballads*.

Yet one question needs to be raised here: What light do the ballads, with their unquestioning acceptance of the Germanic supernatural, shed on the religion of those who composed them, listened to them, and orally transmitted them? Many of these people, but certainly not all, may have called themselves Christians. The threat of being burned at the stake would have seen to that. A brave few clearly set themselves apart from the official creed. Both the Christian writers and the essentially pagan composers of the ballads tended to call these people "witches". But the "witches" portrayed in the ballads are far removed from the traditional image of an old peasant tortured into confessing to Christian fantasies.

For instance, *Northumberland Betrayed by Douglas* is concerned with the aftermath of a 1569 plot to depose Protestant Queen Elizabeth in favor of her Catholic rival, Mary. The two noblemen heading this movement were the Earls of Northumberland and Westmoreland. Lacking money, troops and proper leadership, the insurrection petered out within a month. Lord Northumberland tried to escape to sanctuary across the border. Legal protection should have been automatic, but it was not forthcoming. The Armstrong family stole all of Northumberland's belongings, then handed him over to Lord Douglas who betrayed him for a sum of money. He was beheaded in 1572.

The ballad follows this story closely, but incorporates other details. In particular, it adds another intriguing character to the whole sorry mess. This is Douglas' sister, Mary Douglas. She is the only character the ballad respects. Northumberland is an incompetent, trusting fool. Douglas is a smiling hypocrite who values money more than honor. Mary, however, offers to help Northumberland flee to safety in Edinburgh. The lord replies that he cannot believe Mary's brother would ever betray him. Mary offers to show him what lies in store. He declines, priggishly saying he "never loved no witchcraft", but allows his servant to go to her. Mary instructs the servant to look through the hollow of her ring, and he sees the host of English lords waiting to seize his master. He asks how far away they are. Mary says thrice fifty miles, adding that:

> My mother, she was a witch woman,
> And part of itt shee learned mee;
> She wold let me see out of Lough Leuen
> What they dyd in London cytye.

The distraught servant is unable to convince his master, who goes off blithely and unsuspectingly into captivity and execution. Having done her best to save Northumberland, Mary plays no further part in the ballad.

The magical device of seeing far-off people through a ring doesn't sound at all like humble peasant "witchcraft". It takes us straight back to Saxo, in whose pages Ruta's arm is bent into a ring and, looking through it, Biarco sees Odin on a white horse.

During the period depicted in *Northumberland Betrayed by Douglas*, accusations of "witchcraft" were frequently made against high-born ladies in Scotland and the Borders. Among those accused were the Lady Buccleuch, the Countess of Athole, and the Lady Foulis. The sister of the Earl of Angus, Lady Janet Douglas, was burned for "witchcraft" in 1537.

We should also recall that the composer of the ballad seems to endorse both Mary Douglas' magic and her character. The ballad makes it clear that if Northumberland hadn't been such a fool, Mary would have saved him. Why? Mary wouldn't have called herself an Odinist, and the ballad calls her a "witch", but she is clearly an educated northern heathen of some sort. So why should she bother to try to save the life of a Christian partisan? Heathen horror of treason might explain her motives, or the sacredness of hospitality. But it is tempting to believe that Mary was not acting entirely on her own, and that there was more religious intrigue in the sixteenth century Borders than the main participants, the Catholics and Protestants, were aware of. The religious history of the ballad period needs more study from a modern pagan perspective.

So much for the testimony of the Borderers' own literature. One witness who knew them well, Sir Ralph Eure, complained that theirs was a land of churches "mostly ruined to the ground, ministers and preachers comfortless to com and remaine where such heathenish people are." Another account claimed that hardly any of them could recite the Lord's Prayer. A third credits the Armstrong clan alone "with the destruction of fifty-two church buildings". Another visitor to Liddesdale, noticing the absence of churches, asked whether there were no Christians there, only to be told, "Nah, we's all Armstrangs and Elliotts".

Most interestingly, the Archbishop of Glasgow formally cursed every last Borderer in a proclamation that takes up four modern printed pages. This gentleman made sure to include in his curse "thair wiffis, thair bairns and thair servandis" (their wives, children and servants). Not only were they cursed, but no Christian was permitted to have anything to do with them:

> I forbid all cristin man or woman til have ony company with thaime, etand, drynkand, spekand, prayand, lyand, standand, or in any uther deid doand, under the paine of deidly syn" – (I forbid all Christian men or women to have any company with them, eating, drinking, speaking, praying, lying, standing, or in any other deed, under pain of deadly sin).

Such is the evidence of the ballads and of the Borderers' contemporaries. Now for the laws. Special international laws were enacted for the Borders, more in hope than confidence. At least one of these shows that some traditions persisting on the Anglo-Scottish Borders until well into the reign of Elizabeth I can be traced back directly to the heyday of Germanic heathenry.

This was a 1563 law banning the custom of "bauchling", which meant publicly vilifying an enemy as a detestable man. According to Fraser [71], the bauchler "sometimes made his reproof by carrying a glove on his lance-point, or by displaying a picture of his enemy, and by crying out or sounding a horn blast, indicating that his opponent was a false man and detestable." Bauchling was regarded as being a mortal insult, and could only be defended by combat.

Fraser described this merely as "a delightful local custom", but those of us familiar with Old Norse literature will see at once that it is what the Norse laws knew as *níð*. This was a form of ridicule inviting universal contempt for the victim. *Níð* seems to have involved the suggestion that the victim was both a coward and a passive homosexual. It was often associated with two other words: *ergi*, which meant a (female) nymphomaniac, and *berendi*, the sexual parts of a (female) cow.

Like bauchling on the Borders, in Norse law an accusation of *níð* allowed its victim to "clear" himself by killing his accuser. And just as the bauchler could express himself by "displaying a picture of his enemy", so could the perpetrator of *níð* express himself by carving a statue of his enemy – usually in a position implying passive homosexuality, as several sagas attest. The two characteristics, being a hopeless coward and being the recipient of sodomy, were thought to go together. To be unmanly in one aspect was to be unmanly in all.

This in turn takes us back to Tacitus, who described how heathen German men guilty of *flagitia* ("infamous deeds") were drowned under wicker bundles in muddy swamps. Tacitus describes such men as *ignavos et imbelles et corpore infames*, or "cowardly and unwarlike and infamous with regard to the body". We can therefore be confident that bauchling involved an aspect of sexual vilification, although Fraser failed to explore this topic. The three clues available to us are the glove on the lance, the picture of the enemy, and the derivation of the word bauchling itself.

Gloves were as associated with women then as bras are today. The reivers themselves, who dressed as lightly as possible to spare their horses, didn't even wear gauntlets. Therefore one doesn't have to be particularly Freudian to see a suggestion of sodomy in the image of a leather ladies' glove impaled on a lance. (Remember the Norse word *berendi*.)

We know nothing about the nature of the pictures that were displayed, other than that they somehow depicted the enemy. We do know that the parallel statues in Scandinavia often depicted the enemy in a position of passive homosexuality.

As to the dialect word bauchling, the *Oxford English Dictionary* suggests it may derive from a Norse word meaning "weak, poor, pithless, without substance or stamina". A probably related word, bauchle, means "an old shoe worn as a slipper, or worn down at the heel, which causes the wearer to shamble". Again we have the notion of penetration, this time of a worn-down old object that is practically worthless.

The years in which Christianity was the official religion of our homelands have often been described as the Period of Dual Faith, which will be investigated at greater length in Chapters 25-29. The usual idea is that Christianity prevailed in (most) official circles, continually suffering inroads from intellectual paganism, while heathen Germanic customs lingered on in remote areas and among the (mainly) lower classes. Yet on the Anglo-Scottish borders during the reign of Good Queen Bess a heathen custom that dates back to Tacitus' report was so common that it had to be banned by international law.

Nor are we talking here about a small community on some remote island like St Kilda. Fraser estimates that in the sixteenth century there were probably about 120,000 people in the "English" marches and about 45,000 in the "Scottish" marches. For comparison, the first census in Iceland, in 1703, reported a total population of 50,358. The Borderers were practically a nation of their own, and a reasonably powerful one: on the 24th of November, 1542, 700-800 Border light cavalry ("prickers") routed a Royal Scottish army of 15,000-20,000. This Battle of Solway Moss was the worst military defeat in Scottish history.

It all came to an abrupt end in 1603, on the death of Queen Elizabeth. Her successor was James Stewart, the sixth King James of Scotland who also became the first King James of England. The two kingdoms were united at last, and the old Border marches were now, in James' own words, "the verie hart of the cuntry". He determined to destroy the ancient way of life of the Borders, to disarm the clans, and to impose one set of national laws. As Fraser commented: "There followed one of the most comprehensive and cruel examples of race persecution in British history". From 1603 to 1610 the Borderers were dispossessed, exiled to Ireland and the Low Countries, and hanged in droves. They were permitted to have only work-horses, forbidden to possess weapons, their towers and fortified houses were burned down, many of them were not allowed to leave home for more than two days without a special pass, the laws of inheritance were changed so that younger sons could not inherit and could be (and were) deported. Informers were placed in every town. Gallows were erected all over the Borders. James instructed his officers to make a "quick dispatche", by which he meant execution without trial, of any who did not accept the new order.

This was the same James, styled "by the grace of God, King of Great Britain, France and Ireland, Defender of the Faith, Etc", to whom the most popular English translation of the Bible was dedicated. The translators' opening words read: "Great and manifold were the blessings, most dread Sovereign, which Almighty God, the Father of all mercies, bestowed upon us the people of England, when first he sent Your Majesty's Royal Person to rule and reign over us." Some of the Borderers who survived may have recalled the fate of the Franks at the hands of Constantius and Constantine, of the Roman pagans under Theodosius, of the Frisians, Suebians and Saxons under the Christianized Franks, of the Norwegians under the Olafs. They are unlikely to have regarded James as the earthly representative of "the Father of all mercies".

As a postscript to this chapter we may add that only one song, known as "Teribus", can be unequivocally dated to the pre-Christian Odinist period in Britain. It is therefore a cherished part of our spiritual and cultural heritage. "Teribus" has been recorded from several areas near the modern border of England and Scotland. Most of the surviving lyrics are rather poor, but they all follow essentially the same tune, and they all contain an eroded remnant of the original, pre-Christian, Odinist chorus.

James Murray, the founding editor of the *Oxford English Dictionary* (see Chapter 32), said this [72] :

> The Ruthwell Cross is of course of Christian origin, but a relic of North Anglian heathendom seems to be preserved in a phrase which forms the local slogan of the town of Hawick, and which, as the name of a peculiar local air, and the refrain, or 'overword' of associated ballads, has been connected with the history of the town 'back to fable-shaded eras'. Different words have been sung to the tune from time to time, and none of those now extant can lay claim to any antiquity; but associated with all, and yet identified with none, the refrain 'Tyr-ibus ye Tyr ye Odin,' *Týr hæb us, ge Týr ge Odin!* Tyr keep us, both Tyr and Odin! (by which name the tune is also known) appears to have come down, scarcely mutilated, from the time when it was the burthen of the song of the gleo-mann, or scald, or the invocation of a heathen Angle warrior, before the northern Hercules and the blood-red lord of battles had yielded to the 'pale god' of the Christians.

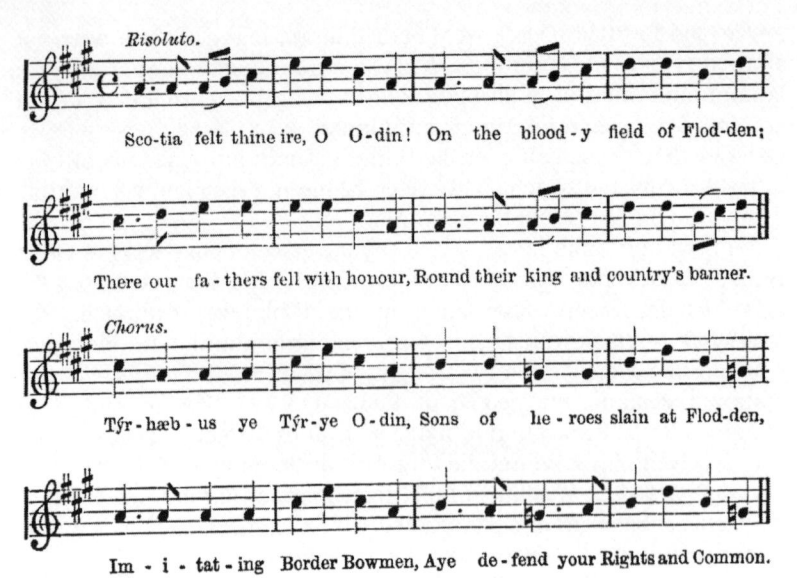

Scotia felt thine ire, O Odin! On the bloody field of Flodden;

There our fathers fell with honour, Round their king and country's banner.

Chorus.

Týr-hæb-us ye Týr-ye Odin, Sons of heroes slain at Flodden,

Imitating Border Bowmen, Aye defend your Rights and Common.

Other Odinist songs have survived in Britain from the period of Dual Faith, but "Teribus" is the only one known to have preceded Christianity.

The Borders were the last European homeland of a large, unified community that was Odinist, albeit in a popular form of our faith. We will soon see that King James' gallows were erected far too late to prevent the resurgence of Odinism among the educated classes of Europe, or to repress its partial survival among the peasants. First, though, we need to see how the Christians typically consolidated their conquests.

24

THE CHRISTIAN ECONOMIC STRATEGY

If I can catch him once upon the hip
I will feed fat the ancient grudge I bear him.

- Shylock, *The Merchant of Venice*

It is the practice of the Apostolic See to decorate with honorable privileges those illustrious men whom it has found prompt and fervent in its service.

- Pope Innocent IV

The property of our churches has come from the proceeds of our crime.

- Peter Adam, the head of Ridley Theological College, Melbourne, Australia, 2009

The ascendancy of Christianity in our northern homelands was based even more on a systematic economic strategy than on military dominance. Since the rot basically started with the Franks, let's briefly recall how the Church deliberately pulled the equivalent of a modern financial scam on the Frankish royal family.

First, it's essential to recall that the Franks were originally a Germanic tribe with pure Odinist values, and their homeland was in what is now northern France (see Chapter 19). They were on a military collision course with the Germanic kingdoms to their south, particularly the Visigoths in Aquitaine, and the Burgundians. In these regions the Germanic upper classes had already converted to Arianism, a "heretical" form of Christianity opposed by the Pope. The underclass over whom they ruled was a generalized "Roman" rabble, whose Christian loyalty was to the Pope rather than to their Arian rulers.

One of the Frankish kings, Chlodwig (often known as Clovis), received overtures from Rome. If he would convert, however superficially, to Roman orthodox Christianity, his southern campaigns would receive the backing of the Pope. The only snag was that he would have to undertake to convert his own people to Christianity. Chlodwig happily agreed to this pact in the year 496.

At first, all went well for Chlodwig and his descendants. The Pope had legions of priests who could travel freely in all the nominally Christian lands, thus easily gathering and passing on military information. This highly efficient spy network was suddenly placed at Chlodwig's personal disposal.

Even better, the underclass in the Visigothic and Burgundian realms were Roman Christians, and they resented their "heretical" ruling class. So when the supposedly Roman Catholic Chlodwig attacked towns like Poitiers, the rabble and their bishops happily opened the gates – and in some cases even mustered up the courage to attack the stockades of their Germanic rulers. In this way, Chlodwig thought that he had conquered Aquitaine and Burgundy, and later other areas.

He was wrong. In reality, the Pope had conquered these Germanic kingdoms, using the half-converted Chlodwig as a puppet.

What happened after that is the really important aspect of the Christian conquest of the originally Odinist Franks, Visigoths and Burgundians. Chlodwig repaid the Pope for his invaluable help by persecuting all "heretics" and heathens in his realm. As they were killed or driven out, many of their lands were given to the Roman church. These gifts were augmented by the Germanic nobility who, for fear of persecution, felt the need to "prove" their Roman Christian allegiance by founding and endowing monasteries.

Only a hundred years after the death of Chlodwig, the church owned one third of all the land in what is now France. (Los, 1968) It paid no secular taxes, and could levy taxes of its own, so the process could only gather momentum. Since land was the main form of wealth, it was merely a matter of time before the church-dominated "kingdom" of the Franks turned on its Odinist neighbors in Frisia and Saxony, where more land could be obtained. Since more wealth bought greater military power, the outcome of the Frankish genocidal crusades against their heathen cousins was assured, despite the heroic resistance of the Odinists.

The economic conquest of the Franks by Christianity had its parallels in all the other northlands. Two snapshots will suffice as examples:

Greenland was pioneered by a tough old Odinist, Eirík the Red, who settled at the Garðar peninsula in about 986. Greenland formally "converted" some time around 1015, and the remains of at least 23 medieval churches have been identified, in addition to a large monastery and nunnery. By 1126 a bishop had been appointed to Eirík's own area of Greenland, Brattahlíð. The bishop's cathedral was 88 feet long by 52 feet wide – massive, by Greenland's standards. As one historian [73] wrote:

> As time went on, the property of the see of Gardar gradually increased, farm after farm being added to the bishopric. By the fourteenth century the whole of the Einarsfjörd district belonged to the bishop, together with a number of large islands lying at the

entrance to this fjord and the Eiríksfjord, as well as extensive hunting-grounds on the east coast ... It is significant that henceforward no more was heard of the chieftain at Brattahlid, who, in the earlier days of the settlement, had always dominated the scene. In the later medieval era the great man in Greenland was undoubtedly the bishop, without equal or second.

It is significant that the bishop's own residence was nearly twice as long as the church, and that one of the biggest outbuildings was a massive stone barn in which he stored the taxes he extracted from the community. That community numbered, according to various estimates, from 3,000 to a little over twice that. They must have worked themselves into early graves enriching the Church and its abbots, priests, monks and nuns.

As a third example, the Odinist kingdom of Northumbria once made up almost a third of mainland Britain. Its power was largely destroyed in the 7th century by a huge coalition of Christian aggressors (see Chapter 18). By the 11th century the most fertile part of this ancient kingdom had become the "County Palatinate of Durham", ruled over by a prince-bishop who held his own parliament, raised his own army, made his own laws and charters, and minted his own coins. This despotic ruler was initially subject to the Norman kings, but before long was answerable only to the Pope in Rome.

The economic history of the Middle Ages is far too large a subject for a book of the present kind, so we will unashamedly view this topic from a purely Odinist viewpoint.

The first point to bear in mind is that, until the ascension of Christianity, the entire wealth of Europe had belonged solely to its pre-Christian, pagan or heathen inhabitants. There was inequality of wealth, of course, and the great civilizations of Greece and Rome had depended on slavery. Even though slavery was assumed to be "normal", the people as a whole, seeing themselves as tribes or nations, believed that in a sense they owned the land and its resources collectively.

Once it was established in a particular area, the Church set itself up as something like a modern corporation, or a proprietary limited company. Its possessions were inalienable. Individuals in the northern lands could lose their property in various ways, but Church property remained with the Church in perpetuity. Every loss to an individual could therefore be transferred to the Church, but the opposite seldom occurred.

At first, in the early part of the Middle Ages, up to about 1050, the secular kings seem to have thought they could control this process. They typically paid off their debts to the Church in deeds like this: "I give to the bishop and monastery of Worcester this piece of land to remain free of all human service till the end of time." [74] Usually, in cases like this, the Church was exempt from secular taxation, but was free to levy its own taxes in the form of "tithes" – a tax of (usually) 10% on the labor of all the people living on its lands. This system was essentially a formula for the perpetual accumulation of wealth.

As the Church fattened itself on the wealth of Europe, the relationship between kings and popes changed. From about 1050 to 1300 monarchs gradually ceded their rights to the Church, and in no field was this more obvious than in law. The Pope claimed to be the supreme judge in all of Europe, and the hapless kings accepted "canon law" – Church law. This form of law became a huge business, with qualified solicitors able to amass fortunes from the "gifts" they received from the litigants they represented before the Pope. Many people from all levels of medieval society were willing to go into debt to pay these lawyers. The fact that the Pope had the power to annul debts owed to money-lenders probably made the investment worthwhile in most cases: the more you paid the Pope's lawyers, the more likely he was to declare you debt-free.

For a time the kings themselves found that it was easy enough to play the new system in their own interests. Furthermore, it could be lucrative. For instance, in 1238 Henry III of England decided to block the will of the monks of Winchester to appoint their own bishop. He appealed to the Pope, and the best lawyers on both sides dragged out the case for over five years. During this time Henry was able to pocket the money raked in by the vacant bishopric – it came to about £20,000, a tidy sum even for a king in those days.

This system worked very well for all but the overwhelming majority of medieval people, the peasants who were fast becoming "serfs". These were essentially slaves, and the Church eventually became the largest owner of actual slaves in Europe. It took until 1807 for slavery to be abolished in the British Empire, but as late as 1864 there were slaves directly and legally owned by the Christian order of the Benedictines in Brazil (Kahl, 1981, p. 33).

As the wealth of Europe passed to the Church, the Church itself became the main employer of the more intelligent section of the community. The first sons of aristocrats usually followed aristocratic careers, but their second sons were often slotted into clerical careers as bishops or abbots. The best and brightest of the lower classes also found that a career within the Church was the best way to "get ahead". It was certainly better than toiling on the fields of the vast farming estates owned by the Church, as millions of serfs did, compelled to wear out their bodies for the glory of Papal Rome.

As the economic interests of the aristocracy and the medieval Church converged, we ended up with the medieval system in which there was no essential difference between "the Church" and "the State". Medieval kings were essentially like the minor tributary satraps of the original Roman Empire, owing obedience to Rome. Their subjects had no choice other than to follow them. This was the political order known as "Christendom": when the Pope was almost as powerful as a modern emperor like Stalin or Mao, and his subjects had no choice but to cloak their thoughts or aspirations in the rhetoric of Christianity

More and more young, intelligent men and women therefore became servants of the medieval Church, in one form or another. The Church was an immensely rich corporation; it was the largest single employer in medieval Europe; it guaranteed legal protection; and it provided the safest career paths. But these intelligent recruits bore with them the seeds of the Church's destruction. They were, after all, the descendants of Odinists, and in many cases their own parents or grandparents were largely "converts" in name only.

It was therefore inevitable that, sooner or later, these young people would subvert the Church from within. They brought to it Odinist values, and eventually those values would challenge the hegemony of the Church's Christian preachings.

But neither of these opposing views of life was destined to prevail. Instead, they came to form a very uneasy hybrid that was the intellectual foundation of "Christendom". This notion of "Christendom" was very useful in opposing the Muslim aggressors who took over much of Spain and most of the Mediterranean islands. Yet it was not really either Christian or Odinist. Christians who actually believed in the New Testament would have accepted the Muslim conquest as part of their god's will. A genuine Odinist would have fought against the Muslims as strenuously as Æthelfrith fought against the Christians. Instead, there was a moral and psychological compromise.

The ethical and intellectual fault-lines of this period were most obviously displayed in a great literary work, the *Song of Roland*, which perhaps dates to the middle of the 12th century. On the one hand, all the "Christian" details about the historical battle – ostensibly between Christians and Muslims – are wrong. On the other hand, the heroism of Roland and Oliver, while delightfully Odinist in tone, is somewhat diminished when we realize that they were really Frankish Christian heroes fighting against their Basque Christian brethren. Even the heroism of this tale is diminished when we recall that the majority of the population was forced to live in virtual slavery, plagued by the illnesses of malnutrition and overwork, in service to a religion that was no longer even that which their forefathers had so bravely resisted.

25

ODINISM IN CHRISTIAN CHURCHES

When Pope Gregory sent Augustine to convert the Odinist Anglo-Saxons, in 597, for once a Christian was instructed not to destroy heathen temples. Instead, the pontiff told his agent:

> Do not pull down the fanes. Destroy the idols: purify the temples with holy water: set relics there, and let them become temples of the true God. So the people will have no need to change their places of concourse, and where of old they were wont to sacrifice cattle to demons, thither let them continue to resort on the day of the saint to whom the Church is dedicated, and slay their beasts, no longer as a sacrifice but for a social meal in honor of Him whom they now worship.

To a large extent, Gregory's instructions were obeyed. Most churches of the Anglo-Saxon period are therefore built on formerly Odinist sacred sites, a process later followed elsewhere.

Four and a half centuries after Augustine's mission, the Normans began to pull down nearly all the Anglo-Saxon churches and erect Norman buildings on the same sites. These churches, and later cathedrals, thus continued to honor the holy places of Anglo-Saxon Odinism. Almost every Norman ecclesiastical building in Britain is therefore built on a site that pre-Christian Odinists considered sacred. The same is true in much of continental Europe.

Throughout Britain, and also many areas of the continent, churches and cathedrals also perpetuated pre-Christian heathen motifs, particularly in their sculpture. A simple introduction to these heathen survivals is provided by Ronald Sheridan and Anne Ross' book, *Gargoyles & Grotesques*.[75] In their introduction, the authors state:

> However we are to interpret the great corpus of gargoyles and grotesques, and other seemingly pagan motifs, which enrich and enliven our European churches, one thing is clear. These strange devices cannot simply be written off as meaningless decorations of purely functional features. It is certain that many of them had a very real meaning for those who created them and for those who worshipped in the structures which housed them or were externally adorned by them. ... The Church in medieval times

had come to be the storehouse of the sub-conscious of people – the lumber-room, as it were, in which were bygone, ancient, half-forgotten, half-formulated beliefs and superstitions, customs and folklore.

Sheridan and Ross divide their book into 23 chapters, each of which contains illustrations from medieval churches of what the authors believe to be depictions of surviving heathen beliefs. Since most of these photos are from English churches, it is unfortunate that the authors determinedly refer to all these survivals as "Celtic". While there was little essential difference between basic Celtic and Germanic beliefs, both being derived from the original Indo-European religion (see Chapter 5), it is a fact that most of the categories of "pagan survival" illustrated by Sheridan and Ross are more amenable to an Anglo-Saxon Odinist interpretation.

We will therefore now examine those Odinist motifs that match the "Celtic" categories described by Sheridan and Ross.

"Giants". The authors cite the Cerne Giant, carved into the hillside above the Dorset village of Cerne Abbas, as a prototype for this motif. This giant has an erect penis and is holding aloft a club. Another gigantic figure associated with this motif is the god Frey. We have an 11th century statuette (supposedly) of Frey from Rällinge in Sweden, featuring an erect penis; and Adam of Bremen said this was a significant aspect of Frey's statue in the temple at Uppsala. Some of the Viking-age stories of Frey state that he lost his sword, which would account for the Cerne Abbas "club": Frey is said to have killed a giant named Beli with an antler, and the weapon held by the Cerne giant has antler-like bulges. The earthwork itself can be dated no earlier than the 17th century, but the 13th century church also contains carved images of giants.

"The Green Man, or Jack o' the Green". Better known as Jack-in-the-Green, this ancient figure personifies the spirit of new life returning after winter. Even today in England he is represented by a man in a wickerwork frame that is covered by branches, leaves and flowers, through which only the occupant's eyes can be seen. He is traditionally a part of the May Day festivities, which still honor Easter (Old English Eostre or Eastre), our goddess of Spring and the dawn.

"Foliate Heads". From *Völuspá* we learn that Odin consults with the severed head of Mímir. Other sources add that Mímir has access to arcane knowledge from other worlds, that his head resides in a well or spring, and that this well is beneath a root of the cosmos-sustaining world-tree, Yggdrasill. Just as a depiction of a crucifixion is an obvious symbol for Christianity, so a severed head from which foliage is sprouting, a head that Odin consults, seems a natural symbol of Odinism.

"Cernunnos". The authors say that Cernunnos was a Celtic horned god. While no surviving myth depicts any of the Germanic gods with horns, there are many depictions of people, presumably priests, wearing ritual horned helmets. Examples of this motif are too frequent to list. Suffice it to say that they nearly always occur in the context of sacred rites. They are found on the runic horn from Gallehus (see the following section), on the tapestries from the Oseberg ship in which two priestesses were buried, in a 7th century Anglo-Saxon grave in Kent, and on the two "dancing warriors" on the Sutton Hoo helmet. H. R. Ellis Davidson suggested that this type of figure represents "an emissary" of Odin. [76]

Horned "dancing warriors" from the early 7th century Sutton Hoo ship burial

"Non-naturalistic severed heads". One example illustrated is a triple head, a tricephalos, at York Minster. The authors say: "The motif was taken into the Christian Church to portray the Trinity; but this device was frowned upon by the Church authorities, and eventually banned." This figure is clearly irrelevant to any Christian myth, but it appears on the fifth century runic horn from Gallehus, north Schleswig, the heartland of Anglo-Saxon migration to the British Isles. On the panels of this horn [77] are scenes that are usually understood to represent heathen rites. The second panel depicts a three-headed "giant" holding an axe in one hand and leading a goat with the other. The goat suggests that the figure is Thor, or one of his worshippers, and the axe became, in later times, the famous "Thor's hammer".

"Fertility". Most of the examples given are of the "Sheela-na-gig" type, sculptures showing a woman with gaping or exaggerated genitals. No-one has been able to explain these figures, and obviously the possession of genitals, whether exposed or concealed, is not a proof of fertility. A better example of fertility would be the figure on the 12th century font at Winterbourne Monkton, who appears to be giving birth. A possible predecessor is the small statuette from Fardål, north Jutland, of a woman in a short skirt who is grasping her right nipple with her left hand and clearly offering her breast. The larger than life-size 3rd century BCE female figure found at Braak in Schleswig, with splayed legs and exaggerated genitals, is more obviously a part of this tradition.

"Nightmares". The examples given by Sheridan and Ross depict a human being clasped and pecked at by monstrous birds and part-reptiles. This motif is very common in Germanic heathen art, two of the best known examples appearing in the first and fourth groups on the Sutton Hoo purse lid. Here the symbolic meaning is complex, with the legs of the humans and the monsters crossing to form swastika-like patterns – presumably a reference to Thor. By the time the motif was taken over by Christianity it had lost all its subtlety, as in the sculpture at Autun of a hanged Judas being menaced by flanking demons.

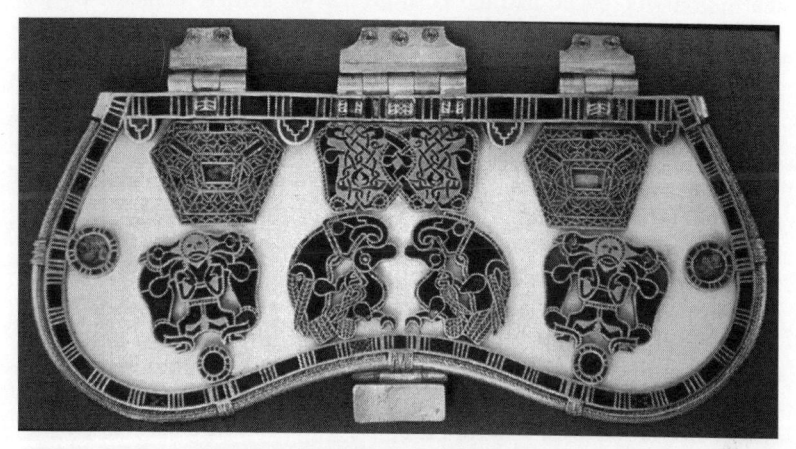

"Nightmare" figures and beaked heads from the English Odinist burial at Sutton Hoo

"Beaked heads and associated pantheon". The authors repeat their usual claim of Celtic origins, but they need have looked no further than the two central images on the Sutton Hoo purse lid, above.

Hermaphrodites. The examples published by Sheridan and Ross are truly grotesque, but have no evident origin in the Bible. They may reflect half-understood fears of heathen priests, since two Christian writers have hinted at some sort of sexual ambiguity (not homosexuality, or they would have said so) among the Odinist priesthood. Adam of Bremen said that Freyr was worshipped at Uppsala with "effeminate gestures", while Bede tells us that Anglo-Saxon Odinist priests were allowed to ride only mares. Ellis Davidson (1974, p. 97) explained Adam's hostility by suggesting rather vaguely that perhaps "some kind of symbolic drama to ensure the divine blessing on the fruitfulness of the season was once performed at Uppsala in Frey's honor". Given the Christian attitude to sexuality (see Chapter 15), it is not hard to imagine heathen fertility rites being reduced to grotesquery by sex-starved Christians.

"Mermaid and Merman". The examples given by Sheridan and Ross are playful and presumably mainly decorative. Yet it is helpful to recall that the word "merman" derives from the Old English word "mere", meaning a lake or pond. The most famous of Anglo-Saxon legendary/heroic figures is Beowulf, whose monstrous opponent Grendel lived in a mere-pool or tarn. Grendel was thus a mere-man. Beowulf then had to deal with Grendel's mother, a *mere-wif mihtig* – "mighty mere-woman", in her lair at the bottom of a deep lake.

"Serpents: St George Motif". It is almost impossible to think of the heroic age of the Germanic peoples without dragons and serpents coming to mind. (The same word was used for both beasts.) They are slain by heroes like Beowulf and Sigurd, they are depicted on items as diverse as the Sutton Hoo shield and the Gosforth Cross, and are depicted on the prows of "dragon ships". They are an enduring image of the Viking age. Even that inveterate Chistianizer, Olaf Tryggvason could not resist naming his flagship the "Long Serpent". In the final battle, Thor and the world serpent will destroy one another. An image so central to Odinism could scarcely fail to pass into Christian imagery.

"The Mallet God". The only illustration of this figure is from a stone pillar at Codford St Mary, Wiltshire. The authors claim this represents Sucellos, but do not explain why he is not depicted with what they call his "goblet of plenty" or his "dog attribute". In fact, the Wiltshire figure is a vigorous male wearing what looks like a typical Anglo-Saxon tunic. In one hand he holds a standard "Thor's hammer", while the other hand reaches up to a tree on which grow fruit resembling apples. This image suggests Thor, the defender of cosmic order, Yggdrasill, the tree that creates that order, and the symbolic apples that keep the gods young.

"Lunar and Solar Heads". The only English example given by the authors is a stucco ceiling from an inn, which looks like a refined version of the sun symbols on the runic horn from Gallehus.

"Centaurs". While these strange creatures, half-horse and half-human, are best known from Ancient Greece, a very clear example is shown on the third panel of the non-runic horn from Gallehus. It is playing some very important role in the Germanic heathen rituals depicted: in the panel above there is a classic Valkyrie with a drinking horn. Three of the images published by Sheridan and Ross provide food for thought. One is from a church at Iffley, Yorkshire. It appears to show a female centaur trampling a sheep beneath her hoofs. In Christian symbolism the sheep, or lamb, is a symbol of Jesus ("agnus Dei"). In the same church there is a carving of a male centaur tearing open the jaws of a griffin, rather as Thor is portrayed as tearing open the jaws of the Midgard Serpent. The griffin was used in Christian symbolism to represent St Mark. In another Yorkshire church, at Adel, a male centaur wearing a Viking-style helmet is firing an arrow at another griffin.

Early 5th century figures from Gallehus, Schleswig. Note the centaur, sun symbols, horned dancers and tricephalos

"Hagodays". These are better known as "sanctuary knockers", rings set on the doors of churches and cathedrals, usually held in the mouth of a fierce beast. It was believed that a fugitive who managed to grab one of these rings would be protected from his pursuers. To grasp a sacred ring was a serious matter in pre-Christian Odinism. Several sagas describe this large gold or silver ring, on which oaths were sworn, as being kept in Thor's temples. H. R. Ellis Davidson (1974, p.77) added: "There is independent evidence that this ring was sacred to Thor, for in Irish sources the 'ring of Thor' is one of the treasures taken from his temple in 995. Earlier than this, in 876, the heathen Danish leaders in England made a truce with King Alfred, and they are said in the *Anglo-Saxon Chronicle* to have sworn oaths to him on their sacred ring."

"Column Figures". These are illustrated by two columns in which a human face is embedded, rather like Ariel embedded in the tree in *The Tempest*, and two in which the columns are suspended on corbels in the form of bearded male heads. In the latter two, another world is symbolically depicted on the capitals. We know that holy columns or pillars that supported the universe were sacred in the Odinist lands. Tacitus mentions one that was standing in his lifetime, perhaps in Frisia. Several writers refer to an *Irminsul* as a central holy object for the continental Saxons. Rudolph of Fulda describes it as a *universalis columna*, a pillar of the universe. A similar column is recalled in the English place-name Thurstable, in Kent. The name means "Thor's column" (from Old English *syl*, pillar). We learn from several of the Icelandic sagas that the main pillars of a house were equally sacred to Thor, just as Thor's equivalent, Indra, upholds the universe in the *Rigveda*. What could be more natural than to carve a pillar in such a way as to incorporate an image of the god with whom it is associated? And how can this bear a relationship to any Christian imagery?

While some of these identifications may be debated, it is still clear that all of these motifs have an obvious Indo-European pagan or heathen relevance, and that any Christian meaning that may be attributed to them is contrived. The fact that heathen imagery survived in churches built on earlier heathen sites shows – at the very least – that Christianity did not destroy all the heathen beliefs of the ordinary people, the masons and other tradesmen who worked on these churches. We shall now see that Odinism continued at much higher levels of society in the Period of Dual Faith.

26

THE PERIOD OF DUAL FAITH: WOMEN

From the beginning of the Christian period it was obvious that two diametrically opposed views of women were locked in conflict. The Indo-Europeans honored women, while the Semitic view regarded females as lesser beings and, largely, blamed women for the presence of "evil" in the world.

We have seen (Chapter 15) that, according to Tacitus, the Germans of his day believed "there resides in women an element of holiness and a gift of prophecy". Tacitus adds that the Germans did not make their women into goddesses. As C. S. Lewis reminded us: "The Norsemen, in fact, treat their women not primarily as women but as people". [78]

A very different view of women was taken by Christianity (see Chapter 15). In particular, it should be recalled that several highly regarded Christian theologians believed sexual reproduction would not have been required at all if Eve had not sinned in the Garden of Eden. St Thomas Aquinas argued that his god must have given Eve to Adam as a "help" for reproduction, since for any other purpose a man would have been better. This attitude continued through to the Protestant period, with Martin Luther, for instance, saying that women were only incubators for children: "If they become tired or even die, that does not matter. Let them die in childbirth – that is why they are there." (*Von Ebelichen Leben,* 1522.) This is consistent with the attitudes expressed in the New Testament. Mary was valued, if at all, as the possessor of a womb that had carried a messiah. When Mary asked her son for help, he replied, "Woman, what have I to do with thee?" (John 2: 1-5) – and in doing so he used precisely the term that he addressed to the "woman taken in adultery" (John 8:10). Not once in the gospels does he use any term of endearment toward Mary, not even "mother".

This attitude to women prevailed in Christian art until the thirteenth century. Women are seldom even portrayed in this art, except for that Mother of all Sin, Eve. We see her perhaps at her worst on the bronze doors of the Romanesque cathedral at Hildesheim (c. 1015). In a hideous scene, two human figures are being expelled from paradise. They are naked and grotesque, pathetically covering up their genitals with leaves. The man, Adam, accepts his lot with bowed head. The woman, Eve, is glancing back at the scene of her crime. If these figures were not so shameful, and naked, they could equally have represented Lot, and his wife (Genesis 19, 8) who looked back with longing on the sinful city of Sodom and was turned by her god into a pillar of salt. Typical of this Biblical misogyny is that the story tells us Lot's daughters then made him drunk so as to have children with him (Genesis 19, 33-36).

In 1903 a ship burial dating to around 850 CE was discovered at Oseberg in Norway. It contained parts of the skeletons of two women, together with a magnificent collection of skillfully crafted grave-goods. These had been naturally preserved due to the chemical composition of the soil. The richly-carved four-wheeled cart has often been compared to the cart in which, according to Tacitus, the goddess Nerthus toured the northern lands of her worshippers.

Few experts have given much thought to the two women who were buried in such luxury, other than to suggest that the elder one, who was buried with the greater distinction, may have been a queen – perhaps Ása, or Alfhild, who played a pivotal role in establishing one of the royal dynasties of Norway. The older woman was about fifty, and the younger one was probably in her early twenties. The younger woman was no mere slave-girl killed to accompany her mistress into the afterlife. She had her own bed, in the burial chamber on the de-commissioned ship, and her clothing and the other appointments of her burial were splendidly crafted. Slaughtered animals placed in the ship included fifteen horses, four dogs, two oxen and a peacock. In brief, both women were of high social status.

There are several indications that the two may have owed this status more to their religious rank rather than to any royal connection. Some scholars have therefore argued that they were both priestesses, devotees of Freya or Frige. One of the reasons for this conclusion is the nature of the grave goods buried with them. These included four looms as well as numerous other tools for making textiles by spinning and weaving, clubs for beating flax, and shears for clipping sheep. Spinning and weaving are closely associated with Frige, while one of Freya's by-names is Hörn, which probably derives from *hörr*, flax. The ship also contained wall-hangings depicting heathen religious rituals and symbols. Furthermore, there was a chest containing hazel-nuts, apples and corn – all of which are well-known fertility symbols.

Of course, ships as such are themselves symbols of both Frey and Freya. (The men in the Icelandic literature said to have received ship-burials were devotees of Frey.) Yet the actual ship in which the women were buried was not suited to open sea voyages, but would have been a perfect vessel to transport priestesses around the fjords to visit their congregations – maybe even carrying with them an image of the goddess.

Perhaps the best evidence that the women were heathen priestesses is of a negative nature. Shortly after the funeral some intruders broke into the burial mound. These were not common grave-robbers, since they did not take the many costly items that we can view today. Their main intention seems to have been to desecrate the burial. The wall-hangings, which presumably decorated the burial chamber, had been torn down and roughly rolled up – as if to prevent the sacred scenes from performing whatever religious purpose they were intended for. The great bed had been hacked to pieces in a seeming frenzy of hatred, suggesting that it may have been resented as symbolizing a divine marriage ritual. Various other objects of religious significance had also been smashed, including the curved serpent on the prow. Both the bodies had been dragged from their burial chamber.

Whoever violated the grave also removed the right hand and the left upper arm of the older woman. Since the aim of the intruders seems to have been desecration rather than robbery, it is unlikely that this was a gruesome theft of her rings and bracelets for mere monetary gain. Probably her jewelry incorporated heathen symbols that enraged the despoilers as much as the great bed evidently did. If that is the case, the removal of her hand and arm was intended more to desecrate her body out of religious antipathy than to rob it. The ultimate earthly fate of the younger woman may have been even more gruesome. Most of her body was removed altogether, so that only a few bones now survive. No reputable scholar seems to have offered any suggestion as to what the violators may have done with her stolen corpse.

As to the identity of the criminals, all those who have considered this question blame Christians who, in H. R. Ellis Davidson's words, must have "objected to the remains of a priestess of the goddess surviving in their neighborhood". It would take a very twisted mentality to break into a tomb solely to smash up religious items in a fit of blasphemous hatred and then to violate the bodies buried there. Something had especially enraged the criminals, and given the prevailing Christian attitudes it may be that the special cause of their outrage was that these were *female* priests. St Paul's words should be recalled here: "I permit no woman to teach or to have authority over men."

From the Odinist priestesses buried in c. 850 to the vile Hildesheim image of Eve in c. 1015, woman in northern Europe had fallen from her place of respect and honor to a position of contempt. Yet the descendants of those Odinists who had been "converted" on pain of death, or actually slaughtered, lived on. Since Odinism reflected their natural view of the world, it could not be eradicated. As we saw in Chapter 24, the Church now owned most of their ancestral lands and wealth. The Church was one of the few employers for young men of intellectual or artistic ability, and of necessity they became its servants. In doing so, however, they were to change Christian teachings and beliefs beyond recognition.

Nowhere was this more evident than in attitudes toward women. By the time of the building of Chartres Cathedral (see Chapter 27) women were being regarded again with a little of their old Odinist dignity. This was the period of the rise of the so-called "Gothic" temperament. Churches were now being dedicated, not to enraged temple-burning saints, but to "Our Lady", *Notre Dame*. Troubadours were extolling fair maidens and the cult of idealized, or "chivalric", or "courtly", love. Madonnas were being carved and painted, or depicted in tapestries, and celebrated in song and romance, and they were ideal versions of woman according to the spirit of the time. ("Madonna" simply means "my lady", and it is often hard to tell whether the artist's real worship was for woman as such or for the mother of Jesus.)

Sir Kenneth Clark made an interesting comment on this new cult:

> Of the two or three faculties that have been added to the European mind since the civilisation of Greece and Rome, none seems to me stranger and more inexplicable than the sentiment of ideal or courtly love. It was entirely unknown to antiquity, Passion, yes; desire, yes of course; steady affection, yes. But this state of utter subjection to the will of an almost unapproachable woman; this belief that no sacrifice was too great, that a whole lifetime might properly be spent in paying court to some exacting lady or suffering on her behalf – this would have seemed to the Romans or the Vikings not only absurd but unbelievable; and yet for hundreds of years it passed unquestioned. [79]

What Clark failed to note was that courtly love was equally alien to Jesus, or his disciples, or his saints. The Jesus who had only harsh words for his mother, the priests who debated whether women were even human, could never have foreseen this development.

It was, of course, a resurgence of the old heathen spirit – but now within the Church. It was not really true to either Christianity or Odinism, but resulted rather from the increasing hybridization of the two radically different faiths. It was a mutant compromise: Odinist respect for women could be projected on to the figure of Mary without the risk of being burned at the stake, and from "Our Lady" it was allowed to radiate out to "My Lady", Madonna, wherever she might be found (or imagined).

The unstable nature of this fusion is well illustrated by a carving that Clark deemed worthy of full-page reproduction in his book: a 14th century ivory of the Virgin and Child from the Louvre. The Virgin in this case is a slender girl who looks pubescent. Her face is childlike, with large eyes, wide cheeks, and the small chin of a toddler. Her shoulders are pathetically slender, and her legs seem short. The "miracle" here is not that of parthenogenesis, but of the idea that such an immature figure could actually survive childbirth. The sculptor knew this too: he deliberately made the Jesus figure much shorter than the age of its face would suggest. In her own way this Mary has a certain delicate charm; but a practical Roman would have scoffed at her unsuitability for child-bearing, while earlier centuries of Christians would have been appalled that any female could become the object of veneration.

The Louvre Virgin is, then, a suitable image for the Period of Dual Faith. This era, an unnatural and uneasy union between incompatible religions, was to last from the early 12th to the 20th centuries. In its course, both Christianity and Odinism integrated to the extent that it is often hard for people living today to disentangle the two strands.

| **Classical pagan (ancient Greek) view of the heroic female torso** | **Christian view of the female body – Eve covering up** | **View of woman in the Period of Dual Faith** |

That disentangling will be the task of much of the rest of this book, but from now on we must bear in mind one self-evident truth. Neither Christianity nor Odinism was dominant during the centuries of Dual Faith. Each religion gave up some of its core beliefs in a necessary but finally unsuccessful union. Each was changed, distorted, in the process. If we can say that Christianity survived, as it did at the formal level, then we must equally say that Odinism also survived, in the form of new core beliefs within the Church that would have been abhorrent to earlier Christians. Alternatively, if it is argued that Odinism ceased to exist during this era, in which its values continued to gain greater (albeit distorted) expression within Christendom, we have to say that Christianity also ceased to exist. The Odinist religious strand would not have been recognizable to Virgil, to Æthelfrith, or to the priestesses of the Oseberg ship. The Christian religious strand would not have been recognizable to Jesus, St Paul, or St Augustine.

27

THE PERIOD OF DUAL FAITH: CHARTRES CATHEDRAL

Alas, Lord, surely thou art great and fair.
But lo her wonderfully woven hair!
And thou didst heal us with thy piteous kiss;
But see now, Lord; her mouth is lovelier.

She is right fair; what hath she done to thee?
Nay, fair Lord Christ, lift up thine eyes and see;
Had now thy mother such a lip – like this?

- Swinburne, *Laus Veneris*

The reader will recall (Chapter 11) that Odinist anthropology begins with three "powerful and loving" gods giving our remote ancestors special gifts: the breath of spirit; mind and feeling; the warmth of life; and a desirable appearance. We have also seen that the god Ríg taught his human son to use runes. Finally, we have stressed (Chapter 9) that Odin's role in the mythology is to acquire knowledge and wisdom, which he shares with his human allies.

By contrast, Christian anthropology has their god creating the first humans. They were his creatures, and at first he gave them just one order: "Of every tree of the garden thou mayest freely eat, but of the tree of knowledge of good and evil, thou shalt not eat of it: for in the day that thou eatest thereof thou shalt surely die." First Eve ate from this tree, then Adam at her urging. Now they knew "good and evil", which must have had something to do with sex, since the initial consequence of their act was that "they sewed fig leaves together" as aprons to cover their sexual parts. God did not kill them as he had earlier threatened. Instead he cursed them and their descendants to lives of misery. In an apparent afterthought he expelled mankind from the garden: "lest he put forth his hand, and take also of the tree of life, and eat, and live for ever".

These two utterly contrasting genesis stories could not fail to have very different psychological effects on the people who believed them. The first promotes confidence in the human use of the mind, of thinking and feeling and the realm of the spirit. It leads to intellectual self-reliance, logic, trust in the potential of human ingenuity, acceptance of human instinct. The other promotes a servile reliance on authority – the authority of a god, or a holy book, or a priesthood, or even just tradition. It necessitates unconditional obedience to the perceived or alleged will of others. In this system the independent use of the mind, personal initiative and even courage can be condemned as "pride", a serious Christian sin, since as Jesus said (John 15, 5), "without me ye can do nothing". Self-reliance is therefore a crime against the god who cursed humanity for seeking knowledge.

The practical results of these two contrasting attitudes were predictable. One view eventually led to the discovery and settlement of a new continent by a handful of British people in fragile sailing ships. The other led to crabbed arguments based on the authority of the Bible, such as St Augustine's [80] proclamation that:

> As to the fabled 'antipodes', men, that is, who live on the other side of the earth, where the sun rises when it sets for us, men who plant their footsteps opposite ours, there is no rational ground for such a belief ... For there is no untruth of any kind in the Scripture, whose reliability in the account of past events is attested by the fulfillment of its prophecies for the future; and it would be too ridiculous to suggest that some men might have sailed from our side of the earth to the other, arriving there after having crossed the vast expanse of ocean, so that the human race should be established there also by the descendants of the one first man.

In other words, the Biblical stories don't conceive of people living in the southern hemisphere, so there can be no such people. The Biblical stories are unconditionally binding, so rational discussion is impossible and impertinent. In 748 Pope St Zachary instructed St Boniface to investigate whether a certain priest was preaching the doctrine that Augustine had dismissed as a "fable", now calling it a "perverse teaching, contrary to the Lord and to his own soul" and adding that if the priest really was preaching such a doctrine Boniface must "expel him from the Church, deprived of his priestly dignity". In total contrast, the heathen attitude would have been to reserve judgment until someone had managed to sail to the southern hemisphere and report back. (That is exactly what men like James Cook did, as soon as the old Biblical dogmas wore thin.)

It is therefore unsurprising that early Christian architecture was based almost entirely on the Roman model the Christians had inherited. The drug of canting adherence to "authority" had poisoned the Western impulse to problem-solving. Still, the pagan Romans had been brilliant engineers, so the Christians were not depriving themselves of much by slavishly copying Roman basilicas for their churches. Yet in 1194 a problem arose for which there were no precedents. The cathedral at Chartres burned down, leaving intact only two towers, the façade between them, and the crypt. There had been fires before, and essentially the church had been rebuilt on the old model, with some updated features. Yet now a whole new style was emerging. It was to become known as the Gothic style. Its basis was the Gothic, or pointed, arch.

The Gothic arch is a far better engineering solution than the round or Roman arch, since the load above is transmitted more directly to the ground and lateral thrust is minimized. Yet the architect at Chartres was obviously instructed to span the entire foundations of the old cathedral, a huge task that even the Gothic arch itself could not accomplish. He solved it by using flying buttresses on a massive scale. The result was a masterpiece, covering over 117 thousand square feet, soaring 370 feet into the skies, and lit by 176 brilliant stained glass windows. The nave alone, where the worshippers sat, was 236 feet long, 54 feet wide and 107 feet high. Chartres was not only an unparalleled achievement from the structural point of view; it was "one of the most remarkable of human achievements ... Now by the devices of the Gothic style ... he [i.e. humankind] could make stone seem weightless: the weightless expression of his spirit." (Clark, 1969)

What did this miraculous building have in common with the Christian complex of ideas? Clearly it would have been unimaginable to the Jesus whose provincial sayings counseled his followers to, for instance: "Take therefore no thought for the morrow: for the morrow shall take thought for the things of itself. Sufficient unto the day is the evil thereof." (Matthew 6, 34) By contrast, Chartres has stood gloriously intact for 800 years. Nor could it have appealed to the Hebrews of the Old Testament, whose "jealous god" allegedly caught them building a high tower, probably envisaged as a sort of stepped pyramid called a ziggurat. According to Genesis 11, 1-9:

> And the Lord said, Behold, the people is one, and they have all one language; and this they begin to do; and now nothing will be restrained from them, which they have imagined to do. Go to, let us go down, and there confound their language, that they may not understand one another's speech. So the Lord scattered them abroad from thence upon the face of all the earth.

Chartres was a supreme example of a people deciding that "nothing will be restrained from them, which they have imagined to do". Chartres was a symbol of the human spirit, which was at last allowed to soar again now that Christianity and Odinism had reached a compromise in the Period of Dual Faith. If the builders had issued a medieval version of a modern prospectus, it would no doubt have been couched in Christian terms, since anything less would have resulted in extreme penalties from the Church. Yet apart from empty words it was scarcely Christian at all. Even the site of the building is said to have been a former pagan shrine. Worse, the succession of Christian buildings on the site were claimed to have contained a tunic belonging to Jesus' mother, and we have seen how unrevered she was in early Christianity (Chapter 26). Worse still, the cathedral at Chartres was actually dedicated to "Notre Dame", "Our Lady", a goddess who was not specifically Christian even in name, and might as well be called Frige or Freya.

Pagan and heathen principles permeate Notre Dame de Chartres. Some are obvious; some less so. Among the latter is the ancient symbol known as the "Vesica piscis". To draw this symbol, take a compass and inscribe a circle. Rule a line from the centre to the circumference. Place the point of the compass on the spot where the two lines join, and inscribe another circle of equal radius. The result is a Vesica piscis, which is often claimed to be a symbol of the female genitals. [81]

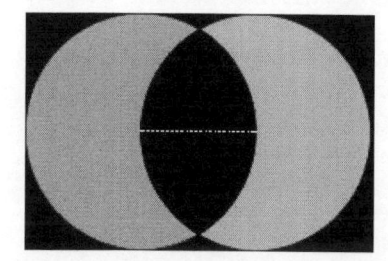

Vesica piscis, incorporating two gothic arches in the centre

Jesus emerging from the central part of a Vesica piscis, in Chartres Cathedral

The area of overlap between the circles contains two Gothic arches sharing a common base line, with one pointing upwards and one downwards, so if the yonic significance of the Vesica piscis is accepted, a female principle is embodied in the very structure of Gothic architecture. Nothing could be less Semitic than this, and we may be reminded of the Braak statue from Schleswig, with her prominent genitals (Chapter 35), or the Sheela-na-Gig figures in rural churches throughout northern Europe. In the centre of the Chartrain West Portal a seated Jesus is depicted emerging from the overlapping part of a Vesica piscis – and if the central portion is indeed to be considered a symbol of the external female genitals, his head and halo occupy a significant position. Since the cathedral itself is a goddess-temple, this symbolism seems plausible.

If that is too esoteric, it is still indisputable that Chartres embodies many other features that are overwhelmingly pagan. For instance, Chartres had a great cathedral school, practically a university, which attracted some of the brightest minds of that era. Its curriculum was based on that of the Roman pagan Varro (116-27 BCE), who had stipulated the "nine liberal arts" of grammar, logic, rhetoric, geometry, arithmetic, astronomy, music, medicine and architecture. By the time of the building of Chartres, medicine and architecture had become professional subjects, so only the first seven of Varro's liberal arts were taught there.

These arts are represented on the West front of the cathedral by statues of eminent ancient philosophers. Music is symbolized by Pythagoras, Logic by Aristotle; Rhetoric by Cicero; Geometry by Euclid; Arithmetic by (probably) Boethius; Astronomy by Ptolemy; Grammar by Priscian. The last of these was a 5th century scholar who based his study of Latin grammar on examples from pagan writers, particularly Virgil (see Chapter 14). Boethius was a 6th century philosopher who was born to an established Christian family but seems to have returned to paganism. According to Arnaldo Momigliano: "... many people have turned to Christianity for consolation. Boethius turned to paganism. His Christianity collapsed — it collapsed so thoroughly that perhaps he did not even notice its disappearance." [82] The other five worthies were all indisputably pagan.

Further decorations at Chartres that seem to have little or nothing to do with anything Jesus and his followers would recognize are the kings and queens of the Royal Portal, the signs of the zodiac and the "great labyrinth" (a pavement maze). The kings and queens are said to represent Old Testament figures, although there is no justification for this; and since they are depicted as wise, benevolent and beautiful the link seems far-fetched. The labyrinth incorporates eleven circuits, at the centre of which was a brass plaque depicting Theseus and the Minotaur. (It has since been replaced with a rosette.) Similar labyrinths, commonly with only seven circuits, were used in pre-Christian Greece and Rome, as well as in heathen northern Europe. Mazes can symbolize many things, and a Christian interpretation is possible, but Theseus is a figure from Greek, not Christian, mythology. (A meditative walk around the eleven circuits might recall the extra dimensions referred to in Chapter 8.)

The men who taught at Chartres were among the best minds of Europe. Their great obsession was to reconcile the ideas of the pagan Greek philosophers Plato and Aristotle. Of course, they tried to drag in Christian doctrines such as the Trinity, which makes that part of their work almost unreadable today. The attempt was a failure. Thus Gordon Leff [83] said of an influential Christian work by Bernard of Silvestris: "This is so much the product of Plato's *Timaeus* that it is hard to see its immediate bearing upon Christianity. That it was closely in keeping with the spirit of Chartres is apparent in its being addressed to Thierry of Chartres." Another Chartrain was William of Conches, who revived the theory of Democritus (5th century BCE), that all matter is composed of atoms. This eventually became the basis of modern physics until the discovery of sub-atomic particles, yet William was referred to the Chancellor for his un-Christian views. Amaury of Bène argued that: "... as light is not seen in itself but in air, so God is not seen by angels or by man in Himself, but in creatures." Leff's comment is delightful: "This immediately negated all the main tenets of Christian teaching: good and evil, sin and merit, the beatific vision or eternal reprobation lost all meaning in a world which was the same as God. There could be no need of salvation, of the sacraments, or ultimately, of the priesthood itself, when everything participated equally in God's nature." Naturally, Amaury was condemned by the Pope, and within four years of his death in 1207 his followers were being burned for heresy.

For a brief time the architects, philosophers and artists of Chartres achieved a synthesis of sorts between Christianity and Odinism. This syncretism, however, left out the major content of both faiths. It could perhaps be represented by the Vesica piscis itself. The area of overlap is in this sense contrived, with the bulk of both circles lying outside it. While it is easy to rejoice in the glory of the cathedral, it is sobering to recall one of the uses to which the maze was put. "Penitents" crawled around it on their knees, begging forgiveness for their Christian "sins".

The Church had encouraged its best thinkers to try to impose on Christianity an intellectual coherence. Given their heads, they had built a magnificent temple to a fertility goddess, had set up an international school to teach pagan philosophy, and had philosophically abolished the Christian god and all his tenets. In retrospect, they cannot be blamed for their ultimate failure. Neither the revelations claimed by a tribe of desert marauders, nor the homespun wisdom of a wandering fakir, could be reconciled to the demands of logic, or to the spiritual instincts of a people who were mainly still Indo-European, or to the claims of empirical reality. Christianity was a religion for people such as the zombie-like followers of St Cyril (Chapter 16), not for pagan intellectuals like Hypatia or caring ministers like the priestesses of Oseberg.

The Church therefore had no option but to resort to coercion. For the next few centuries heretics were persecuted, crusaded against and killed; witches were burned; absurd civil wars devastated Europe, reducing the population of Germany by maybe two-thirds; Catholics burned Protestants when they had the upper hand, and vice versa; intellectuals like Bruni and Galileo were persecuted or burned; and in all this time the vast mass of the people was deliberately kept in a state of health-destroying poverty and soul-destroying ignorance. Swinburne referred accurately to: "… all the blackness of darkness, rank with fumes of blood and loud with cries of torment, which covers in so many quarters the history, not romantic but actual, of the ages called the ages of faith". It is a testament to the relevance of Odinism to the European soul that a residue of it not only continued at a popular level, albeit lacking in sophistication, but in fact gradually ousted the alternative activities promoted by Christianity for the common people. In view of the persecutions, it is surprising that any of the old Odinist folk-customs survived at all. In the next chapter we will therefore examine just a few of those survivals.

Meanwhile, there is much Odinist symbolism in Chartres and other great cathedrals that is still largely unremarked – and certainly not properly studied. One of these is the use of heathen sacred mathematics.

In 2001 a mathematician at the University of Queensland, Dr Joan Helm, apparently cracked a code embedded in the manuscript of Chrétien de Troyes' 1170s poem, *Lancelot*. When Dr Helm laid out facsimiles of the manuscript on her floor, she noticed an ornate illuminated capital E at line 4401 – for no reason that is obvious in terms of the poem's structure. She noticed that the poem has 7118 lines, and when this figure is divided by 4401 the result is 1.6173596, or as close as was possible in that manuscript to 1.618. This is the figure known to the ancient Greek heathen philosophers as "the golden ratio".

The golden ratio occurs when you divide a line into two lengths, such that the whole line bears the same ratio to the longer segment as the longer segment does to the shorter. Today we represent the golden ratio as φ, "phi", which is the Greek letter representing the first syllable of the Parthenon's main architect, the sculptor Phidias. It can be the basis of geometrical shapes such as rectangles and triangles, can generate spirals, and may be expressed as 1.6180339989 ... etc.

According to Plato, the gods ordered the universe according to this geometrical ratio. It has been argued that almost every aspect of the Parthenon is based on it, and since the Parthenon was dedicated to the goddess of wisdom, its sacred geometry should be of special interest to Odinists.

Dr Helm was convinced that Chrétien de Troyes (or his scribe) had embedded the "forbidden" heathen ratio into his manuscript as a way of preserving it so that readers who had progressed beyond the ignorance of the dark ages could benefit from it, while the enforcers of that period, the Christian priests, wouldn't have a clue.

In the 13th century a mathematician called Fibonacci "discovered" a sequence of numbers that begin: 1,1,2,3,5,8,13,21,34,55,89, etc. In addition to all sorts of other interesting properties, each succeeding number in this sequence is the sum of the previous two. Curiously, if you divide a larger number by its predecessor, the answer comes closer to φ, 0.168, the further you get into the Fibonacci sequence.

Equally, modern biology has shown that many life-forms are structured very like the Fibonacci sequence, in that the more examples you measure, the more the average approximates to φ. This applies, for instance, to leaves on many twigs, to the spiral structure of nautilus shells, and so on. It starts to seem as though Plato may have been right: the gods may well have organised much of the universe according to this sacred heathen ratio.

Interestingly, it has been argued [84] that Virgil consciously used Fibonacci numbers in the structure of his *Aeneid*, which as we have seen is the most comprehensive surviving Western account of the heathen afterlife (Chapter 14).

One geometrical form that potentially contains an infinity of φs is the pentagram. If you analyse the illustration below, you will see that AD divided by AC equals φ, as does AC divided by AB, and so on.

Furthermore, another pentagram can be constructed within the first, as indicated by the starting line C to C^1. Within that new shape another can be nestled, and so on. Medieval Christians suppressed heathen knowledge that was not sanctioned by the Bible. In particular, they hated the pentagram, which they associated with their "dark god" called Satan.

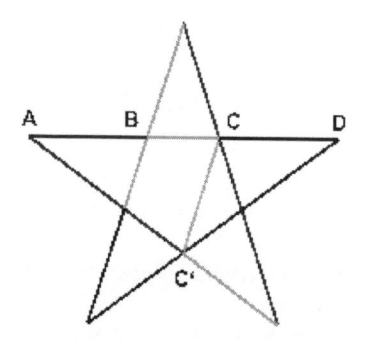

The pentagram can contain an infinity of golden ratios

Yet according to many writers on the subject, there are pentagrams in various features of Chartres Cathedral. One possibly extreme theory even claims the basic plan of the building is based on pentacles (pentagrams in circles) overlapping so as to form a vesica piscis, as shown below.

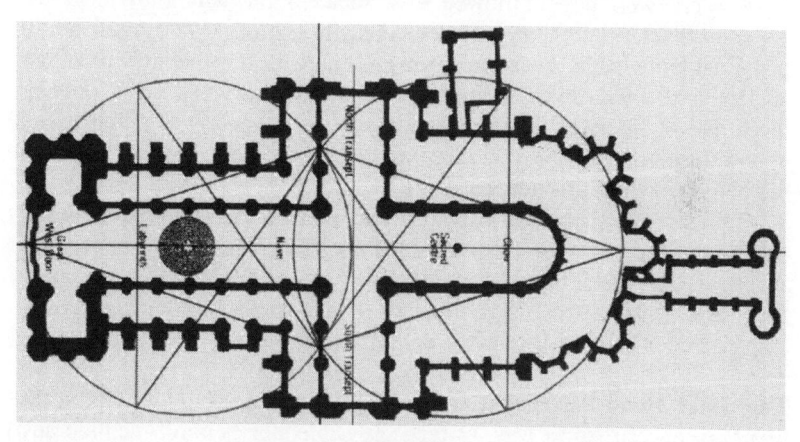

source:
http://members.home.nl/peregrine/TheGothicCathedrals.html

Without necessarily endorsing this particular theory, it is obvious that the great Gothic buildings of the Period of Dual Faith require much more study from a clear-eyed Odinist perspective. So far, there have been far too many wooly speculations about the alleged influence of ancient Druids or Knights Templar, and far too little logical or scientific analysis.

28

FOLK CUSTOMS: YULE

However subdued the people may have appeared there was always the active pagan instinct at work just beneath the surface.

- Stubba CG, Hidden Gods: the Period of Dual Faith

Every year as December approaches, articles, letters and blogs are published questioning the relationship between the customs of the season and the core values of Christianity. Some writers claim that at least some of the festive customs really can be linked to Christianity. Gift-giving, for example, may recall the tradition of the "Three Wise Men". Others claim the opposite, often indignantly. To these writers, gift-giving is secular and materialistic, and it encourages greed rather than spiritual purpose.

Readers who have followed this book so far will know that the apparent discrepancies can be resolved easily enough with a modicum of historical knowledge. In essence, what has happened is that aspects of our ancient and much-loved Odinist customs have survived on a popular level, and at the same time an equally simplistic version of an alien and opposed religion has been crudely grafted on to them. Neither tradition has benefited from this unnatural union.

Odinists can therefore stand up and reclaim our popular seasonal traditions. They are ours; not those of the Christians. They reflect our ancestral values; not those of the Middle East. And they will not recover their true spiritual significance until their origin in Odinism is re-emphasized. The brief list below, concerning Yule, may help in this task.

The date. Many unsophisticated modern Christians believe that Jesus was born on Christmas Day. In fact, the Bible stories don't mention any month or day. This caused problems for the early Christians, and until the 4th century CE all sorts of dates were used for Christmas. December 25 was eventually chosen, not because any new information had come to light, but because Odinists held our great mid-winter festival of Yule at mid-winter. Roman pagans also had their version of Yule, the seven-day Saturnalia. This festival was held at midwinter as a celebration of fertility and continuing life, even at the most barren time of the year, when the sun is at its lowest and weakest. It symbolizes the wheel of the seasons, which itself is related to the wheel of the ages (see Chapter 12). Julius Caesar's calendar, introduced in 45 BCE, was inaccurate by just over 11 minutes a year, and by the 4th century CE this incremental error meant that the shortest day was officially on the 25th of December.

The gifts. Surviving accounts of Yule in northern Europe are scanty, but we know a lot about its southern equivalent, the Saturnalia. Pagan Romans gave each other gifts at this time, choosing them very carefully for their intrinsic luck. For instance, honey was a popular present, given to ensure a year of sweetness. Gift-giving of this sort is an assertion of the human will to influence the future to the benefit of others, and is the opposite of Christian dependence on the will of a capricious god.

The mysterious gift-giver. It should be noted that the early church banned Christians from giving or receiving presents at this time of the year, believing it to be a heathen practice. According to folklorists, they were right. Today's Santa Claus is largely an advertising creation, but the tradition of a mysterious gift-giver is based on "Odin, riding through the Yuletide nights to distribute rewards and punishments to his worshippers", according to Christina Hole [85]. The surviving untarnished accounts do not show Odin "punishing" anybody – that is merely a Christian intrusion – but it is certainly fitting that the bringer of the gifts of knowledge and wisdom to humanity should be celebrated by a figure whose costume indicates that he is not of our normal world or our conventional time.

The greenery. Holly, ivy and mistletoe were special to our heathen ancestors because they were powerful life symbols, being evergreen and also bearing fruit at the most desolate time of the year. They were brought indoors at Yuletide as life-affirming decorations, and also hung as garlands on doors. For centuries the church banned these practices. That ban is long gone, except in one respect. In Christian tradition, mistletoe is never allowed inside a church. That is because it is sacred to Odinism as the weapon used to "kill" Balder – and it is therefore the apparently insignificant instrument that will ultimately bring about the regeneration of the earth after Ragnarok. The English-speaking peoples have shown their attitude to this church ban by creating a custom of kissing under the mistletoe.

The feast. Communal feasting and drinking of alcohol, in front of roaring fires, were central to the Yule festivities. Until the days of central heating, people remembered this by burning in their open fires a huge log of oak (for Thor), ash (for Odin) or fruit-tree wood (for Frey), called the "Yule Log". In many areas it was traditional to retain a portion of last year's log to be added to the new Yule fire, thus celebrating the cycle of the year. The great annual feast was also a joyful acknowledgement of our ancestors' sense of tribal community. Its Christian antithesis was the Last Supper, a furtive meal held by Jesus and his last twelve followers, one of whom had already decided to betray him.

The tree. This is another evergreen that was brought into houses at Yuletide as a life symbol. It seems to have been suppressed at an early date everywhere except in Germany, suggesting that it was a domestic-scale reminder of the Odinist sacred pillar (Chapter 25). From Germany the custom was spread to America by German settlers and soldiers, and subsequently to England in the 1820s. (Prior to that the English used a "Kissing Bough" suspended from the centre of the ceiling. It was just as decorative, but it provided more boisterous fun.) The tree as a central symbol of Odinism is a reminder of the joy of life, which is why maypoles were often banned by Christian priests. Their alternative symbol was the cross on which criminals were miserably crucified.

The candles. These are based on what was known as the "Yule Candle", indicating its sacred origin. It was a large candle, usually colored red, blue or green, and decorated with evergreens – mainly holly. It symbolized the light of the returning sun, the fuel for all life on earth. Christianity made its own use of the candle, of course. Sacred candles are burned in Catholic churches for the benefit of the souls of the bodily deceased, which reveals the contrast between the Odinist emphasis on life and the Christian emphasis on death.

The candle itself is a domestic reference to the great symbolic architecture of our ancestors in the Neolithic era. Tombs from that period, such as those at Newgrange, Clava and Maes Howe, were engineered so as to be pierced by shafts of sunlight on the shortest day. [86]

The carols. Communal singing was no doubt part of the old Yuletide festival. We can assume this from the fact that some early "Christmas" carols are clearly Odinist in spirit, with a later Christian veneer clumsily smeared on. Probably the best-known is the *Boar's Head Carol*, still sung every Christmas at Queen's College, Oxford, and accompanied by a thinly-disguised Odinist ceremony. (The boar is sacred to our god Frey, and its head often appeared on warriors' helmets.) Furthermore, many carols, and early songs such as *Sumer is icumen in*, are in the Ionian Mode, which was hated by the Church and labeled *Modus Lascivius* ("the Wanton Mode"). That they survived attests to their popularity.

The office party. From peasant Yuletide customs that survived in Britain and northern Europe until the last century, and from Roman accounts of the Saturnalia, we know that people dressed in various disguises at this time of the year – and that, being ritually unrecognizable, they indulged in a lot of horseplay. Modern versions of this behavior include the office party, the family Christmas get-together, and the various New Year's Eve functions, at all of which the usual limits of acceptable behavior tend to be relaxed. The closest Christian alternative is the midnight mass, when participants deliberately segregate themselves from the broader community in an austere declaration of their difference from the rest of the people.

The silly hats. During the Saturnalia, slaves were allowed to do and say almost whatever they liked. That included wearing the pointed hats that were normally forbidden to all but freemen. These hats are the ancestors of those we find today in Christmas crackers. Among other things, they symbolize the organic nature of the Odinist folkish community: even those who find themselves in a lowly social position are important members of a living tribe.

The Queen's Speech. In the Commonwealth countries, a modern tradition is for the Queen to make an annual televised speech. Although the actual content of these speeches is usually banal, the idea of a monarch making a special address to his or her nation at a consecrated time of the year harks back to our ancestral tradition of **sacral kingship**.

Over a hundred years ago the historian E. A. Freeman [87] noted that:

> The ancient English kingship was elective ... Among a people in whose eyes birth was highly valued, it was deemed desirable that the king should be the descendant of illustrious and royal ancestors. In the days of heathendom it was held that the king should come of the supposed stock of the Gods. These feelings everywhere pointed to some particular house as the royal house, the house whose members had a special claim on the suffrages of the electors. In every kingdom there was a royal family, out of which alone, under all ordinary circumstances, kings were chosen; but within that royal family the Witan of the land had a free choice.

Freeman perhaps overstated the clarity of the heathen English law, but his argument bears repetition today, when we are so used to the concept of "constitutional monarchy" with its clear-cut order of royal succession. To re-state it in simple terms: the heathen Anglo-Saxons recognized that the blood of Wóden flowed strongly in certain families, and it was from these families that the Witan could appoint the king. (The Witan was a form of parliament, and its name embodies the ideas of "knowledge" and "wisdom", thus recalling Wóden himself.)

It is in appropriation of this ancient context that the current occupant of the throne of Britain makes annual royal pronouncements.

In examining these popular customs we have descended a long way from the great philosophers associated with Chartres cathedral, but that is inevitable. For hundreds of years the lives of most Europeans only intersected with religious belief when they were about to be burned or hanged or whipped. The European serf was trapped in a grim struggle to survive, and simply lacked the time, energy and education to engage in theology. Still, the ordinary men and women of those fearful centuries knew by instinct what rites and rituals suited their own spiritual needs. Despite their outward and token compliance with the Christian oppressor, they subverted even the "holiest" day of Christianity to the point that it is now far more Odinist than Christian. That is an astonishing achievement!

29

ANGLO-SAXONDOM AND COGNITIVE DISSONANCE

Sometimes it is hard to believe that there was a time, not all that long ago, when profound questions of the relationship between ethnic and religious identity could be discussed rationally and civilly. One such open-minded discussion can be found in *Racial Origins of English Character* by R. N. Bradley [88]. Bradley seems to have vanished down a memory hole since writing this book, but in his day he was both an archaeologist and an insightful psychologist. His 1926 book was one of the first to explore the relationship between Christianity and the Anglo-Saxon character. We are used to such discussions nowadays when it comes to Islam and the "Arab temperament", but they are mere psychobabble compared with Bradley's lucid, restrained and very English reflections.

Bradley's main thesis was that Christianity in his time was not inherently "good" or "bad" in itself, but could only be assessed as a tool for the maintenance of the Nordic element of the English nation – specifically in England, but by inference including the worldwide Anglo-Saxon diaspora. If Christianity succeeded in that task it was useful, according to Bradley; if not, it was a waste of effort.

We need to project ourselves back in time to understand Bradley's concern. In 1923 a Princeton University professor named Carl Brigham estimated that about 80% of the population of England belonged to the Nordic sub-group of the white race, so when Bradley was writing Nordics were not yet under immediate threat in England itself. Yet the Empire was unraveling rapidly, and many of the best young Englishmen (both home-bred and colonial) had recently been killed in yet another insane, fratricidal war. Bradley was trying to assess whether Christianity would bolster or undermine the position of the survivors.

Bradley believed that the upper classes in England were almost entirely Nordic. (The far more numerical lower classes must also have been mostly Nordic to sustain Brigham's 80% estimate for the *total* population.) A glance at their portraits today confirms that he was probably correct. Even some of the most depraved of the upper classes were fine-looking physical specimens.

However, even the comparatively primitive biology of Bradley's era had already revealed that some Nordic genetic characteristics are recessive. Only a few generations of interbreeding with an initially small number of non-Nordics would be enough to reduce the Nordic percentage of England's population to potentially unsustainable levels.

Bradley analyzed Christianity as an instrument of social control. Whatever the veracity or otherwise of its teachings, his aim was to evaluate it as a tool for the maintenance of the dominant English class and sub-race. His conclusion was that the spirit of Christianity was antithetical to the spirit of Nordic humanity – or, as stated earlier, to the spirit of 80% of the English in his day.

Bradley went even further than this. He concluded that Nordics had only freely embraced Christianity in the past when it was useful to them: "Historically speaking it was only by a fiction that the greater part of the Nordic race accepted Christianity at all; and it has been maintained by a continuation of these fictions..." Bradley tried to be more specific:

> It is due to a most elaborate fiction that the squire has sat for centuries of Sundays under the parson and heard that the only way to salvation is to sell all that he has and give to the poor, or that the path of the rich man to heaven is as difficult as it is for a camel to pass through a needle's eye. The fiction is that the doctrine does not apply to squires or that it is a kind of parable with a heavenly meaning and not intended literally; and to this fiction every well-bred person subscribes. But there is absolutely no evidence that Christ did not mean what He said. The fact is that the Nordic is not a Christian but a ruler; he holds practically none of the tenets of Christianity. Yet he finds the Church useful for many reasons; it bolsters up his class, his rule and his traditions; on the other hand it both contents the people and keeps them in subjection .... It has been said that its first acceptance among the Jews was due to the fact that in a time of hopelessness and bitter persecution it offered the only possible consolation – happiness and glory in a future life; hence its great appeal to the poor and suffering. It is not the religion of the eugenist but the dysgenist; the poorer, more miserable, more suffering a person was, the greater his future reward ... The Nordic is essentially eugenic and ... un-Christian. Quite apart from the purely religious aspect of the mission and teachings of Jesus Christ ... the question must ultimately arise ... which is to survive, the Nordic spirit, or the Christian?

Bradley thought that people create their idea of gods based on their idea of themselves:

> God and religion to the Nordic are a useful form representing order, stability, and proper hierarchy; God and King whom they

outwardly honour are inwardly the mainstay and support of their class ... Thus its support of King, Constitution and Church is in large part a matter of self-support.

To Bradley, Christianity was a tool, bereft of spiritual significance:

[Humanity] needs some form of religion mainly for disciplinary purposes and Christianity serves as well as any other so long as it is treated as a formality.

But the tool of Christianity was useless when it came to the moral underpinning of the British Empire:

Christianity is no religion for the Nordic, and it breaks down at once as soon as he comes to deal with subject peoples. If he treats them as equals, as his Bible tells him he should, his empire vanishes in smoke.

Anyone who is interested in the relationship between religion and national character would find stimulating nuggets in the pages of Bradley's book. Apart from its antiquarian interest, perhaps we also need to remember that the world's current military superpower is the most avowedly Christian of all modern nations. If Bradley was right, America's Christianity is like a moral landmine that could destroy not just imperialist America, but also its allies. In all the recent US-inspired talk of the "clash of civilizations", few commentators seem to be pointing out that Islam is in many ways becoming more fanatical, and Judaism likewise, and also Christian America – but that meanwhile the founding peoples of countries such as the UK, Ireland, Canada, Australia, New Zealand, Germany and the like are becoming increasingly post-Christian.

Bradley's thesis is perhaps the clearest example of one myth that is still common among some members of our older generations: that Christianity provided a sort of "social glue" which held the West together. In fact, it seldom did. From the Thirty Years War of 1618 to 1648, to the various crusades against "heretics" and "pagans", from the Inquisition and the almost endless witchcraft trials and burnings, right through to the Scopes "monkey trial" of 1926, Christianity was a thorn in the flesh of the West. Christianity was invoked as a motivating factor on both sides in the American Civil War (in which at least 618,000 of Bradley's cherished Nordics perished), in World War 1 (at least 8,758,000 dead) and in World War 2 (at least 54,800,000 dead). The "social glue" argument is refuted by the numbers of our fallen heroes and civilians on all sides in an endless series of futile genocides.

What Christianity did to the soul of our people was to set up a "cognitive dissonance". Our human species finds it hard to hold two conflicting ideas at the same time, and perhaps northern Europeans are the least able to do so. Having two contradictory "cognitions" (usually ideas) often causes stress once the "dissonance" is noted, and this leads to negative emotions such as guilt, shame, anger, anxiety and so on. The sufferer then typically either reduces the tension by changing one of the competing ideas (or activities), or else tries to rationalize it.

An example that occurred in Bradley's time was the moral conflict between British imperialism, which for many was a source of pride, and imperial oppression. However mild that oppression may have been in 1926, it was hardly justifiable by quoting St Paul: "...there is neither Greek nor Jew, circumcision nor uncircumcision, Barbarian, Scythian, bond nor free: but Christ is all, and in all." (Colossians 3, 10-11). The cognitive dissonance in this case could be resolved by rejecting Christianity, by rejecting the Empire, or by attempting to rationalize the conflicting beliefs.

In the end the dissonance was largely resolved by abandoning the Empire, although there are many in Britain and the former White Commonwealth who still feel "guilt" over the imperial deeds of their ancestors. However, this was not before advocates for the Empire had done their best to "justify" it.

One such was Rudyard Kipling, who received the 1907 Nobel Prize for literature "... in consideration of the power of observation, originality of imagination, virility of ideas and remarkable talent for narration which characterize the creations of this world-famous author." Kipling tried to justify the Empire in two different ways. First, its colonial subjects were "lesser breeds without the law", as stated in his poem *Recessional*. That placed them on the same level as the pagans whom early Christianity regarded as essentially subhuman. (See Chapter 15. The rhetoric comes from Biblical "books" such as Deuteronomy.)

Kipling's second justification was that, through the Empire, British people were bringing enlightenment and Christian virtues to benighted savages. This was "The White Man's Burden", which he urged Anglo-Saxon America to adopt toward the Philippines, in a poem which begins:

Take up the White Man's burden –
Send forth the best ye breed –
Go bind your sons to exile
To serve your captives' need;
To wait in heavy harness,
On fluttered folk and wild –
Your new-caught, sullen peoples,
Half-devil and half-child.

The viewpoint of this poem, it may be necessary to add, is entirely Christian. No proponent of the ancient Athenian Empire would have needed to justify imperialism in such half-hearted and essentially masochistic terms.

We have glanced at the basic cognitive dissonance arising from Christian imperialism only because it was relevant to the time in which Bradley was writing. One way of attempting to resolve the almost endless cognitive dissonances of the Period of Dual Faith had been tried by many Western intellectuals before Bradley, and that was to jettison Christianity. Usually this response led simply to atheism, or to a vague pantheism – particularly among those who could see that Christian dogma was illogical, or that Christian teaching was in conflict with empirical science, or simply those who objected to the conduct of organized Christianity. However, some of the people who chose this path were knowledgably sympathetic to their ancestral Odinist spirituality without realizing that heathen views could provide an intellectually and morally coherent alternative to Christian dogma.

Thinkers in this last group are known today as "proto-Odinists". They rejected Christianity although sometimes they complied with its rituals through devotional tokenism, usually as a result of social compliance. They were imaginatively attracted to the world view of their ancestors, but they were incapable of progressing to the stage of seeing Odinism as a genuine alternative. Their thinking was sometimes confused, but they took a necessary first step away from the cognitive dissonance that had made the Period of Dual Faith in Western culture so self-destructive.

The next few chapters will examine five of these proto-Odinists. The list could be expanded at much greater length, but the five we will consider make the situation clear.

30

A PROTO-ODINIST PRESIDENT: THOMAS JEFFERSON

Thomas Jefferson, 1743-1826

Thomas Jefferson, the third president of the United States (in office from 1801-1809), was a genius. When President John F. Kennedy welcomed 49 Nobel Prize winners to the White House in 1962, JFK said: "I think this is the most extraordinary collection of talent and of human knowledge that has ever been gathered together in the Executive Mansion – with the possible exception of when Thomas Jefferson dined there alone." He may well have been right. By occupation Jefferson was a lawyer, politician, diplomat and farmer. By way of hobbies he was a skilled violinist, linguist (expert in Greek, Latin, French, Old English and Scots Gaelic), inventor, architect, founder of the University of Virginia, astronomer, archaeologist and author.

Jefferson was a complex man, and no aspect of his character is more mysterious than his religious views. Christians certainly don't know what to make of "the Sage of Monticello". The dominant view seems to be that he was a "deist", which in terms of his era can mean almost anything.

The problem for the Christians is that on the one hand, Jefferson regularly attended the Anglican church. On the other, he wrote words like the following:

> You say you are a Calvinist. I am not. I am of a sect by myself, as far as I know.
>
> *Letter to Ezra Stiles Ely, 25 June 1819*

> As you say of yourself, I too am an Epicurean. I consider the genuine (not the imputed) doctrines of Epicurus as containing everything rational in moral philosophy which Greece and Rome have left us.
>
> *Letter to William Short, 31 October 1819*

> It is between fifty and sixty years since I read it [the last book of the Bible, Revelation], and I then considered it merely the ravings of a maniac, no more worthy nor capable of explanation than the incoherences of our own nightly dreams.
>
> *Letter to General Alexander Smyth, 17 January 1825*

> I concur with you strictly in your opinion of the comparative merits of atheism and demonism, and really see nothing but the latter in the being worshipped by many who think themselves Christians.
>
> *Letter to Richard Price, 8 January 1789*

> But it does me no injury for my neighbor to say there are twenty gods or no God. It neither picks my pocket nor breaks my leg.
>
> *Notes on Virginia*, 1782

> Millions of innocent men, women, and children, since the introduction of Christianity, have been burnt, tortured, fined, and imprisoned; yet we have not advanced one inch toward uniformity. What has been the effect of coercion? To make one-half the world fools and the other half hypocrites; to support roguery and error all over the world.
>
> *Notes on Virginia*, 1782

While it would be easy to add to this list of Jefferson quotes, there would be little point in doing so. We can deduce from them that Jefferson believed he belonged to a "sect" of his own, that he felt an affinity with the pagan philosopher Epicurus, that he thought Revelation was insane, that the being worshipped by "many" self-proclaimed Christians was actually a demon, and that polytheism was as acceptable as other forms of faith. Yet there is still something missing. To understand Jefferson's religious views we must examine some of his actions.

One of the three achievements that Jefferson proclaimed in his own epitaph was his *Bill for Religious Freedom*, passed by the Virginia General Assembly in 1786. Its crucial section read:

> No man shall be compelled to frequent or support any religious worship, place, or ministry whatsoever, nor shall be enforced, restrained, molested, or burdened in his body or goods, nor shall otherwise suffer, on account of his religious opinions or belief; but that all men shall be free to profess, and by argument to maintain, their opinions in matters of religion, and that the same shall in no wise diminish, enlarge, or affect their civil capacities.

Another achievement of which Jefferson was justifiably proud was his University of Virginia, founded in 1819. Jefferson was its architect. A survey of members of the American Institute of Architects once voted Jefferson's design the most significant work of architecture in America. Its most innovative feature is that all the faculty buildings are centered on a library rather than a church. Not even a chapel was included in Jefferson's original plans. Clearly, then, Jefferson had more faith in the principle of knowledge and wisdom than the god of the Bible. Whether he was aware that Odin is the god of wisdom is another question.

As a lawyer and legislator, Jefferson was clear-eyed about the origin of modern common law in the ancient laws of Odinist England. In a letter to Thomas Cooper on February 10, 1814 he wrote:

> For we know that the common law is that system of law which was introduced by the Saxons on their settlement of England, and altered from time to time by proper legislative authority from that time to the date of the Magna Charta ... This settlement took place about the middle of the fifth century. But Christianity was not introduced till the seventh century; the conversion of the first Christian king of the Heptarchy having taken place about the year 598, and that of the last about 686. Here then, was a space of two hundred years, during which the common law was in existence, and Christianity no part of it ... that system of religion could not be a part of the common law, because they were not yet Christians ...

This is fair enough, as far as it goes. Yet we learn even more from a 1944 book [89] :

> In his youth, [Jefferson] had studied Anglo-Saxon, and while he also followed the suggestions of Montesquieu, Locke and various others, he based his affirmation of human rights on the laws of the Saxon forefathers. For he found that the Anglo-Saxons, when they settled in England, were fully aware of the natural rights of man and that their common law proclaimed the principles of liberty which he proposed to vindicate as a racial birthright. They had established these principles indeed before Christianity appeared in England, and Jefferson conceived American freedom as a restoration on a new soil of the 'happy system of our ancestors', as he called it. This was the reason why, as John Adams remembered later, Jefferson suggested that the great seal of the country should bear on one side the images of Hengest and Horsa.

With this mention of Hengest and Horsa the trail to Jefferson's religious views suddenly grows clearer. Now we can understand the background to his letter to Major John Cartwright, of 5 June, 1824:

> ... the common law existed while the Anglo-Saxons were yet pagans, at a time when they had never yet heard the name of Christ pronounced or knew that such a character existed.

So here we have Jefferson, the brilliant lawyer, clearly attributing his beloved common law to the *"pagan"* Anglo-Saxons. The Cooper letter only said that the founders of our modern western law "were not yet Christians". The Cartwright letter, by contrast, openly accepts that they were pagans. If we add to this the claim that Jefferson wanted the seal of the US to bear the images of Hengest and Horsa, whom Jefferson knew to be heathen Odinists, the mists begin to part.

In 1995 Michael Lind, then a senior editor of the *New Republic*, [90] identified America as a series of three republics, with a fourth one in the offing. The first is the one that interests us here. This was "Anglo-America", born of the Revolution of 1776 and killed by the Civil War. Jefferson is defined as its greatest spokesman. From Lind's book we learn that he wanted his great new university to train:

> ... the "natural aristocracy" of North America, students from all classes selected by rigorous examination and admitted without any reference to family income, [to] study ... natural history ... with special emphasis on the hereditary mental and moral superiority of the Germanic peoples ... and Anglo-Saxon laws and institutions, ancient and modern. Every graduate must be proficient in Anglo-Saxon ... as the New World's learned tongue.

Let's summarize. Thomas Jefferson, the only genius ever to be elected US President, thought that many Christians actually worshipped a demon. He therefore built what he called a "wall of separation" between the Church and the new Republican State. He designed a university on architectural principles that honor Odin, but neither Jehovah nor Jesus. He believed that the best of laws dated back to the pre-Christian Odinist period of the Anglo-Saxons. He wanted the great seal of the US to depict the heathen Odinist leaders who brought the Anglo-Saxons to England, Hengest and Horsa. He wanted Old English, the language of Hengest and Horsa, to be "the New World's learned tongue".

The "Sage of Monticello" probably didn't know the word "Odinism", since its first recorded use wasn't until 1848, but he should certainly be respected as much as any other proto-Odinist by his kinsfolk today. The fact that Jefferson's America was swept away in a Civil War that broke out 35 years after his death is no deterrent to including Jefferson in our toasts to our sacred ancestors.

31

A PROTO-ODINIST POET: ALGERNON CHARLES SWINBURNE

Before truth causes her triumphant light to penetrate into the depth of the heart, poetry intercepts her rays, and the summits of humanity shine in a bright light, while a dark and humid night still hangs over the valleys.

- J. C. Friedrich von Schiller

Algernon Charles Swinburne, 1837-1909

It is hard for us today to imagine just how tightly nineteenth century thought was strait-jacketed by Christianity. When, however, we read of the superstitious horror that Christians expressed toward the theory of evolution we gain even greater admiration for thinkers like Darwin, Wallace, Huxley and Lyell, and for statesmen like Jefferson, who defied the strait-jacket and the intellectual madhouse from which it derived.

Yet the scientists, at least, all had hard geological and biological facts to sustain their positions. How much more difficult it must have been for a poet in that age to tackle Christianity head-on from a clear-eyed pagan perspective. This was the era in which the most widely read of all English poets was Tennyson, whose religion extolled:

> That God, which ever lives and loves,
> One God, one law, one element,
> And one far-off divine event,
> To which the whole creation moves.

No writer was to be a greater affront to this strand of Christian fundamentalism than Algernon Charles Swinburne. Swinburne was only 29 years old when his *Poems and Ballads* burst, in all its erotic, lyrical and pagan splendor, on a prudish public. Despite his youth, though, he knew exactly the reaction he could expect from the moral guardians of the age. As he later wrote, the sanctimonious imagined him "stalking triumphant through the land and displaying on every Hearth and in every Home the banner of immorality, atheism, and revolution." Swinburne's choice of words here was sardonic: in 1866 authors and publishers could be jailed for immorality or atheism. *Poems and Ballads* was not atheist. It was purely heathen. Any "immorality" that the prurient discerned in it arose directly from their misunderstanding of the old pagan conception of joy, and its consequent affirmation of life in all its forms.

In the ancient pagan tradition, activity that is harmonious with nature is virtuous, even if it may be defined as "sin" in some Christian tract. Thus all the characters in Swinburne's poems are judged in terms of the fullness of their response to one another and to the natural world.

The outcry was immediate. Swinburne's publisher was threatened with prosecution, and the poet himself received obscene physical threats. Something of the mood of the time comes through in a letter to Swinburne from Winwood Reade, author of *The Martyrdom of Man*. From America Reade wrote: "To Algernon Swinburne, Pagan, suffering persecution from the Christians, greeting. Your book is making a furore in this continent." Reactionary Christians hated the book. As Mr Justice Archibald said, if *Poems and Ballads* "had not been written at all, or had been committed to the flames it would have been much the better".

On the other hand, the youth of the time found the liberation of *Poems and Ballads* (and its successor, *Songs Before Sunrise*), intoxicating. According to one biographer [91], Cambridge undergraduates "joined hands and marched forward, clearing the pavements before them as they shouted the morally offensive stanzas of *Dolores* or the politically unnerving lines of *A Song in Time of Revolution* into the unwilling ears of their elders." *Poems and Ballads,* recalled Gosse, "took the whole lettered youth of England by storm with its audacity and melody".

Swinburne's pagan philosophy began with a sense of the beauty and majesty, the glory and the joy of the pre-Christian world. Addressing the "pale Galilean" directly, the poet recalls the splendor of an earlier religious conception:

> Of the maiden thy mother men sing as a goddess with grace clad
>   around;
> Thou art throned where another was king; where another was queen she
>   is crowned.
> Yea, once we had sight of another: but now she is queen, say these.
> Not as thine, not as thine was our mother, a blossom of flowering seas,
> Clothed round with the world's desire as with raiment, and fair as the
>   foam,
> And fleeter than kindled fire, and a goddess, and mother of Rome.
> For thine came pale and a maiden, and sister to sorrow, but ours,
> Her deep hair heavily laden with odour and colour of flowers,
> White rose of the rose-white water, a silver splendour, a flame,
> Bent down unto us that besought her, and earth grew sweet with her
>   name.
> For thine came weeping, a slave among slaves, and rejected, but she
> Came flushed from the full-flushed wave, and imperial, her foot on the
>   sea.
> And the wonderful waters knew her, the winds and the viewless ways,
> And the roses grew rosier, and bluer the sea-blue stream of the bays.
>
>   from *Hymn to Proserpine*

By contrast, the Christian god, whom Swinburne characterizes elsewhere as "the lord of darkness", has brought nothing but blight and misery. His incense is the smell of burning human flesh, and his feet "threaten and trample all things and every day". The very world "has grown grey from his breath". This position underlies all of *Poems and Ballads* but is clearly encapsulated in the *Hymn of Man:*

> O thou that hast built thee a shrine of the madness of man and his
>   shame,
> And hast hung in the midst for a sign of his worship the lamp of
>   thy name;
> That hast shown him for heaven in a vision a void world's
>   shadow and shell,
> And hast fed thy delight and derision with fire of belief as of
>   hell;
> That hast fleshed on the souls that believe thee the fang of the
>   death-worm fear,
> With anguish of dreams to deceive them whose faith cries out in
>   thine ear;

> By the face of the spirit confounded before thee and humbled in dust,
> By the dread wherewith life was astounded and shamed out of sense of its trust,
> By the scourges of doubt and repentance that fell on the soul at thy nod,
> Thou art judged, O judge, and the sentence is gone forth against thee, O God.

So vile is this "lord of darkness" in Swinburne's eyes that in *Anactoria* he has the pagan poet Sappho swear:

> Him would I reach, him smite, him desecrate,
> Pierce the cold lips of God with human breath,
> And mix his immortality with death.

Wherever the "pale Galilean" has triumphed over the great heathen gods in men's hearts, the result is human misery and degradation. The effect of Christianity on the human heart is like a withering salt wind:

> It was for this, then, that thy speech
>   Was blown about the world in flame
> And men's souls shot up out of reach
>   Of fear or lust or thwarting shame -
> That thy faith over souls should pass
> As sea-winds burning the grey grass?
>
> It was for this that men should make
>   Thy name a fetter on men's necks,
> Poor men's made poorer for thy sake,
>   And women's withered out of sex?

The lines above are from *Before a Crucifix*. In a gleeful inversion of the Christian propaganda associated with the desecration of sacred heathen trees and statues, Swinburne posits a towering, ghastly cross, casting its corrupt shadow over humanity:

> And mouldering now and hoar with moss
>   Between us and the sunlight swings
> The phantom of a Christless cross
>   Shadowing the sheltered heads of kings
> And making with its moving shade
> The souls of harmless men afraid.
>
> It creaks and rocks to left and right
>   Consumed of rottenness and rust,
> Worm-eaten of the worms of night,
>   Dead as their spirits who put trust,
> Round its base muttering as they sit,
> In the time-cankered name of it.

The core of *Poems and Ballads* is *Laus Veneris*. The title of this highly complex poem is a wry twist on the Latin phrase *Laus Deo:* "Praise be to God". It tells the story of the Christian knight Tannhäuser, held captive by the charms of Venus. To understand the full self-awareness of Swinburne's subversive intent, it is important to realize that the opening line of the poem alludes to the last words of Keats' *Ode To A Nightingale.* "Asleep or waking is it?" Tannhäuser asks, directing attention from the outset to the object of his passions.

On one level the poem is a psychodrama in which the knight, a darkly medieval figure, orthodoxly Christian, confronts his own decadent wish to deny ethereal beauty and sensation in favor of a sterile ideology. In his monologue he reflects on the history of Venus-worship, particularly as it exalts its devotees. Although still retaining a Christian viewpoint, he is unable to refrain from exultation:

> Lo, she was thus when her clear limbs enticed
> All lips that now grow sad with kissing Christ

Gradually the poem becomes an attack on the life-denying religion that tyrannizes the knight, until in the last four stanzas he turns to the glorious goddess and joins his fate with hers, rejecting the sterile "bliss" of being "High up in barren heaven before his [God's] face".

That is the story of the poem at one level. It is also, as one critic has described it, "a dramatization of the battle between Blakean contraries within the wracked mind of Tannhäuser", in which body and soul, virtue and sin (and their rewards), fruitfulness and barrenness, love and happiness, all contend." [92]

The poet is also an actor in this drama. In a way that would suggest post-modernism if it were a contemporary production, Swinburne insists on the literary nature of his work. It is introduced by the words of a fictitious medieval scribe, which forces attention to the shaping hand of the poet himself and his ability to evoke all previous and possible articulations of the central myth.

Furthermore, the beauty of the goddess is embodied in the poetic vehicle. "The beauty of the poem," said the critic mentioned above, "recapitulates, transmutes and makes permanent the beauty of otherwise ephemeral erotic sensations". If this sounds too modern for a poem written over 140 years ago, consider these lines:

> Outside it must be winter among men;
> For at the gold bars of the gates again
>   I heard all night and all the hours of it
> The wind's wet wings and fingers drip with rain.

Very little poetry as terse and "natural" as this was written until well into the 20th century. Just as the poem affirms Venus by embodying her beauty, so it also asserts the intellectual progressiveness of paganism.

Swinburne had no doubt as to how the gods should be worshipped:

> I seek not heaven with submission of lips and knees
> With worship and prayer for a sign till it leap to light:
> I gaze on the gods about me, and call on these.
>
> I call on the gods hard by, the divine dim powers
> Whose likeness is here at hand, in the breathless air,
> In the pulseless peace of the fervid and silent flowers,
> In the faint sweet speech of the waters that whisper there.
> Ah, what should darkness do in a world so fair?

To a thinking heathen poet like Swinburne, his religion inevitably raises theological questions. These are addressed in different poems. In the early *Felise,* the narrator adopts a Stoical pagan agnosticism:

> We know not whether death be good,
>   But life at least it will not be:
> Men will stand saddening as we stood,
>   Watch the same fields and skies as we
>   And the same sea.

A similar note of resignation is struck in *The Garden of Proserpine*:

> From too much love of living,
>   From hope and fear set free
> We thank with brief thanksgiving
>   Whatever gods may be
> That no life lives for ever;
> That dead men rise up never;
> That even the weariest river
>   Winds somewhere safe to sea.

The last thought here, the mystical reference to the sea as the ultimate goal of the individual spirit, provides the key to the poet's philosophy. Throughout Swinburne's works, "the sea" is the source and end of the soul. It is a symbol of what is known in the *Vedas* as the "Brahman", the absolute reality, and the goal of the individual spirit, or "atman". The purpose of the human soul in this heathen tradition is liberation from the cycle of rebirth and suffering, leading to ecstatic knowledge of reality and union with the Brahman. (See Chapter 2 for the relation of this blissful state to the name of Odin.)

We know, from a letter written in 1865, that Swinburne also thought reincarnation a logical explanation, rather than merely a matter of belief. Later, on the death of his fellow-poet Rossetti in 1882, he was to write:

> Albeit the bright sweet mothlike wings be furled,
>   Hope sees, past all division and defection,
>   And higher than swims the mist of human breath,
> The soul most radiant once in all the world

>Requickened to regenerate resurrection
>Out of the lightness of the shadow of death.

Another spiritual possibility that Swinburne expresses is even more mystical, an extended existence in a state of "deathless life and death". Thus Merlin in *Tristram of Lyonesse* is rapturously integrated with all living things without losing his individuality. The still-existing wizard "hears in spirit a song" that is "shed" from "the mystic mouth of Nimue / like a consecration". Merlin is at once discreet and incorporate, and he:

>... knows the soul that was his soul at one
>With the ardent world's, and in the spirit of earth
>His spirit of life reborn to higher birth
>And mixed with things of elder life than ours.

This pagan mysticism is completely alien to anything in Christianity, since its epiphany depends on a sense that all of life is one rapturous unity. Nature is not the *ex nihilo* creation of a capricious god, and separate from humanity, but something which always subtends our conscious life. In our highest moments the highest among us can participate ecstatically in this unity, as when Tristram, before his final battle, swims in the sea:

>And like the sun his heart rejoiced in him,
>And brightened with a broadening flame of mirth:
>And hardly seemed its life a part of earth,
>But the life kindled of a fiery birth
>And passion of a new-begotten son
>Between the live sea and the living sun.

This acceptance underlines the pagan attitude to change. Unlike the Christian, who sees change leading to death and the end of things, the pagan is reconciled to the facts of Fate, so that change and death are just aspects of the beneficent world-force, parts of the process of integration and transformation that is life itself. As Swinburne writes in *Genesis:*

>For the great labour of growth, being many, is one;
>>One thing the white death and the ruddy birth;
>The invisible air and the all-beholden sun,
>>The barren water and many-childed earth.

>For if death were not, then should growth not be,
>>Change, nor the life of good nor evil things;
>Nor were there night at all nor light to see,
>>Nor water of sweet nor water of bitter springs.

This heathen tradition always leans toward monism, which has been defined as the doctrine that mind and matter are formed from, or reducible to, the same ultimate substance or principle of being. This is the position which Swinburne favored in what he considered his most significant poem, the majestic *Hertha*. Here the Germanic goddess of the earth, mystically identified with the world tree, announces:

> I am that which began;
> > Out of me the years roll;
> Out of me God and man;
> > I am equal and whole;
> God changes, and man, and the form of them bodily; I am the soul.

> Before ever land was,
> > Before ever the sea,
> Or soft hair of the grass,
> > Or fair limbs of the tree,
> Or the flesh-coloured fruit of my branches, I was, and thy soul was in me.

Hertha points out that she is our "mother, not maker", and before stating that the "twilight" of the Christian god "is come on him", laments:

> O my sons, O too dutiful
> > Toward Gods not of me,
> Was not I enough beautiful?
> > Was it hard to be free?
> For behold, I am with you, am in you and of you; look forth now and see.

Hertha is a long, complex and moving poem. To do justice to it would require a separate chapter of this length. Interested readers will find it in the 1871 volume of poems called *Songs Before Sunrise*.

Swinburne, the first great pagan poet of the modern age, died in 1909. His executor, Theodore Watts-Dunton, had promised the poet that no Christian rites would be read over his corpse. Too ill to attend the burial, Watts-Dunton sent instructions that the mourners were to gather around the grave in silence, throw flowers into it, and then disperse. The priest in charge of the churchyard where Swinburne was to be reunited with his ancestors had other ideas. As the mourners listened to his graveside address, he could not help using phrases from the Anglican *Book of Common Prayer*. At least one of the mourners protested vociferously.

Swinburne's reputation suffered in the first half of the 20th century, partly because of the general reaction against all things Victorian, and partly because his exquisite lyrical skills tended to overshadow the depth of his thought. Furthermore, his profound sympathy for the human condition was uncongenial to twentieth century angst. The last few decades have seen the beginning of a significant reappraisal of Swinburne's work, and several major studies have ensured his continuing relevance as a great poet and a figurehead of modernity in both literature and morality.

It is now time for the heathen community to reassess Swinburne's contribution to our religious position. Although he failed to make the full transition to modern Odinism, those of his poems that address religious matters express almost every nuance of heathen thought that was conceivable in his lifetime. It should also be noted, in conclusion, that he was one of the two or three greatest experts on and exponents of the Border Ballads (see Chapter 23), which he often emulated in new and entirely heathen works of his own.

32

A PROTO-ODINIST SCHOLAR: JAMES MURRAY

The Murray family
*Left to right, standing: Aelfric, Wilfrid, Oswyn, Elsie;
seated: Hilda, Harold, James Murray, Ada Murray, Ethelbert,
Ethelwyn;
front row: Arthur, Gwyneth, Rosfrith.*

Toward the end of the Period of Dual Faith, many educated men and women began to reject Christianity entirely. Most did not have the knowledge, much of which is of very recent discovery, to see that a re-embracing of our original faith was intellectually viable and responsible. Still, take Christianity out of our traditional Western culture and all that is left are the heathen elements, as the rebellious Swinburne clearly saw.

But what of the men and women who were truly representative of the Period of Dual Faith? Those who treasured our pre-Christian past but couldn't bring themselves to make the final break with Christianity? How did they think? We may never really know what was in the minds of the lower socio-economic classes, since few of them left any written records. Even so, we get glimpses – sometimes more than that – through their surviving folk culture. Yet to truly understand the Dual Faith mentality we need to study the recorded lives and writings of educated people.

There was none more rewarding of study than James Augustus Henry Murray (1837-1915). James was born near the town of Hawick, in Teviotdale, on the Scottish border. His father was a tailor. Despite having a brilliant and precocious mind, James had to leave school early owing to lack of money. He tried to follow his father's trade, but while still in his teens he became a schoolmaster. From that time on he educated himself, eagerly, in many subjects – but especially in languages, philology and above all, lexicography (dictionary making).

By 1867 he was applying for a position at the British Museum. The surviving draft of his letter reveals that he had achieved an astonishing breadth of linguistic knowledge, particularly when we know from many other sources that Murray was a modest man who would never exaggerate his own abilities. The only way to convey his achievement is to quote at length from his letter:

> I possess a general acquaintance with the languages & literature of the Aryan and Syro-Arabic classes – not indeed to say that I am familiar with all or nearly all of these, but that I possess that general lexical & structural knowledge which makes the intimate knowledge only a matter of a little application. With several I have a more intimate acquaintance as with the Romance tongues, Italian, French, Catalan, Spanish, Latin & in a less degree Portuguese, Vaudois, Provençal & various dialects. In the Teutonic branch, I am tolerably familiar with Dutch (having at my place of business correspondence to read in Dutch, German, French & occasionally other languages,) Flemish, German, Danish. In Anglo-Saxon and Moeso-Gothic my studies have been much closer, I having prepared some works for publication upon these languages. I know a little of the Celtic, and am at present engaged with the Sclavonic, having obtained a useful knowledge of Russian. In the Persian, Achaemenian Cuneiform & Sanscrit branches, I know for the purposes of Comparative Philology. I have sufficient knowledge of Hebrew & Syriac to read at sight the O.T. and Peshito; to a less degree I know Aramaic Arabic, Coptic and Phoenician to the point where it was left by Gesenius.

It should be remembered that all this was achieved by the son of a poor tailor, and entirely through his own efforts while working full-time to support himself and his growing family.

Let's now look at James' religion. He was definitely some sort of Christian, holding daily prayer sessions at the family dining table. Yet he was a very strange Christian. He was a member of the Congregational church, which proudly traced itself back to the Scots who had resisted – at great personal risk – Charles I's attempt to inflict his new prayer book on them. So Congregationalism was very closely linked to Scottish patriotism, which may well have been its main attraction.

Despite the family prayers, Murray refused to celebrate Christmas, usually taking the family for a long walk in the snow while others attended church. By contrast, he encouraged the children to make turnip lanterns for Hallowe'en, at which time the girls usually rode around the house on broomsticks. He was also an accomplished amateur geologist, but seems to have been unperturbed by the clash between Christian doctrine and the recent discovery of vast geological time.

It was a blow to Murray when his son Aelfric decided to become an Anglican priest. "I myself abhor the priest and all his claims", he thundered to the errant child. As he grew older he began to notice that Christianity in practice favored the profusion of the unfit, asking "… what will become of unthinned humanity?" On the outbreak of WW1 he called the dreadful conflict "a lamentable outcome of centuries of Christ's teaching".

On the other hand, Murray was a proud Scottish Borderer, from a region that was still mainly heathen in the time of Shakespeare (see Chapter 23). In Murray's day it was not uncommon for Borderers to have the "second sight", and the Murrays were no exception. In 1872 they went on holiday to Hastings. Murray walked out on a long reef, accompanied by a stray black dog. The tide seems to have nearly cut him off. He suddenly had a panic attack. According to his grand-daughter:

> Getting to his feet he hurried, slithering on the wet, sea-weed covered rocks, back to [his wife] Ada, without attempting to cross the channel. When he got near her, Ada called to him, "It's all right, the man who was with you while you were out there spoke to me as he passed and told me that you could get across the channel." "My love", said James, "there WASN'T ANY MAN WITH ME ON THAT ROCK!" And looking out over the wide deserted shore it was true, neither man nor dog was anywhere to be seen.

This was not the only time that James and Ada experienced – and happily accepted – "supernatural" experiences that clashed with normal Christian beliefs. Given all this evidence, it seems his Christianity may have been emotionally deep, but was intellectually very shallow.

The 19th century saw the publication of the first scientific dictionaries. In France, Émile Littré had spent thirty years compiling a dictionary of 4,000 large quarto pages. In Germany, the Grimm brothers and their team of assistants were working on a monumental dictionary of German. As far as English dictionaries went, perhaps the best available was the one by the American, Noah Webster (compiled from 1828 onwards), but it was smallish in scope and riddled with errors. English needed a comprehensive dictionary at least as good as the German and French ones, but the English universities were then in such a reactionary state that they were subject to a Royal Commission in 1850.

As the great historian E. A. Freeman wrote of Oxford: "It, or at least a majority of it, will have nothing to do with English or any other Teutonic tongue ... their ignorance is not that negative darkness which consists in the mere absence of light ... It is an aggressive contempt for all wise learning." Greek and Latin were taught, of course, since Greek was the language of the New Testament and Latin was the traditional language of the church. In 1870, Henry Sweet, the future great scholar of Anglo-Saxon and Icelandic, told Murray that Oxford dons "are hardly aware of the existence of Shakspeare & Chaucer yet".

In short, no-one at the great English universities was qualified to compile a comprehensive and scientific dictionary of our own language. If anyone was to do it, he would have to be an outsider. The only outsider who was up to this massive task was James Murray.

Various forward-looking scholars twisted the arms of both a reluctant Murray and Oxford University's unimaginative publishing house. In 1877 Oxford and Murray signed a contract that led to the production of the most influential dictionary the world has ever seen, the supreme authority on the English language. Murray was still working on it, often for twelve hours a day and more, when he died. He sometimes had to take out large personal loans to finance the research. It was not finished until thirteen years after his death. Yet Murray was the man who solved all the lexicographical problems, and the man without whom this superb achievement – all 59 million words of it – could never have succeeded.

What sort of a man, then, was this self-taught genius of the Age of Dual Faith? More particularly, how did such a man view the tension between the imposed, official religion of his nation and the underlying Odinist nature of its cultural foundations?

James Murray clearly thought of himself as a Christian. Yet as we have seen, he believed in the second sight, he refused to celebrate Christmas, he enjoyed celebrating Hallowe'en, he abhorred Christian priests, he was untroubled by the growing geological evidence against the Bible, and he had grave doubts about the dysgenic impact Christian teachings were having on the human future.

Murray was a great family man, and whenever he despaired of his life-task his main worry was that his family was suffering from the *Dictionary* work's low pay and immense stress. So it is reasonable to look for hints of Murray's deeper attitudes in his family affairs.

James gave his children relatively uncommon, mostly Germanic and entirely heathen names: Aelfric, Wilfrid, Oswyn, Elsie, Hilda, Harold, Ethelbert, Ethelwyn, Arthur, Gwyneth and Rosfrith. He explained his thinking in an article in 1863, when he referred to the "... fine old Saxon names [of the] hardy northern tribes from which we boast our Anglo-Saxon lineage ... like themselves, hardy, rough and bold." These "fine old" names he contrasted with the Georges, Anthonys, Denises and Michaels who "flourished in the legendary saint-lore, with which wily priests fed the ignorant love of the marvellous, and deepened the gloom of the middle ages." He later complained when his eldest son chose "nasty Pictish names" for his own sons – Donald and Kenneth.

It would not have been the done thing for a Victorian scholar to write, "Christian priests made the dark ages even darker by telling lies about legendary saints with outlandish, foreign names". Yet that is how we might paraphrase Murray today. The astonishing thing is that although Murray's views were unguarded by Victorian standards, no-one seems to have taken offence. There were no calls for him to retract. No-one moved to expel him from his church. It seems that, at this stage of the era of Dual Faith, the educated classes agreed with him, or else didn't care very much – as long as he did not cross the border to overt paganism.

Nor did anyone object when Murray wrote of *Teribus*, the song of his home-town, Hawick, (Chapter 23) that it:

> appears to have come down, scarcely mutilated, from the time when it was the burthen of the song of the gleo-mann, or scald, or the invocation of a heathen Angle warrior, before the northern Hercules and the blood-red lord of battles had yielded to the 'pale god' of the Christians.

Nor did anyone object when he included in his great *Dictionary* the word "Odinism".

It seems that Murray's attitude to Christianity was essentially a pragmatic one, accepting it as the official faith and trying to find what good (that is, what Odinist values) there might be in it. In Murray's case a degree of Scottish patriotism also entered the picture. Strikingly, though, something similar seems to have been the case with many intelligent, educated people of his day. They could not make a full break with the official religion, no doubt for a variety of personal reasons, yet they can be counted as proto-Odinists, since without their strong pride in our people's pre-Christian achievements the 20th century Re-Awakening of Odinism would have been delayed. The "human nature" of the Nation of Odin doesn't seem to have changed much over the millennia, so perhaps James Murray's attitudes were typical of many others about whom we know far less. Meanwhile, Murray fixed in the amber of our recorded language millions of words that tell us more about our ancestral faith than all the censorious texts of priestly figures like Bede and Sturluson.

33

A PROTO-ODINIST COMPOSER: RICHARD WAGNER

Richard Wagner, 1813-1883

Richard Wagner was both a great musician and a great proto-Odinist. His most significant compositions are the epic German heathen operas of *The Ring of the Nibelungs*, and perhaps the most erotic and most mystical opera ever written, *Tristan and Isolde*.

These works amounted to a revolution in European music – and European culture in general. It is beyond the scope of this book to examine Wagner's influence on the 19th century, so one quotation will have to suffice. In a letter to the composer Debussy, the eminent French symbolist poet Pierre Louÿs wrote: "We recently had a very serious conversation on the subject of Richard Wagner. I merely stated that

Wagner was the greatest man who had ever existed." Many people at that time would have agreed.

In 1849 Wagner became an exile from the German state of Saxony as a consequence of his involvement in the liberal and nationalist revolutions of that and the previous year. In 1849 he also wrote an essay called *Die Kunst und die Revolution* ("Culture and Revolution"), from which the extract below is taken. It is reproduced here because a genius' insights into aesthetic matters can and should provide inspiration for contemporary Odinist artists. Essentially, Wagner here explains why Christian art from its inception was so morbid, in the sense of life-denying. Here is how Wagner saw things:

> Christianity adjusts the ills of an honorless, useless, and sorrowful existence of mankind on earth, by the miraculous love of God; who had not – as the noble Greek supposed – created man for a happy and self-conscious life upon this earth, but had here imprisoned him in a loathsome dungeon: so as, in reward for the self-contempt that poisoned him therein, to prepare him for a posthumous state of endless comfort and inactive ecstasy. Man was therefore bound to remain in this deepest and unmanliest degradation, and no activity of this present life should he exercise; for this accursed life was, in truth, the world of the devil, that is, of the senses; and by every action in it he played into the devil's hands. Therefore the poor wretch who, in the enjoyment of his natural powers, made this life his own possession must suffer after death the eternal torments of hell! Naught was required of mankind but faith – that is to say, the confession of its miserable plight, and the giving up of all spontaneous attempt to escape from out this misery; for the undeserved Grace of God was alone to set it free.
>
> The historian knows not surely that this was the view of the humble son of the Galilean carpenter; who, looking on the misery of his fellow men, proclaimed that he had not come to bring peace, but a sword into the world; whom we must love for the anger with which he thundered forth against the hypocritical Pharisees who fawned upon the power of Rome, so as the better to bind and heartlessly enslave the people; and finally, who preached the reign of universal human love – a love he could never have enjoined on men whose duty it should be to despise their fellows and themselves. The inquirer more clearly discerns the hand of the miraculously converted Pharisee, Paul, and the zeal with which, in his conversion of the heathen, he followed so successfully the monition: "Be ye wise as serpents"; he may also estimate the deep and universal degradation of civilized mankind, and see in this the historical soil from which the full-grown tree of finally developed Christian dogma drew forth the sap that fed its fruit. But thus much the candid artist perceives at

the first glance: that neither was Christianity art, nor could it ever bring forth from itself the true and living art.

The free Greek, who set himself upon the pinnacle of Nature, could procreate art from very joy in manhood: the Christian, who impartially cast aside both Nature and himself, could only sacrifice to his God on the altar of renunciation; he durst not bring his actions or his work as offering, but believed that he must seek His favor by abstinence from all self-prompted venture. Art is the highest expression of activity of a race that has developed its physical beauty in unison with itself and Nature; and man must reap the highest joy from the world of sense, before he can mould therefrom the implements of his art; for from the world of sense alone can he derive so much as the impulse to artistic creation. The Christian, on the contrary, if he fain would create an artwork that should correspond to his belief, must derive his impulse from the essence of abstract spirit, from the grace of God, and therein find his tools. What, then, could he take for aim? Surely not physical beauty mirrored in his eyes as an incarnation of the devil? And how could pure spirit, at any time, give birth to a something that could be cognized by the senses?

All pondering of this problem is fruitless; the course of history shows too unmistakably the results of these two opposite methods. Where the Greeks, for their edification, gathered in the amphitheatre for the space of a few short hours full of the deepest meaning, the Christian shut himself away in the lifelong imprisonment of a cloister. In the one case, the Popular Assembly was the judge: in the other the Inquisition; here the state developed to an honorable democracy: there, to a hypocritical despotism.

Hypocrisy is the salient feature, the peculiar characteristic, of every century of our Christian era, right down to our own day; and indeed this vice has always stalked abroad with more crying shamelessness, in direct proportion as mankind, in spite of Christendom, has refreshed its vigor from its own unquenchable and inner wellspring, and ripened toward the fulfillment of its true purpose. Nature is so strong, so inexhaustible in its regenerative resources, that no conceivable violence could weaken its creative force. Into the ebbing veins of the Roman world, there poured the healthy blood of the fresh Germanic nations. Despite the adoption of Christianity, a ceaseless thirst of doing, delight in bold adventure, and unbounded self-reliance remained the native element of the new masters of the world. But, as in the whole history of the Middle Ages we always light upon one prominent factor, the warfare between worldly might and the despotism of the Roman Church: so, when this new world sought for a form of utterance, it could find it only in opposition to, and strife against, the spirit of Christendom.

The art of Christian Europe could never proclaim itself, like that of ancient Greece, as the expression of a world attuned to harmony; for reason that its inmost being was incurably and irreconcilably split up between the force of conscience and the instinct of life, between the ideal and the reality. Like the order of chivalry itself, the chivalric poetry of the Middle Ages, in attempting to heal this severance, could, even amid its loftiest imagery, but bring to light the falsehood of the reconciliation; the higher and the more proudly it soared on high, so the more visibly gaped the abyss between the actual life and the idealized existence, between the raw, passionate bearing of these knights in physical life and their too delicate, etherealized behavior in romance. For the same reason did actual life, leaving the pristine, noble, and certainly not ungraceful customs of the people, become corrupt and vicious; for it durst not draw the nourishment for its art impulse from out of its own being, its joy in itself, and its own physical demeanor; but was sent for all its spiritual sustenance to Christianity, which warned it off from the first taste of life's delight, as from a thing accursed. The poetry of chivalry was thus the honorable hypocrisy of fanaticism, the parody of heroism: in place of Nature, it offered a convention.

Only when the enthusiasm of belief had smoldered down, when the Church openly proclaimed herself as naught but a worldly despotism appreciable by the senses, in alliance with the no less material worldly absolutism of the temporal rule which she had sanctified: only then commenced the so-called renaissance of art. That wherewith man had racked his brains so long he would fain now see before him clad in body, like the Church itself in all its worldly pomp. But this was only possible on condition that he opened his eyes once more, and restored his senses to their rights. Yet when man took the objects of belief and the revelations of fantasy and set them before his eyes in physical beauty, and with the artist's delight in that physical beauty – this was a complete denial of the very essence of the Christian religion; and it was the deepest humiliation to Christendom that the guidance to these art creations must be sought from the pagan art of Greece. Nevertheless, the Church appropriated to herself this newly roused art impulse, and did not blush to deck herself with the borrowed plumes of paganism; thus trumpeting her own hypocrisy.

Worldly dominion, however, had its share also in the revival of art. After centuries of combat, their power armed against all danger from below, the security of riches awoke in the ruling classes the desire for more refined enjoyment of this wealth, they took into their pay the arts whose lessons Greece had taught. "Free" art now served as handmaid to these exalted masters, and, looking into the matter more closely, it is difficult to decide who was the greater hypocrite: Louis XIV, when he sat and heard the Grecian hate of tyrants, declaimed in polished verses from the boards of his court theatre; or Corneille and Racine, when, to win the favor of their lord, they set in the mouths of their stage heroes the warm words of freedom and political virtue, of ancient Greece and Rome.

The horned helmets and other falsely "Viking" clichés of Wagnerian stage productions are apt to detract attention from the depth of Wagner's intellectual, moral and religious opposition both to Christianity at its best, and also to the increasingly sentimental and shallow Christianity of his era. Modern Odinist artists could do worse than to reflect on this 19th century genius' own artistic manifesto.

Yet despite his intellectual brilliance, and despite the grounding of his greatest works in the northern European heathen literary tradition, even Wagner himself was unable to justify his rebellion against Christianity in any terms other than those of pre-Christian Greece and Rome. Only those of us who have since benefited from the insights of people like Jefferson, Wagner, Swinburne and Murray can see that the northern European spiritual genius has also been there all along, simply waiting for us to rediscover it and allow it to complement the other forms of our ancestral tradition.

34

A PROTO-ODINIST ART MOVEMENT: AUSTRALIAN "PAGANISM"

Rayner Hoff, 1894-1937, "Idyll: Love and Life"

In the 1920s there was a prominent artistic circle in Sydney, Australia, known to modern art historians by the alternate names of "Heroic Vitalists" and "paganists". Its followers believed that Australian art was on the verge of a "Renaissance", as they termed it, that was beyond the capacity of war-weary Europeans. They also worked diligently to bring about their Renaissance, believing that it wasn't something that would just happen. According to their pagan theories great achievements could only be attained as a consequence of active spiritual struggle.

The elder statesman of this school was the artist and author Norman Lindsay (1879–1969). Lindsay believed that Christianity had corrupted our morality through its hostility to the human body and to sexuality. It was his view that "in Creative art one must find the direction of life"; but art was not free to explore this direction because of Christian constraints. Art could therefore only progress by returning to pre-Christian heathen attitudes. In 1924 Lindsay summed up his vision of the art of the future. "Art where it touches the most vital of all issues, which is sex, the stimulus of life's rebirth, will be frank, licentious, shameless ... adoring the naked body, surrounding it with emblems of happiness, strength and courage." Typically, when once asked to illustrate the Bible, Lindsay quipped: "Oh, no, no, no! Couldn't think of it. It's a very dangerous book. Had a very bad influence."

A literary magazine called *Vision* served as the vehicle for paganist views. Its editors were Norman Lindsay, his son Jack, and the young Kenneth Slessor (1901-1971). Slessor is now considered by some to have been Australia's finest poet – and has been voted the most popular.

To the paganists Australia was a new Arcadia. Its climate, its light, and even the seaward orientation of its habitable parts suggested ancient Greece. They also felt that the healthy outdoors lifestyle which most Australians then lived was itself leading to a Classical and athletic perfection of human form. Thus Rayner Hoff, the leading sculptor of this group, was outraged when another artist claimed that his 1927 torso *Australian Venus* was idealized rather than being (as it was) a realistic depiction of a radiantly healthy flesh-and-blood Australian woman.

Because the genial climate of coastal Australia was so Mediterranean, the paganists tended to honor the gods in their Greek, rather than Northern, manifestations. The All-father was here more likely to wear the skirt of Zeus than the heavy cloak of Odin; any Australian sacred site would obviously resemble Delos more than Uppsala or Yeavering; and the woods, valleys and streams of Australia seemed a natural home for the dryads, nymphs, satyrs and similar creatures of ancient Greece. (So much so that Frank Lynch's 1924 *Satyr* was furiously condemned as "a pagan work" by killjoy Christians.)

The paganists' focus on the Aegean did not blind them to the Northern form of our religion. Slessor wrote of Valkyries as comfortably as he wrote of Pan; and Lindsay's *Walpurgis* is one of his best works. Nor were they unaware of the underlying unity between the Mediterranean and Northern expressions of Indo-European spirituality.

Rayner Hoff (1894-1937) became in some ways the main spokesman for the paganists – or "Heroic Vitalists". A brilliant young English artist, winner of the Prix de Rome, he arrived in Australia in 1923 to teach sculpture and drawing. He created a new Australian sculptural tradition – expressing heathen values through an Art Deco style. His students were to form the core of the next generation of Australian sculptors, including Frank Lynch, Barbara Tribe, Lyndon Dadswell, Jean Broome, Eileen McGrath, Vic Cowdroy, Elizabeth Conlon and Liz Blaxland.

Rayner Hoff: "Australian Venus".

By contrast, Henry Moore: "Seated Woman"

The paganists rejected Christianity outright, but without making a fuss of it. Christianity was to them a dried-up superstition of the past, one in which no-one with a leaping heart and coursing blood could believe. Their attitude was perhaps summed up in Slessor's vision of what would happen if Rubens' cherubim could "vault in these warm skies":

> Down to our spires their lusty whooping,
> Fanfares of Paradise, would speed,
> Far down to dark-faced clergy stooping
> Round altars of their doleful creed.

The paganists aimed for an art that was life-affirming, sensuous, joyful and optimistic, and for subject they focused on the heroic human form. Hoff's marble relief, *Idyll: Love and Life*, is a good example. The figures are lovingly and superbly modeled. The man and woman are treated equally. Despite the artistic difficulties involved, Hoff has managed to avoid anything static in their embrace: it is energetic and sinuous. Their love has obviously borne fruit, in the form of the child held aloft. They embody the spirit of Norman Lindsay's ideal of artistic creation as "the spirit of fecundity which loves to see the sap rise ... Its spirit is a wild thing called joy, its body naked as the deathless gods".

It is important to recall that Hoff's lovers here are not idealized. They are real flesh-and-blood Australians. As to their physical appearance, Hoff himself wrote: "I doubt if ever the Ancient Greeks produced better examples of physical beauty and grace ... the call of the sun, surf, great open roads and wonderful bush is all too strong for any to resist. Hence we are active, virile and well." So virile and well that, according to the paganist poet William Baylebridge, the world should be over-run by "strong, hot-necked natural" Australian men and women!

Direct allegory is rare in the works of the paganist school, even though all but the youngest of these artists had cut their teeth on a diet of Symbolism. When allegory does appear it has none of the dreamlike stasis of artists like Moreau, nor of the bombastic lifelessness of German works from a decade later. Usually, though, the Australian paganists avoided allegory. Works like Barbara Tribe's *Caprice*, which bore the full brunt of Christian condemnation, aimed to portray life directly as the pagan artists saw it. In Tribe's case, her nude girl is shown simply experiencing a sudden start. Nothing more is intended. The paganist emphasis was on the response of higher-order humans to life as it really is, and not as Christians – or any other nay-sayers – said it should be.

One other aspect of the Australian paganist movement deserves mention. In an age when art by women was often seen as something of a weekend hobby, the paganists were very serious about the achievements of their female colleagues. For instance, a book about Rayner Hoff's "star pupil", Eileen McGrath, was published as early as 1932.

The works of the Australian paganists mostly survive, and both public and critical appreciation of them increases yearly. Historically, though, their artistic movement was swept aside by "abstract expressionism", which was the aesthetic flag-bearer of New York cultural imperialism. But as more and more Westerners are shaking off the heritage of the Judeo-Christian cult, we will need to find new artistic ways of expressing our own rediscovered spirituality. We could seek no better starting point than the vibrant, energetic, yet true-to-life works of our forebears in the paganist or Heroic Vitalist movement. Nearly a century later there will of course be differences, but the artistic energy and integrity of the paganists should provide inspiration for 21st century heathen artists – regardless of the medium they choose to employ.

35

THE LIMITS OF PROTO-ODINISM

'Nowadays' is a civilization in which the prime emblems of poetry are dishonoured. In which serpent, lion and eagle belong to the circus-tent; ox, salmon and boar to the cannery; racehorse and greyhound to the betting ring; and the sacred grove to the saw-mill. In which the Moon is despised as a burnt-out satellite of the Earth and woman reckoned as 'auxiliary state personnel'. In which money will buy almost anything but truth, and almost anyone but the truth-obsessed poet.

- Robert Graves, *The White Goddess*

Robert Graves identified some of the serious spiritual problems facing our modern world, yet we are entitled to ask, as he himself asked of Aldous Huxley: "What has he to offer in its place?" Reduced to its essence, Graves' long and often turgid book [93] suggests that we should turn from the unquestioning worship of a patriarchal father-god to that of a matriarchal mother-goddess – and he even suggests that individual earthly women, in whom his moon-goddess may manifest herself for a while, embody "supreme glory, power, wisdom and love".

His answer is merely a mirror-image of what he wishes to refute. There is no balance in Graves' proposal. From what we know of healthy Germanic societies in pre-Christian times, men and women complemented each other in an earthly reflection of the complementarity of our many gods and goddesses. Yet to be fair to him, Graves was working largely from Christianized Welsh poems which he could access only in translation, and he seems to have been almost unaware of the Germanic religious tradition – otherwise, he could hardly have failed to notice that Odin is (among other things) a god who is "obsessed" with truth and is therefore the patron of poets.

In a similar way, the proto-Odinists referred to in the last few chapters failed to see that there was to hand a complete alternative to the Christianity that they rejected or (in Murray's case) subverted from within. As with Graves, they cannot be blamed for this weakness in their thinking. They had little to go on other than 18th and 19th century re-tellings, almost always by Christian writers, of what became known, slightingly, as "Norse myths". They did not have the benefit that we enjoy of decades of sound scholarship into the cogent and coherent beliefs of our ancestors. Brilliant though these proto-Odinists may have been, the society in which they lived knew almost as little about the Odinist legacy that informed its vital culture as it knew of sub-atomic particles.

Thomas Jefferson (Chapter 30) was fully aware that Anglo-Saxon heathens gave us the basis of his beloved common law. He did not take the next step, which would have been to ask what else we might learn from them.

Of all Victorian poets, Swinburne (Chapter 31) was the most open to Odinist mysticism. The sense of heathen ecstasy was often conveyed in his poetry, and only he could enshrine the human quest in terms such as: "... fain to reach, beyond all bourne of time or trembling sense" (*Tristram of Lyonesse*). Yet for a lesser poet than Swinburne this could easily have degenerated into what Robert Graves called Ramakrishna's *samadhi*: "... a psychopathic condition, a spiritual orgasm ... the most refined form of solitary vice imaginable". Furthermore, Swinburne's central poem, *Hertha*, collapses at the end into a predictable Victorian monism. Once again, Swinburne, like the others, was limited by his era, which had little idea of the comprehensiveness of Odinist beliefs.

James Murray (Chapter 32) managed to enjoy a life relatively untroubled by the great religious struggle that was becoming obvious in his lifetime. According to some of the standard histories, this was a tussle between the vigor of Victorian Protestantism and the sensuous candles-and-incense appeal of a form of Roman Catholicism that seduced the likes of Oscar Wilde. According to others, such as C. P. Snow in his 1959 lecture *The Two Cultures*, the gulf was between scientists and "literary intellectuals". In reality, it was neither of these things. It was a split between any form of Christianity that was worthy of the name, and the resurgence of the old Odinist spirit of our ancestors.

It would be wrong to criticize Murray for going no further. His lifetime achievement of documenting the history of our language has preserved popular Odinist thought better even than Francis James Child's *The English and Scottish Border Ballads*. If Murray had gone any further in an Odinist direction he would have been marginalized and his life-task could not have been completed. He paid lip-service to the dominant religion of his time, and we are all richer for his patience.

Wagner (Chapter 33), likewise, can be forgiven for almost anything. Much of his life was spent "on the run" in consequence of his revolutionary activities; and his opposition to Judeo-Christianity earned him few friends – least of all in the Jewish community that dominated music in his era. Despite its aesthetic beauty, his last great opera, *Parsifal*, was seen by Friedrich Nietzsche as "... a work of perfidy, of vindictiveness, of a secret attempt to poison the presuppositions of life –

a bad work ... I despise everyone who does not experience *Parsifal* as an attempted assassination of basic ethics."

Perhaps Wagner was merely tired and ill when he completed *Parsifal*, although from a purely musical point of view he was still at a creative peak. (The opera was first performed a year before his death.) Like Swinburne, he could not quite see that fully-fledged Odinism could be an intellectually sophisticated and spiritually fulfilling alternative to 19th century Christianity. Even so, the glories of his music live on.

The Australian "Heroic Vitalists" (Chapter 34) were largely what they were also called: pagan-*ists*. There was a faint air of dilettantism about their works, despite their artistic success and their honesty to nature. In their two dominant decades, Australia was mainly populated by Anglo-Saxons and closely related people. It was, in the end, an evasion to populate the Australian "bush" with Arcadian mythological figures, since these were not the particular manifestations of the gods that the direct ancestors of the Australian population would have found most immediately relevant to their spiritual needs.

More importantly, though, whatever their personal views may have been, in terms of how they lived their lives the proto-Odinists might as well have been atheists. Even Swinburne's exquisite openness to all of experience would not be beyond the ability – at least in theory – of someone who had never heard of Indo-European spirituality.

Many critics of Christianity in the era of the proto-Odinists tended toward atheism. Atheism as such does not necessarily lead to either good or bad behavior. Knowing that someone is an atheist does not tell us anything about how that person will lead his or her life, or what he or she will consider to be valuable, admirable or even necessary to mature self-actualization. Atheism does, however, limit the capacity of the individual to experience the human condition at its highest and most autonomous level. It does so in three obvious ways.

First, all human beings have needs. Many thinkers have tried to analyze these needs, and because his logic is exceptionally clear we will look briefly at John Merritt's famous hierarchy of needs [94]. Merritt argued that our most basic needs are physical: food, water and the like. Then comes what he called the "respondent" level: the need to interpret the outside world through our senses. A third level he called "operant": the need to move in and manipulate our environment. A fourth was "co-operant": the need for relationships with other humans. Then comes the "epistemic" need for knowledge, learning and thinking. Finally, and most significant, there are our "evaluative" needs, which enable us to resolve conflicts between the earlier and more purely physical urges by building up consistent preferences, discriminations and moral values.

That last level brings us into the realm of religious thinking. Only religions can offer a consensual world-view about the point and purpose of human life. Without religion, Merritt's "evaluative" needs can only receive ideological answers that are socially determined on behalf of specific social groups or classes. The individual in this case becomes an agent, conscious or not, of a class or group struggle. Moreover, without religion, there can be no consistency at all in terms of our "evaluative" needs. The ever-changing individual is likely, in the face of different circumstances, to espouse one set of values at a given life-stage, then another in a few years' time – rather than to delve deeper and deeper into the meaning of things.

A second way in which atheism limits our development as self-actualizing humans is that it denies – or is at least indifferent to – one of our basic forms of human thinking. Many theorists have proposed that knowledge is made up of an identifiable number of discrete disciplines, or "forms of knowledge". We have seen (Chapter 27) that Varro codified the idea of there being nine "liberal arts", and that the Chartrain school reduced these to seven. More modern scholarship has clarified this idea by arguing that there are seven distinct "forms of knowledge", each of which has its own unique (a) concepts, (b) logic, (c) way of testing its statements against experience, and (d) methodology. According to one exponent of this view, Paul Hirst [95], these different forms of knowledge are: mathematics, physical science, human sciences, history, religion, literature and fine art, and philosophy.

Whether or not we accept this view in the precise form stated by Hirst, it is clear that the grammars of the various forms of knowledge are quite different, and that to transpose elements of one to another makes little sense. For instance, physical science depends on the theoretical possibility of falsifying hypotheses. Mathematics depends on deductive reason. We can therefore say "Darwin's theory of evolution could be disproved by new evidence", or "Two plus two equals four", but not "Two plus two could be disproved by new evidence". Equally, we can say "The gods and goddesses are benevolent", or "Artists applied the laws of perspective in the Renaissance", but not "The laws of perspective are benevolent".

Given that there are approximately seven discrete forms of knowledge, and that humans throughout the millennia have worked out the rules that govern these different forms, it follows that people who are not "open" to all these different forms of knowledge are limiting themselves to a restricted level of human existence. It would be rather odd if an adult were to reject the notion of, say, history. To do so would not be to dispute the accuracy of previous historians, but rather to argue that history does not or should not exist: effectively, that yesterday did not happen. In a similar way, atheists deliberately exclude themselves from one aspect of human thinking, the aspect that finds an ultimate meaning in life's struggles, that allows us to attain the deepest wisdom and the most searing beauty.

A third difficulty with atheism is that it limits human understanding to what we are capable of expressing *in language* at this stage of our evolution. The more we try to talk about gods and goddesses, the more we are forced to refine our language to the point that it can describe a deity in terms that apply only to a deity. If we were ever successful in doing so, it could only be in a language that we ourselves cannot understand – since we are, ourselves, all too human. Simple humility therefore suggests that atheistical arguments based on words alone need to be balanced by the transcendent apprehensions of the deities in many centuries of music and the other arts.

The proto-Odinists were not atheists, and in some cases we know that they had strong religious or spiritual beliefs. Their only problem was that they were blind to the notion of "coming home" completely to the spiritual path of their own heathen ancestors. The next stage, however, had been intellectually prepared. All that was required was for people to step forward and advocate a return to the full range of Odinist thinking and feeling. Several people subsequently did just that, and they are known today as "Odinist pioneers".

Many such pioneers are still alive, but for reasons of privacy this book will mention only five of those who are no longer with us: Rud Mills and Evelyn Price, Ann Lennon, and Else and Alec Christensen. As yet, there are no full-scale biographies of these people, so the following chapters will be short, informal sketches rather than developed portraits.

36

ODINIST PIONEERS: RUD MILLS

Alexander Rud Mills, 1885-1964. Photo taken c. 1935.

Odinists come in many different sizes, shapes, and political allegiances. Yet this author has never met one who believes that the power of the State should prevail over the rights of individuals. The call to the individual conscience that is a keystone of Odinist morality is tolerated, nowadays, in times of peace. But when the State, that "coldest of all cold monsters", feels itself to be under threat, it is quick to turn on all who do not meekly accept hand-me-down opinions. Odinists are not exempt.

The modern world's first prominent Odinist, Alexander Rud Mills, attended Melbourne University as a classmate of Robert Menzies, the future Prime Minister of Australia. Mills became a lawyer and a poet, and his free-thinking nature was probably encouraged by his friendship with W. D. Cookes, the Director of the Rationalist Association of Australia. In the spirit of Odinist inquiry, Mills travelled with Sidney Webb to the Soviet Union, but he was disgusted by Soviet collectivism and contempt for individuality. He then visited Germany, but despite arranging a meeting with its Roman Catholic leader, Adolf Hitler, he was unable to interest the Fuhrer in Odinism.

As his spiritual confidence in our ancestral religion matured, Mills published a series of books on Odinism. One of his earliest texts was *Hael! Odin!*, published in 1933 under the name Tasman Forth. From the same year came a discussion of the Christian ethic in politics called *And Fear Shall be in the Way*. Probably his best-known work was *The Call of our Ancient Nordic Religion* (1957).

In the 1930s Mills was openly advocating the establishment of an Odinist church, the "Anglecyn Church of Odin". He was recruiting converts to the re-awakening faith, and according to one historian [96], by about 1934 "up to 120 members [i.e. Odinists] used to practice 'the Ritual' every Thursday evening and hold Odinist ceremonies on Mills' land at Croydon". The future of Australian Odinism seemed assured.

With World War II looming, Australia itself looked to be threatened. There were several possible attitudes that people might take. One was that Australia's long-term security was bound up with the fate of the British Empire. This was the view of the Prime Minister, Mills' old classmate, Sir Robert Menzies. On the 3rd of September 1939 Menzies broadcast that Australia was now a participant in a war he described as a "tragedy", a "wanton crime", and an "agony".

Some took a different attitude. The war in Europe didn't affect Australia directly, and Australia's armed forces might well be required to defend their homeland if Japan advanced southward. The chief proponent of this isolationist position was the Australia First Movement, which urged that: "Australia should look to its own interests without regard to the total allied strategy". This movement was supported by the poet Ian Mudie, novelist Miles Franklin, Sir Thomas Gordon, Adela Pankhurst Walsh of the famous suffragette family, and the Women's Guild of Empire. It was led by Percy Reginald Stephenson (1901-1965).

"Inky" Stephenson was a prominent man of letters. He had been taught Latin at Maryborough Boys' Grammar School by the famous anthropologist Gordon Child, and gone on to study arts at the University of Queensland, where he became a close friend of Jack Lindsay and Eric

Partridge – and also became the 45th member of the Australian Communist Party (later denouncing communism as "only banditry disguised as a political philosophy".) In 1924 he gained a Rhodes Scholarship, and after his studies at Oxford he became manager of the Franfrolico Press. Here he published authors like Aldous Huxley, Jack Lindsay, Hugh McCrae and Kenneth Slessor. He translated and published Nietzsche's *The Antichrist* in 1929, and after moving to the Mandrake Press he published D. H. Lawrence's paintings, the first English edition of *Lady Chatterley's Lover*, and works by Aleister Crowley. On returning to Australia in 1932 he became managing director of the Australian Book Publishing Company, bringing out works by Norman Lindsay, Banjo Paterson, Henry Handel Richardson, Eleanor Dark, Randolph Hughes and Xavier Herbert – all household names today in literary circles.

Stephenson was therefore no lightweight, and no disgruntled "outsider" figure. All his life he had advanced the careers of new, and particularly Australian, writers. It was probably inevitable that he would adopt the isolationist position with regard to the war in Europe. In September 1941, Stephenson launched the Australia First Movement.

At the outbreak of the war the Federal Government had passed a "National Security Act" giving the authorities sweeping powers to rule by regulation. In effect, Australia, like Britain under Churchill, had moved close to being a dictatorship. By 1942 there were 6,780 people held in Australian concentration camps, including foreign nationals and people perceived as political dissidents. A parliamentary faction led by Abram Landa and S. M. Falstein began agitating to have the leaders of the Australia First Movement incarcerated.

Rud Mills had had some contact with Inky Stephenson. To start with, he had sent another Odinist, Les Cahill, to Sydney to try to convert Stephenson to Odinism. He had also written articles for Stephenson's monthly, *The Publicist*. Finally, when Stephenson came under government suspicion, Mills wrote a letter offering him legal advice. The letter was intercepted.

At the urging of Landa and Falstein, Stephenson was arrested on the 20th of March, 1942, and interned for three years, five months and one week. With him in the concentration camp, guarded by machine guns and barbed wire and starved of rations, were about twenty other members of Australia First. These people were prisoners of conscience in the strictest Amnesty International sense of the phrase. Not one was ever charged with a single offence.

Soon to join them was Leslie Kevin Cahill. He had enlisted on the 20th of January 1942, and served as an army private. For having tried to convert Stephenson to Odinism, he was arrested on the 10th of March. He ended up at Loveday concentration camp in South Australia, where he was held until the 6th of February 1944.

Now it was the turn of Rud Mills. On the 10th of March, 1942, Major Ted Hattam of Military Intelligence and Sub-Inspector Birch of the

Victorian CIB Special Branch called at his flat in Canterbury, Melbourne. Apparently believing that Mills' faith in his Anglo-Saxon ancestral gods would somehow make him support a Roman Catholic like Hitler, they searched his premises but found nothing incriminating. He remained free until the 7th of May, when he was taken under armed guard to a detention camp in Broadmeadows. From there he was sent to Loveday.

Mills was forced to appear before a military tribunal in July 1942. Despite having been systematically starved of rations for three months, and despite having at least once been beaten with a rifle by a sadistic camp guard, he still put up a decent showing. The tribunal recommended that he be released without restriction. On the 17th of December 1942 he walked out of Loveday concentration camp as a free man.

In 1944 the Attorney-General, Dr Evatt, set up a Commission of Inquiry to investigate the detention without trial of Australian citizens. Rud Mills was grilled for three days in the witness stand, but failed to crack. In its report, the Commission concluded that: "after the outbreak of war he [Mills] had not disclosed in his conduct any hostility to the allied cause". One might wonder why they thought he would. After all, the Prime Minister, Sir Robert Menzies, had also done everything he could to avoid the war. Even as late as the 18th of August 1939 he had argued that the British and Germans "have more in common than not, and the things we argue about are mere froth on the surface".

This was a point that Mills had also been making. But Mills' internment showed that what was an acceptable opinion in the mouth of a Christian politician was unacceptable from the pen of an Odinist poet.

Others took the hint. Most of the Odinist circle faded away. The Anglecyn Church of Odin went deeply underground. Les Cahill vanished from public life so completely that no photo of him is known to survive. Rud Mills fought for compensation for his unjust imprisonment, but received nothing. The book that he planned to write about his incarceration never appeared, and exhaustive searches in recent years have failed to locate its manuscript.

Mills' writings are not always clear, largely because he was trying to express what had scarcely been thought before; but they are reasonably consistent. One persistent theme is that the Indo-European spiritual tradition was everywhere vital, active and joyful, but that it became distorted following the immigration of alien peoples to our ancestral homelands. In particular, the rot became deadly in the multi-racial Athenian empire under the teachings of Socrates and Plato, which subsequently provided the spiritual defect at the heart of Christianity:

> The Plato-Socratian thinking produced unforeseen results. It brought disaster to Greece and Rome, and yet it became the basis of the Christian religion. This basic attitude judged by immediate temporalities seemed to some people harmless enough; but, like

the untrue foundations of a building, it must eventually bring about a collapse of the entire structure. [97]

The irony of the police suspicion of Rud Mills is that his co-religionists in Germany suffered similar fates. There were millions of heathens in Germany before the Third Reich, so it was not surprising that the new regime utilized the ancient and sacred Odinist symbol of the swastika in an attempt to harness the healthy instincts of German cultural patriots.

National Socialism may have borrowed some of the trappings of Odinism, but it was officially opposed to our religion. Alfred Rosenberg, the philosopher of National Socialism, declared bluntly that "Odin is dead!" Meanwhile, Adolf Hitler proclaimed that although Nazis must "reject the intellect ... this must not take the form of a revival of the worship of Odin" (whatever that was supposed to mean!). Since Nazism was largely a Roman Catholic phenomenon it tended toward a worship of whatever hierarchy was in power at the time – and at that time, the favored hierarchy was the Corporate State. It had no more room for the spirit of Odinist individualism and free inquiry than the Australian government that incarcerated Rud Mills, Les Cahill and others.

The last German religious census taken just before WW2 found that Germany (excluding Memel) had 31,944,000 Roman Catholics, 42,636,000 Evangelicals, 308,000 Jews, 1,208,000 people "without belief" and 2,746,000 "neo-pagans" [98]. Most of these "neo-pagans" would have been heathens of some sort within the Germanic tradition. After the war there were hardly any of them left – or at least hardly any who dared to admit it on an official census. Perhaps they were all dead: no-one has yet bothered to investigate their fates.

From the beginning of the Third Reich, heathens were persecuted. For instance, in 1933, Rudolf von Sebettendorff was arrested and exiled. The works of heathen writers such as Lanz von Liebenfels, Ernst Issberner-Haldane and Reinhold Ebertin were banned. Former membership of a heathen congregation disqualified anyone from holding rank or office within the N.S.D.A.P. Things quickly became worse. In 1936 Friedrich Barnharb Marby, a runic enthusiast and follower of von List, was arrested and sent to a camp at Flossenberg; he was released from Dachau in 1945. He was not alone. But the full power of the state was not focused on religious minorities until the 9th of June 1941 when the head of the security police, Heydrich, banned a large number of spiritual practices. Among the victims were followers of Rudolf Steiner, followers of von List, and traditional heathens. "Their organisations were dissolved, their property confiscated, and many of their leaders arrested" [99]

Australian Odinists and German traditional heathens were both persecuted by their governments, and both for the same reason. Western nation-states of the mid-20th century were still essentially Judeo-Christian in outlook, and viewed our Indo-European spiritual tradition with suspicion and hostility.

37

ODINIST PIONEERS:
EVELYN PRICE, THE "FIRST LADY" OF ODINISM

Evelyn Louisa Price, 1888-1973

Evelyn Price was an Odinist as early as the 1920s. After a long and romantic courtship, in 1951 she finally married Rud Mills, the father of the Odinist Re-Awakening. By then they were both in their sixties. Evelyn is therefore very much the "First Lady" of Odinism.

An extremely generous relative of the Price family has written the following personal memoir, and has given permission for its publication here:

I had seen her several times when I was a child back in the 1940s, a kindly lady, who was an aunt, the elder sister to my father. We lived in Geelong, Victoria, but she in Canterbury, Melbourne, so there were only fleeting visits.

In the mid 1960s I came to live in Melbourne and as one does, visited. She was living in Upwey at the time, in a solid but sparse, timber residence that had been built for a previous premier of Victoria, Sir Thomas Bent. She was alone, her husband Alexander Rud Mills having deceased in 1964. It was always my disappointment that I had never met him in the flesh. Evelyn Louisa Mills, born Evelyn Price to parents Frederick Andrew Price and Helena Louisa Rogers, looked forward to my visits, which through the late 1960s and early 1970s became increasingly frequent. We passed the time in the seemingly lost art of conversation, either out on the broad verandah under the gums on summer afternoons and evenings, or inside before roaring log fires during winter's bleakness.

Slowly, I began to know and appreciate her. She was the epitome of my family's heritage, and I have not seen the likes of her since and doubt that I ever will again, though some upcoming and possibly enterprising teenagers of early twenties grand-nieces may prove me wrong in time.

Evelyn's mother, Helena, had died in childbirth in 1903 at Geelong – a caesarean operation that failed. Thus Evelyn became the surrogate mother at the age of 14 to her five siblings. Her long struggles through decades to ensure that the family stood on solid ground faced many hurdles. She was accepted by the Victorian Education Department as a junior teacher at Chilwell Primary School in Geelong, Victoria, prior to World War I and after retirement was offered the position of headmistress for a time at Mitcham State School. In between these times she had travelled through much of Victoria teaching in remote towns, though two of her mountain-top experiences in teaching were at Bright and at Parkville, Melbourne.

Aunt's romance with Alexander Rud Mills spanned approximately 30 years. Family problems on both sides, and it seems Fate, conspired to keep them from marrying. They managed to become engaged but it was called off because of the pressure of family relationships and it was not until 1951 when both were in their sixties that they were able to tie the knot. In the late 1920s Evelyn became interested in Rud's philosophies and attended the many Odinist festivals with him in the Victorian countryside. Some years after Rud's death she handed to me many of his books and some writings, stating at the time that some of these were given to the State Library of Victoria. An investigation led me to discover that they were not on public show but were held away from view on a restriction order. Fortunately this is not the case today and Rud's books may be called down for research purposes.

Several months prior to her death in 1973 Evelyn handed to me a marked copy of Rud's *The First Guide Book to the Anglecyn Church of Odïn* and requested that the Order for the Burial of the Dead be read at her funeral. I was very pleased to do this for her. She had made a few changes to make it more amenable for the Christians in the congregation but over-all it was an Odinist order of service. It was accepted well by those present with the exception of the funeral director – who was, I believe, a Methodist lay preacher – and who could not hide his discomfort.

Aunt was a remarkable woman, the driving force behind her younger siblings and undoubtedly of great comfort to Rud over the years. I am the richer for having known her and possibly a little poorer for not having personally known her husband.

38

ODINIST PIONEERS:
ANN LENNON, REBEL WITH A CAUSE

What is morality? Morality is physical, intellectual and moral fitness, a healthy mind, a healthy body and a healthy soul; above all, a joy in virility, wisdom and beauty. The Christian Church anathematised these three, basing its dogmas upon the doctrines expounded by Christ in *The Sermon on the Mount* and by St. Paul in his *Epistles*. Poverty is exalted, marriage decried, evil is not to be resisted, and no thought is to be taken for the morrow. Not only did these subversive doctrines go far towards wrecking the Roman Empire, but today ... they are likely to wreck Western civilisation more certainly than famine, plague and war.
- Major-General John Frederick Charles Fuller
The Dragon's Teeth: A Study of War and Peace

Ann Lennon's immediate ancestors were a mix of Irish Catholics and Ulster and English Protestants. Crucially, she was mainly brought up by her Irish Catholic mother. Therefore she was able to learn at first hand the hypocrisy of organized Christianity.

Growing up in a large Liverpool slum family, she was a quick learner. One of her earliest "political" memories was of her Uncle Sam, who gave the youngsters of the family a history lesson after they were taken to see the remaining "slave-stands", "where the negroes once were brought in chains from Africa to be auctioned off to wealthy Christian gentlemen":

Sam "snorted in disgust," then said:

> Slaves? We've had white slaves right here in England and Ireland. Farm-workers have been slaves for years – so poor, they've lived on crusts of bread and potatoes and hardly known the taste of meat. So they've poached! ... The poaching farm hands do is snaring small birds and animals like hares to make a meal for their family. The woods they catch them in belong to the rich folk, you see, and if you're caught taking any wild life living free in them, then you were hung for it. I read of a young labourer who was asked how he lived on 2/6 a week and he said he didn't. He poached. 'Better to be hanged for it than starve to death' were his words. ... Then if they weren't hanged, they'd be

transported to America. After their War of Independence from England the Yanks wouldn't take any more convicts so they were sent to Australia. So don't any of you think that the only slaves were black ones. And there were other sorts of slaves too. Chimney sweeps were slaves to their masters. The coal mines employed slaves – not only men but women and children too. The cotton mills kept thousands of slaves for years. ... Remember that, you young uns!

Ann Lennon, 1905-1992

Ann's family was worse off than most African slaves who ended up in America. After all, no-one owned the Lennons of Liverpool, so no-one cared about them. Like all the rest of the family, young Ann had no option but to beg for food. (Her father was a sailor, and his meager wages only came through to the family after his latest voyage, by which time there was usually another hungry Lennon mouth to feed.)

When Ann's mother could see no future at all for the family, she attempted suicide. The children were then sent to a grim Catholic orphanage, separated from their siblings, and forced to abuse their immature bodies by working like adults for starvation rations. As a result of childhood malnutrition, Ann never grew taller than five feet. Her mind, however, was always alert. She observed Irish Catholic priests in Liverpool blessing Irish terrorists:

> Our dad didn't like Mum's devotion to her Church and I suspect that this was the cause of many of their disputes. It was a time when there was much activity in the Irish Sinn Fein movement (now known as the I.R.A.) When any of its members attended church for confession, the priest gave them full absolution for any killing that might follow, with the promise of entry into Heaven should they themselves be killed!

Despite her clear-eyed view of the moral corruption of Christianity, young Ann might possibly have stuck with her mother's Irish Catholic faith. What turned her around was that she obtained a scholarship to attend a Catholic secondary school, Mt Pleasant Convent. Toward the end of her first year, the Mother Superior called in Mrs Lennon and told her that:

> ... she did not consider it right and proper that I should receive any further education that would unfit me for the kind of life that God had ordained for me! ... Poor Mum began to cry. My own thoughts whirled around in confusion. As Mum tearfully said how well I'd been getting on, the Mother Superior halted her with a raised hand. ... 'No, please listen to what I offer. We are prepared to give you £20 if you remove Ann from here at once with no further fuss or bother'.

So ended Ann's academic education, at the age of thirteen. She then ran away from home and found a menial job in a "Soldiers' Home for Incurables" in Stockport. She was soon promoted to ward duties, with the prospect of training as a nurse – which in those days was a career reserved mostly for girls of the middle class. She wrote to her mother to tell her that all was well and there was no need to worry. Ann's mother replied that:

> ... Father Hanlon [the parish priest] said that I must go home at once. I was needed there and that was my proper place. Indeed, if I did not return he himself would come to Stockport and fetch me back!

Being still well under the "legal" age, Ann was forced to return home. She eventually managed to talk her mother into standing up to the priest, and was allowed back into the repatriation hospital. At last, turning 18 in 1922, she was able to start nursing training.

Four years later she had almost finished her studies. Meanwhile her mother, Nell, had given birth to three more children. Then word came from her sailor-father, to say that he was stuck in Adelaide, South Australia, and could not return to England. The Waterside Workers Union in Adelaide had been striking for better wages and conditions, and Chief Steward Jim Lennon had walked off his ship in solidarity with them – and promptly been sent to prison with them, as well as being black-balled from serving on British ships ever again. In those days the Unions looked after their own. They found Jim both work and a decent place to live. He invited his family to come out to Australia and join him. Ann's UK training was complete, and there were no prospects for the younger children in the slums of Liverpool, so they emigrated.

Ann then had to do another year's training to comply with Australia's different regulations. In one of the hospitals she met a patient, Arch Lapthorne, whom she was eventually to marry. Significantly, he was a member of the Rationalist Association. Arch and Ann moved to Sydney just as the Great Depression began to bite. Like many of the unemployed, they spent afternoons in the Sydney Domain, listening to the soap-box orators. As she commented later: "It was a cheap and pleasant way to spend our limited time together".

One day a particular speaker infuriated her by mocking those – like her own mother – who had been duped by Christianity. Ann had words with him. The crowd sided with the little red-haired girl, dragged the speaker off his own box and installed her on it. Ann spoke tenderly of her own mother, then told the crowd:

> They aren't to blame. It's those at the top of the hierarchy who have power and money, who are to blame, and who permit conditions of poverty and misery to continue.
>
> I reminded them that there were thousands of unemployed people like themselves the world over who were quietly suffering just as they and their families were. And why? Because of the failure of the banking system, which took more note of figures in a ledger than it did of human flesh and blood. I said that man was his own worst enemy because he wouldn't think rationally. He read what the papers printed and believed that ninety percent of it was true, instead of only ten percent as truth. I said that until they woke up and began to question, in an organised way, those part-truths, they would continue to be exploited by the state and church, by those in authority who told them there would be plenty of pie-in-the-sky waiting for them, if they were patient and obedient to authority.

So began Ann's career as a public speaker. The Rationalist Association supported her weekly talks, which were increasingly reported in the press, and the crowds grew. Here is her own summary of part of a speech she gave on "The Problem of the Unfit":

> As we all know in the Great War thousands were sent by our nation and many others, of their best manhood – all to fight and be sacrificed on the altar of national sovereignty. As we also know, they were the flower of the nations who sent them and they paid the price for their bravery. Today we have to breed from second and third rate stock. My plea for eugenic reform

will no doubt upset a number here today. But we must prevent the continued procreation of the unfit, for the sake of the future generations.

Particularly upset by Ann's speeches was a group of Catholic "ladies" who threatened her eyes with their umbrellas. Arch and his Rationalist friends had to save her "by moving in close around me as a guard from further onslaught of these gentle Christian maidens!" Soon, her speeches began to take a new turn. Here is Ann's summary of one of them:

> I said, How can we reasonably teach our children to love and revere the God, depicted time and again in the Old Testament as requiring animal and human sacrifice. This God may be a Jewish God, believed in by a primitive race thousands of years ago, but he cannot be one we Aussies can believe in! ... an angry deity who brought down dreadful punishment upon the people if they disobeyed him – a fearful Jehovah who ordered thousands of innocent men and their women to be put to the sword. What sort of a God was this? He must have been a real He-Man kind of God!

After this, Ann noticed that the police were attending her speeches, jotting down her phrases in their note-books.

In 1932 one Australian worker in three was unemployed. Evictions for non-payment of rent were common. One day Ann saw the police evicting an unfortunate family and she heard:

> ... a child screaming from behind the front door. Standing there pressing it back was a big policeman. I could see a small foot poking out from beneath the door and I ran forward calling out, 'Don't you know there's a child pinned behind that door?' ... [T]he policemen ignored me, I rushed at him, pushed him aside and released the sobbing child.

She was charged with assaulting a policeman. The charge was dismissed, presumably because the thought of a five-foot girl assaulting a burly Australian policeman was ludicrous. But worse was to come.

On October 23 of the same year Ann made a public speech to an audience of 600, and was promptly arrested on a charge of blasphemy. This was a serious matter. The only precedent under the current laws had been that of G. W. Foote, in 1856, who had been sentenced to twelve months' hard labor. The part of Ann's speech that apparently caused most offence to the police complainants was this:

> [Jehovah] loved bloodshed and the smell of burning flesh ... This God of you Christians is a Jewish god, not an Aussie god, not a fair-dinkum Aussie God, just a Jewish god with his money bags around his neck.

Probably fearful of being seen to over-react, the establishment reduced the charge to one of "infringing the Domain by-laws ... by addressing an assembly in an unseemly manner, amounting to blasphemy". Ann conducted her own defense in the Central Summons Court on December 20, 1932. She was convicted, and she appealed.

The unemployed people in the Domain passed around the hat, collecting money for Ann's defense. Her Rationalist friends, and others (of whom more later), sought influential help. The appeal case ran from 6-8th of January, 1932. Ann was represented by the former Justice Piddington, an appointed judge to the High Court of Australia, and Clive Evatt, a fiery Labor KC. The appeal was heard by a half-deaf judge. His Honor made it clear that in his opinion Ann's crime was far worse than merely "unseemly". He would have liked to treat it as outright blasphemy. Unfortunately, he could only impose the maximum penalty for the charge that had been laid. That was 21 days hard labor, or a fine of £10.

Ann, who had been living from hand to mouth like so many others in the Depression, did not have £10 to her name, and she had no hope of raising it. A policeman began taking her down to the cells below the court. At the last moment an angry man stormed up shouting: "Constable, take your hand off Miss Lennon! She is now free to leave!" This benefactor had paid her fine. The benefactor was Billy Miles.

William John Miles was a public accountant and businessman who founded in 1912 what later became the Rationalist Association of New South Wales. He regularly spoke at the Domain against conscription in the First World War, until the conscription proposal was finally defeated by referendum in 1917. In 1936 Miles funded and edited a new monthly magazine called *The Publicist*. In that year the Melbourne-based Rud Mills (Chapter 36) was living in Sydney. The two were friends. Also living in Sydney in 1936, and closely associated with Miles, was Les Cahill, another Odinist from Melbourne. Mills wrote for *The Publicist*, and Miles supported Mills' bid for Parliament in the election of 1940.

Ann Lennon's criminal conviction does not seem to have dampened her ardor, although she now confined her speeches to "private" meetings of Miles' Rationalist Association – of which she became Secretary. At least one speech she gave attracted so many people that they had to hire the Brisbane Football Stadium to accommodate the crowd. A sound system was installed so that those milling outside could hear her words.

War was looming. The authorities were keeping a close watch on people who had expressed pacifist sympathies, or even merely opposed Australia's involvement in a European conflict. Ann Lennon's pacifist speeches had been widely reported. Miles, the ex-communist Cahill, and Mills were all publicly arguing that Australian troops should be kept at home to defend Australia against Japan – the very policy that was later enacted by Prime Minister John Curtin.

In a series of mass arrests, those who opposed the conduct of the war were swept up in March 1942 and sent to concentration camps. Miles himself was beyond arrest – he had died on 10 January. Ann Lennon (now Mrs Ann Lapthorne) was also out of reach. She had been invited by the New Zealand Rationalist Association to give a lecture tour in that country. She arrived just in time, and there she remained safely until the war was over. She and Arch then returned to her family in Adelaide.

There an event occurred that seems to have ended any thoughts Ann may have retained of resuming her speaking career. Her brother Chris, whom she had "mothered" back in Liverpool, was employed as a beach patroller. There was a large number of displaced Yugoslavs (including Muslims) in Adelaide at the time. They hung around the beaches, often making inappropriate approaches to the local girls. The girls complained to Chris, who explained to the Yugoslavs that things weren't done that way in Australia. This led to at least one fist fight. Then Chris was murdered on the beach at Semaphore, Adelaide.

Ann's life became a private one after that, and before long the health of her older husband began to decline. He died in 1969.

Most of the above information comes from a memoir that Ann wrote for her family, *Born a Rebel*. In it she downplayed parts of her life that may have distressed her relatives. "Ann" seems to be the correct spelling of her name, but she sometimes signed herself "Anne". An elderly lady who attended, as a child, Rud Mills' Odinist meetings, provided this author with further information about Ann – who was apparently called "Annie" in Odinist circles. None of these further adventures has yet been verified. All were entirely reputable, but it is easy to see why Ann may have thought them too difficult to explain to her family. In particular, the elderly lady insisted that Ann was present at a town hall lecture in Sydney when the novelist Miles Franklin, the main speaker, had to be rescued from some armed communists who had invaded the meeting. A mixed group of pacifists, Rationalists and Odinists rescued Franklin by forming a ring around the ladies, forcing their way into a back room, and shoving Franklin and the other women out to safety through a window. If the informant's memory was accurate, Ann Lennon was one of them.

39

ODINIST PIONEERS: ELSE CHRISTENSEN, "THE FOLKMOTHER"

> Liberty is a duty not a right.
> - *motto on Ezra Pound's notepaper*

A young Else Christensen, 3rd from right

T-shirt design to raise money for Else's release after false imprisonment

What follows is a personal memoir written by the author of this book on the death of Else Christensen (1913-2005):

Else Christensen, known to Odinists around the world as The Folkmother, died on the fourth of May this year.

While I was never able to meet Else face to face, I was honored by a rich and rewarding correspondence with her for over thirty years, starting in 1972. With a letter-writer as gifted and as generous as Else was, it is possible to know the other person better than one will ever know many workmates, neighbors or even family members. One aspect of Else's character that was contagious, even through the medium of letters, was the profound delight that she found in even the simplest aspects of life.

No matter how trying the circumstances, Else was irresistibly light of heart, and much of this quality arose from her boundless curiosity. Few of us could see any bright side to being wrongfully convicted of a serious crime, but Else wrote from prison – with almost child-like sincerity – that she could not be other than happy, given that she now had the opportunity of learning so much from a class of girls with whom she had never before had the opportunity to mix.

The woman who became revered as The Folkmother was born in Esbjerg, Denmark in 1913. She was confirmed into the Lutheran faith as a child, but "dropped out of Christianity", to use her own words, at the age of fifteen.

Else and her husband (see Chapter 40) emigrated to Toronto in Canada, where she became manager of the X-ray department at a local hospital until her retirement.

After turning her back on Christianity, she considered herself an "agnostic" until the 1960s, when she discovered the writings of Rud Mills. It was a meeting of two joyful minds, and from that moment the purpose of the rest of her life became clear.

In 1969 she founded the first Odinist association in North America. This organization was very loosely structured and went through several name changes, including The Odinist Movement, The Odinist Fellowship and The Odinist Community.

As far as the historical sequence of the Re-Awakening is concerned, it is important to remember that Else's discovery of Odinism preceded that of various well-known individuals in America, of Stubba in England, of Sveinbjörn Beinteinsson in Iceland, and of the Melbourne University group in Australia – all of which took place in the early 1970s, in a strange example of synchronicity. It is also vital to recall that Else clearly saw herself as following in the path of Rud Mills, whose writings she frequently reprinted.

In August 1971 she began publishing *The Odinist*, which continued without a break until her malicious legal prosecution at the age of 79.

In the late 1970s Else moved to Crystal River, Florida, where she lived on a small acreage with a creek-front. I recall many delightful letters from that idyllic period in her life, when she was particularly taken with an alligator that lived in the creek and occasionally waddled ashore to scrutinize her.

This period of frith came to an end when Else received a 30-month prison sentence on trumped-up charges of transporting soft drugs across state lines. The background to this prosecution was that she had established a very successful prison outreach ministry which was, of course, a threat to the establishment.

After serving out this unjust sentence in her usual blithe spirit, she was deported back to Canada. Rescued by the good folk of Wodanesdag, she lived in British Columbia in a caravan, with an annex full of boxed archives, amid an idyllic landscape. Her letters from that period were uniformly joyful and serene, her only regret being that she might not live long enough to catalogue all her books, papers, photographs and other archives.

In my view Else very much deserves her title of The Folkmother. Only she had the wisdom to pick up the baton that Rud Mills tried to pass to us in the 1930s. Most of those who have since come to the Re-Awakening probably would not have done so had it not been for Else Christensen.

Our spiritual path, Odinism, does not have a founder. It has been with us for as long as our people have existed; and it has never been lost, even during the long Period of Dual Faith. In the 19th century there were many people who glimpsed aspects of our renewed spiritual dawn despite the remaining darkness, and these people are known to us as proto-Odinists. Yet one man, and one alone, can be called the Father of the Re-Awakening: Alexander Rud Mills. His eventual wife, Evelyn Price, is indisputably the "First Lady" of Odinism.

Similarly, there can be no other claimant to the title of The Folkmother than Else Christensen.

40

ODINIST PIONEERS:
ALEC CHRISTENSEN: AN UNSUNG HERO

We're all more or less caught up in the speed trap of modern society. We have just witnessed the Olympics where a fraction of a second makes the difference between a win or a loss. But in life you're not in competition with anybody but yourself, you're not out to win medals; you're here as a member of your folk, and your efforts are not counted in seconds in competition with other people, but rather in the quiet and continuous influence you have in the overall future in the life of our folk.

- Else Christensen, 1992

Alec Christensen, 1904-1971

The following memoir of Alec Christensen was written by his wife, the late Else Christensen, and is reproduced with the permission she granted this author in 2002.

Aage Alec Christensen was born September 14, 1904, in Copenhagen, and grew up in a working man's home. His father was a candy-maker who unfortunately died when Alec was 10 years old. A 15-year-older brother was just about to leave home, so Alec was alone with his mother, who without much schooling herself put all her energy into giving her son a proper education. As Alec didn't have any special preferences, his mother found him an apprenticeship with a family friend who was a wood-carver. As it turned out, this was a good choice as Alec had a talent for drawing which stood him to good use in his new trade, and he became an excellent craftsman.

As a journeyman young Alec went 'travelling on his trade' as it was called and often done by those who wanted to see a little more than their own backyard. All were, of course, union members, and the local office would help any young journeyman to find jobs and accommodation. Alec went as far as France, learning more tricks of his trade, and in between even won a few bouts as an amateur boxer.

On the way back through Germany he experienced the total break-down of the German economy which came a few years after the end of WW1. He told stories about the devaluation of the German mark, of the workers having to be paid twice a week to keep up with the swiftly rising prices, then paid each day to get at least a few items for their wages. He also told how he and the man in whose house be was studying, on Sundays went outside the city begging potatoes from the farmers. When the situation became too severe all foreign workers were told to leave, and just inside Denmark Alec had to get money from the Union to buy a ticket back to Copenhagen.

All along the young wood-carver was passionately interested in politics and the various swingings of the political scene caused by the Russian Revolution, the formation of the USSR, the fight within the different small socialistic groups and the rising nationalism of the workers of Germany. On arriving home this interest was in no way forgotten, and Copenhagen was abuzz with political discussions in the coffeehouses and meeting halls; and you could often find Alec in the middle of a fierce argument.

In the meantime his first marriage where a daughter had been born went on the rocks; he moved out of the house. His mother had died and his older brother had his family to care for. So Alec stayed around with friends or in rented rooms. Wherever he was, he was arguing for fair pay for the workers, for freedom of choice and for protecting his country and its ways against the internationalism of most of the socialistic parties.

This was how I met Alec. I, too, was very interested in politics and on the rather radical side of the issues. We started going to meetings together, hanging out in the same bars, and before long our liaison took on a permanent nature. Shortly after, Denmark became occupied by the German forces, and we decided to remain neutral. We liked the social program of National Socialism, but we were Danes, not Germans, so to stay out of the events seemed to us to be the better policy. Since we were known as political activists, Alec was later picked up together with other such individuals and taken to the local concentration camp; luckily this happened so early that the camp had not yet been moved to Germany. Alec was able to persuade the German political police that we did not intend to participate one way or the other, and after about half a year he was let go. Later we were both picked up for questioning as it became known that we had weapons. The investigators only knew about the handguns, so when they were handed over and we had been duly interrogated, we were let go after a couple of hours; and we experienced no further problems.

The many restrictions during the occupation had gotten under our skin, so when things again became closer to normal we took advantage of the freedom. At the time we had acquired a 9-ton yawl, so after talking plans over, we decided to pack up most of our important belongings, sell the rest which we could not take with us and see how far we could get. The boat was strong enough for crossing the Atlantic; but somehow the weather gods did not like that idea. For such a crossing you have to pick up the trade winds at the Azores at a certain time of the year. Various problems delayed us and we were too late to reach the islands in time, this was in '48. We tried again the following year, but again there were delays and the storms came early that year too. Finally we gave up the great plan, sold the boat in England, got immigration papers to Canada and arrived in that country in February of 1951 with forty bucks between us.

I had some school English, we had spent almost half a year in England, Alec spoke a little French, so we made out all right. He had of course taken his tools with him, so we found work and accommodation, and began to get used to the Canadian way.

To our disappointment Toronto was politically dead, nobody seemed interested in what the politicians were doing with the people's money. The Socreds *[presumably Social Creditors]* were most alive but even they were not able to attract much activity. We finally met some other Europeans who, like us, were politically aware, and we were discussing ways of getting people interested in the political scene.

Nothing really happened until we accidentally came across a fellow who had the books written by A. Rud Mills and didn't know what to do with them. Alec right away grasped the idea

Mills had developed. He had earlier come upon the idea to promote British pre-Christian beliefs. WWII interrupted his efforts, but after the war he again gathered a small group of friends who celebrated the seasons, read the few books available dealing with Norse mythology and, mostly, British history.

The fellow gave us the books sensing that we were interested and we began holding meetings, exploring the idea of picking up where Mills had left off; he had died in the mid-fifties *[Here Else was wrong. Rud Mills died on the 8th of April, 1964.]* The more we read, the more enthusiastic we became; here, finally, was something solid we could put before our Folk to replace barren Christianity with its concepts of sin, death and spiritual stupor, something that would bring new emotions to our people and give us back our forgotten spiritual heritage.

We tried, as a feeler, to send out a small publication, poorly done for we did not yet really know what we were doing, only groping; however, we also soon realized that we needed to study the past more before we would be able to do anything realistically.

Unfortunately Alec developed heart problems, and had several heart attacks which caused activities to be put on hold. He died in May '71, but the idea of going back to our past to regain our future stayed with us; a few friends in Toronto and southern Ontario decided to go ahead.

We brought out the first issue of *The Odinist* in August '71 – the rest is history.

41

THE LIMITS OF EARLY MODERN ODINISM

"I fancy we have had enough of Jerusalem," she said [looking at a diaroma of the 1st century city] "considering that we are not descended from the Jews. There was nothing first-rate about the place, or people, after all – as there was about Athens, Rome, Alexandria, and other old cities."

  - Sue Bridehead in Thomas Hardy's novel, *Jude the Obscure*

The limits of the thinkers discussed in the last five chapters were largely those of era and circumstance. For instance, with the exception of Rud Mills, none had the opportunity to publish book-length accounts of their beliefs. They were limited to speeches, magazine articles and pamphlets, which did not allow them the luxury of presenting their views systematically or completely. In the case of Mills, he was attempting something that no-one had done before. Even the meticulously considered masterwork of Charles Darwin required amendment by later scientists, so it would be unfair to chide Mills for not writing the book he might have written were he alive today.

Another problem they faced was that the material on which they had to rely was firmly in the hands of university professionals who may have been good linguists, or good comparative religionists, or good cultural historians, but who didn't realize that these skills were inadequate. At worst the academics were hostile to their sources; at best, with a few brave exceptions, they had no psychological or spiritual connection with the subject over which they claimed some sort of academic "ownership". Their books and articles therefore recall the conversation of Shakespeare's characters:

Antonio: He misses not much.
Sebastian: No. He doth but mistake the truth totally.

In recent years a new generation of scholars has begun to arise, men and women who are genuinely heathen and can approach the historical sources with honesty and imaginative, yet critical, sympathy. This task, unfortunately, is far from complete.

These problems apply also to the book you are reading. It was written at a particular time, by a mere human, and a new archaeological or scientific discovery, even the recovery of a "lost" manuscript from some library, might change some of the conclusions that have been drawn so far.

Furthermore, the future is unknowable. We are still in the stage of "early modern" Odinism, and no-one can say how this spiritual adventure will develop. However, in the opinion of this writer, Odinism as it is today needs to address many issues. Several of these are listed below, together with examples. The list is far from complete, and other Odinist writers even today would place their emphasis elsewhere. If this book stimulates them to do so it will have been worth the effort.

Odinism must become more **rational and coherent**. It needs to be developed according to an intellectual architecture based on consistent principles and basic ideas, so that any purportedly Odinist statement can be subjected to relevant tests of validity. For instance, there are many commercially-produced books in New Age shops that purport to explain the runes, or to lay down Odinist rituals. Most Odinists treat these pot-boilers with scorn, but on what precise basis could we say that such-and-such a book "is not really Odinist at all"?

Odinism must be **contemporary**, meaning both that it is compatible with current knowledge and that it engages with current intellectual issues. For instance, in mainstream physics the dogmatic pronouncements of Albert Einstein are still accorded the obeisance that Christians formerly gave to the pronouncements of Popes. If Einstein's belief in the Big Bang as a "singularity" is correct, then the heathen alternative of eternal recurrence is incorrect – and vice versa. Modern scientific cosmology is therefore very much an Odinist concern.

Odinism must be **socially relevant**. It needs to provide values and techniques that enable us to analyze and resolve current social issues. For instance, Odinism is a nature-based religion. Humans, like our deities, are a part of nature, not somehow set above it. We therefore understand that natural resources such as forests should not be destroyed for short-term financial gain. But most habitat destruction today is an almost inevitable result of human overpopulation. To "save" a forest may be a worthwhile act, but it is only treating the symptom, not the problem. Odinism needs to provide us with a rational and coherent way of analyzing and then addressing problems of this kind.

Odinism must become **action-oriented**, meaning that it must provide us with guidance as to how we approach our tasks and goals in this current life. For instance, many Odinists today are at least highly competent artists or musicians. A sincere Christian composer such as John Stainer knew exactly what he was doing when he wrote his great work, *The Crucifixion*: he described it as a "Meditation on the Passion of the Holy

Redeemer". Odinist artists must be able to be guided by their faith, not to "illustrate" it in the manner of Stainer, but to create music or visual art that is recognizably Odinist – rather than, say, atheist or Muslim.

Odinism must be **broad and balanced**. It needs to be able to express diverse views, without any antagonism, but within the criteria listed above. For instance, the worst mass-killer in Australian history was a man with the IQ of a child. He is currently serving a life-sentence in prison and will probably never be released, since there is no way to raise his IQ to the point that he can become responsible for his actions. He is reportedly being abused, horrendously, by his fellow-prisoners. From an Odinist perspective, how should society deal with people like this? And how can a range of diverse answers be raised without generating the sort of knee-jerk acrimony that is more suited to Judeo-Christianity?

Odinism must be **spiritually and emotionally meaningful**. It cannot be confined to some sort of historical re-enactment, not even a mere re-statement of the pre-Christian views of our ancestors, and it needs to address the transcendental issues that humans seek from any other religion. For instance, Odinism encompasses the idea of reincarnation. But what does it mean to us – in this life – that most of us will be reincarnated? How does it affect the way we live on a day-to-day basis? How does it influence our choice of careers, or marriage partners, or hobbies, or what we will choose from a restaurant menu?

Odinism will need to be **organized** in some way, but this must be in accordance with the nature of Odinism itself and not based on earlier and alien models. In particular, we must avoid what Walter Pater [100] called, "those mechanical *arcana*, those pretended 'secrets unveiled' of the professional mystic, which really bring great and little souls to one level".

Odinism must therefore never be thought of as embodying a **secret knowledge**, of the type that may be passed from initiates to novices as in a Christian Gnostic cult. The knowledge aspect of Odinism is equally available to all of us, like the rules of chess or tennis. What is not equally available is the ability to put these rules into action. That is why Odinism stresses the "nine noble virtues", which are: courage, fidelity, industriousness, discipline, self-reliance, honour, hospitality, perseverance and truth. Broadly speaking, these are also the qualities of the gods. As the pagan philosopher-king Marcus Aurelius pointed out: "… it will greatly help thee, if thou rememberest the gods, and that they wish not to be flattered, but wish all reasonable beings to be made like themselves". All of us are free to meditate on the qualities of the gods.

Odinism must recognize that **all Odinists are intrinsically equal**. Even though we have different temperaments, abilities and skills, we can all make a valid contribution. Even though some of us have lived longer than others, in this lifetime or in the past, we are all participating in the Odinist Re-Awakening in our own ways. An Odinist who is a superb athlete is every bit as valuable to all of us as one who can ask the great questions and blithely accept either the answers or the silences; or a great artist; or a musician or architect or scientist of genius. An Odinist who can be a good parent, measured in terms of how the children develop, is doing better than that great philosopher-king, Marcus Aurelius, whose son was a Christian-loving monster.

A gold medal for Jake Wetzel, third from left, wearing his Thor's Hammer at the Beijing Olympic Games

These are just some of the issues that need to be addressed. They are certainly not the only ones that should or will occupy us, and some would say that other issues are already more important. The conclusions that Odinists will draw, as more and more of us return to our spiritual home, cannot be predicted at this stage in our emergence from the Period of Dual Faith.

Even so, the final chapters of this book will suggest some guidelines that may help to ensure that we approach whatever the future may hold with both confidence and joy.

42

THE ODINIST TRANSVALUATION OF VALUES

The Matrix is a system, Neo. That system is our enemy. But when you're inside, you look around, what do you see? Businessmen, teachers, lawyers, carpenters. The very minds of the people we are trying to save. But until we do, these people are still a part of that system and that makes them our enemy. You have to understand, most of these people are not ready to be unplugged. And many of them are so inured, so hopelessly dependent on the system, that they will fight to protect it.

- Morpheus in the 1999 film, *The Matrix*

When we, as modern Odinists, look back on the vile mob that so cruelly murdered Hypatia (Chapter 16), it is hard not to feel raw anger. Hypatia, an embodiment of all that was beautiful, noble, wise, healthful, was cut to pieces by a degenerate rabble who wished to impose their own miserable nature on the rest of humanity. St Cyril's thugs were motivated by an unthinking rage, based on resentment of everything in life that is higher than themselves. It was fuelled by a conviction that a god who shared their own brutish nature would reward them. In Shakespeare's imagery, it was the vile monster Caliban licking the feet of his unworthy "god", Stephano, in *The Tempest*.

Within a short time creatures like Cyril and Caliban overturned the main values of the pagan world. The qualities that pagans had always considered important in the making of a good person (Chapter 15) were maligned, except when it was useful for propaganda purposes to deny them to non-Christians, or when they formed such an essential part of Indo-European human nature that they could not be entirely extirpated. An instance of the latter is the feeling of compassion. There is space here to look at only one example of heathen compassion.

Leprosy is a disease caused by a bacterium and spread by droplet infection. It probably originated in India, but how and when it first reached our northern Odinist homelands is a mystery. It was certainly present in Anglo-Saxon England in heathen times, although it was probably very rare. During the heathen period lepers were buried in ordinary graveyards. If they were high-status individuals, they were buried with high-status objects. Since they were interred side-by-side with non-lepers it therefore seems that sufferers lived within their ancestral communities, and were regarded as they had been before they fell sick. One example is the funeral of a probable princess at Barrington, Cambridgeshire. She was buried in a bed, and accompanied by rich grave goods. Furthermore, since the disease is debilitating, in the later stages of their illness lepers must have been tended by their families and friends. This tallies with accounts we have from the literary sources of sick heathens being looked after in their family homes.

The story revealed by Anglo-Saxon graves changes with the Christian take-over in England. Before long there were whole cemeteries given over solely to diseased people, many of them lepers. For instance, there were 35 lepers buried at the Norwich cemetery of St John the Baptist. This graveyard was beyond the city gates, which suggests the lepers were forced to live outside the town, in their own little outcast colony. They were considered unfit to be buried with their non-diseased kinsfolk.

Unlike Odinists, who looked after their sick, Christians tended to regard obvious diseases like leprosy as an outward manifestation of "sin". As early as 549 CE the Council of Orleans, as Christina Lee [101] tells us, "curbed the social intercourse of lepers with non-lepers". So if the lepers could not be tended by their families, they would have had few options but to beg for food. By 583 the Council of Lyons even banned them from begging. It was therefore unsurprising that in 643 the *Edictus Rothari* declared that lepers were "dead to the world". Leprosy had become what Lee called "a living purgatory endured for sinful living". And of course, the particular "sin" that gave rise to leprosy in the Christian mind was lust. Here is Pope Gregory: "Those have permanent scabs who are overcome by wantonness of the flesh without respite ... if the heart's temptation leaps forth into action, without doubt the secret intoxication breaks out all the way into scabs of the skin ..." A Greek Christian named Aretaios Cappalogue even stated that one symptom of leprosy, that outward sign of moral depravity, was "permanent erections"!

The modern sentimental form of Christianity claims that compassion is a Christian virtue, but as Jesus is supposed to have said: "A good tree bringeth not forth corrupt fruit; neither doth a corrupt tree bring forth good fruit" (Luke, 6:43). As far as compassion is concerned, Anglo-Saxon graves show that the "fruit" Christianity brought forth was not "good". Archaeology shows us that practical compassion, as distinct from sanctimonious cant, was an Odinist virtue.

It has been necessary to spend more than a few lines on the subject of illness and compassion here because it is too easy to take modern Christian spokesmen at their word. After all, the facts that refute their claims are not well known, and in many cases have only recently been brought to light. One otherwise brilliant thinker who fell for some of the Christian claims was Friedrich Nietzsche (1844-1900). Nietzsche noted how quickly the Christians had inverted Indo-European values, and proposed that for the sake of human health and the survival of worthwhile culture the Christian values should themselves be overturned. He called this task "The Transvaluation of all Values".

Nietzsche was not, and could not be, aware of two factors that were critically important to his project. First, many heathen values had survived throughout the Period of Dual Faith. Second, the modern Church, unable to wipe out these heathen ideals, had been forced to re-label them as "Christian" values. The Christians claimed, falsely, to be "moral"; Nietzsche therefore called himself an "Immoralist". The Christians claimed, falsely, to believe in heathen virtues such as compassion and charity; Nietzsche therefore poured scorn on even pragmatic compassion and charity. The Christians claimed to hate one of their gods called Satan; Nietzsche therefore assumed an air of Satanism. His grand project thus came to resemble a Christian Mass mumbled backwards.

Nietzsche was more of a psychologist than a philosopher. He was far more interested in making people healthy than in developing a consistent set of beliefs. In his view, Europeans of his day were decadent, and he defined decadence in terms of a disgust with life, with pleasure, with joy. His Europeans were spiritually cancerous with a life-denying weariness, obsessed with theory to the extent that their obsession became hostility to life itself. This decadence, a negativity in the heart and the soul, had begun with Socrates – a vulgar, argumentative hater of music, poetry, art and human instinct itself, a man so coarse that he could not even comprehend the healthful, joyous beauty of ancient Athens but instead strove to destroy its legacy, to drag Greece down to his own vulgar level.

Socrates: the would-be destroyer of the Athenians?	*Nietzsche: wanted to heal Western decadence*

It was not on a whim that the Athenians condemned Socrates to death, or that Rud Mills blamed him for side-tracking Western culture. Socrates partially corrupted Plato, and probably Athens, but did not impose much damage on the health of the rest of the world until Christianity adopted his anti-life attitudes.

The consequence of centuries of Socratic and later Christian corrosion of the Western soul was Nietzsche's starting-point. For as long as Christians could maintain some intellectually meaningful belief in a Jehovah-type god, the schizophrenic tension between European human nature and Socratic/Christian life-denial could be reconciled, just – but in Nietzsche's time Europeans had "killed" their god: "God is Dead", he famously wrote.

Erich Heller [102] summarized, better than this writer could, Nietzsche's diagnosis of the spiritual sickness that had to ensue:

> They knew not what they had done, but He who could forgive them is no more. Much of Nietzsche's work ever after is the prophecy of their fate: "The waters of religion," Nietzsche writes at the time of *Zarathustra*, "recede and leave behind morasses and shallow pools ... Where we live, soon nobody will be able to exist." From now onwards they will *hate*, Nietzsche believes, however many *comforts* they will lavish upon themselves, and hate *themselves* with a new hatred, unconsciously at work in the depths of their souls. True, there will be ever better reformers of society, ever better socialists, and ever better hospitals, and an ever increasing intolerance of pain and poverty and suffering and death, and an ever more fanatical craving for the greatest happiness of the greatest number. Yet the deepest impulse informing their striving will not be love and will not be compassion. Its true source will be the panic-stricken determination not to have to ask the question "What is the meaning of our lives?", the question which will remind them of the death of God ... Rather than have that question asked, they will do everything to smooth it away from the face of humanity. For they cannot endure it. And yet they will despise themselves for not enduring it, and for their guilt-ridden inability to answer it: and their self-hatred will betray them behind the back of their apparent charity and humanitarian concern. For *there* they will assiduously construct the tools for the annihilation of human kind. "There will be wars," Nietzsche writes, "such as have never been waged on earth." And he says: "I foresee something terrible. Chaos everywhere. Nothing left which is of any value; nothing which commands: Thou shalt!"

If the test of a prophet is the accuracy of his predictions, Nietzsche passes with flying colors. The last century has suffered wars more terrible than any psychologist but Nietzsche could have foreseen, waged with weapons that the best scientists of his day could have not have imagined.

The European "self-hatred" that he diagnosed has now reached such a point that the West has surrendered its borders and, under the secularized Christian dogma of "multiculturalism", many of its chief spokespersons in politics, business, the media, the churches, the universities, even what remains of the arts, are gleefully promoting the extinction of their own kind.

As to Nietzsche's "I foresee something terrible. Chaos everywhere. Nothing left which is of any value", one has only to look at postmodernist philosophy; or what currently passes for architecture, art, or serious music; or the sociological phenomenon of consumerism; or the vast bulk of American television, film and other "popular culture"; or the Christian-style hatred of humanity by the extreme "environmentalist" movement. Aggressive decadence – hatred of life – is the overwhelming motif. As another perceptive poet, W. B. Yeats, wrote in *The Second Coming* (1920):

> Things fall apart; the centre cannot hold;
> Mere anarchy is loosed upon the world,
> The blood-dimmed tide is loosed, and everywhere
> The ceremony of innocence is drowned;
> The best lack all conviction, while the worst
> Are full of passionate intensity.

The "best", who "lack all conviction", are currently going under. Just like the prominent self-haters who "are full of passionate intensity", they are suffering from fatal lifestyle choices. Some of their illnesses may be related to specific problems of late capitalism, such as environmental pollution or impure foods, but it is symptomatic of Western decadence that rates of suicide are increasing in most nations of formerly Odinist stock; and so are the numbers of people being labeled with psychological "syndromes"; and so are divorce rates, youth homelessness, violence in our cities, crime in general, and just about every other measure of a dysfunctional society and people.

Nietzsche bequeathed to us a way of approaching the problems besetting modern humans. We live a century after his death, and have access to far greater knowledge than was available to him. We are therefore able to recognize the strange and unhealthy synthesis of Christianity and Odinism that constituted the Period of Dual Faith and led to our present social ills. Unlike Nietzsche, we can easily identify the specifically Christian ways of thinking, mostly secularized nowadays, that are keeping Western men and women unhealthy, decadent, depressed and all too often suicidal, and certainly unable to achieve their destiny. Once these are recognized for what they are they can be "transvalued" quite logically and clinically.

Before we attempt to do so, it is necessary to stress once again that it is not enough merely to re-affirm the old, pre-Christian values and beliefs, no matter how serviceable they were in their time. Odinism is a living religion, and here we need to be reminded once more of the legal definition of Odinism as: "the continuation of ... the organic spiritual beliefs and religion of the indigenous peoples of northern Europe ... *as they have found expression in the wisdom and in the historical experience of these peoples"*

The "wisdom" and "historical experience" of our people includes the Period of Dual Faith, which as we have seen was as much Odinist as it was Christian. The Christians may own the title deeds to Chartres Cathedral, or Durham, but the inspiration of these temples owes far more to Odin's quest for knowledge than to the wandering fakir of the Christian Gospels. The "historical experience" of our people also includes brilliant proto-Odinists like Jefferson or Wagner, as well as sturdy Odinist pioneers like Mills and Christensen.

Nietzsche was an atheist, with all the problems that implies (see Chapter 35), but atheism was a more tenable position in his day. He knew nothing about modern physics (Chapter 8); or the "fields" that Rupert Sheldrake attributed to morphic resonance (Chapter 13); or the astonishing correlation between the views of our ancestors and modern science (Chapters 11 & 12); or the technological brilliance of our ancestors (Chapter 15); or even the survival of our spiritual traditions at a popular level (Chapters 23, 25 & 28). Nor should he have suspected the modern separation of forms of knowledge into distinct logical divisions (Chapter 35). Equally, the discipline of comparative religion was not sufficiently advanced in his time for awareness of the fact that religions which believe in cyclic time usually posit a long-term upward spiral.

Yet working with the materials to hand, Nietzsche applied his brilliant intellect to the problem, daring to pursue pure logic wherever it might take him. If eternal recurrence meant that we must re-live every one of our days over and over again, then there was only one logical course of action: we must live each day, each hour, each minute in such a way that we would *wish* to live it again and again. But who is capable of doing that? Not the Europeans of Nietzsche's time, or so he said, because they were too decadent. But some time in the future a new form of human would arise, one filled with such joy and strength and inner power that he or she could live as Nietzsche prescribed – and more: "be a glory to life itself", as his sister aptly wrote. Even the very best living humans cannot yet aspire to this state for themselves, but they can be "an arrow of desire" for the next form of humanity. He called this future being the "Superman". Because of later misuse of this term, we will refer instead to the Higher Man, which of course includes women.

Nietzsche was never entirely clear as to what he meant by the Higher Man, and there has been much debate over whether he really believed in such a being in any literal sense. That debate would not have disturbed him, since he believed in a different form of "truth" to that of the logic-chopping Socrates and his medieval theological followers who thought it was legitimate to ask how many angels could dance on the head of a pin.

He thought a desire for truth of *that* sort was a sign of pathology: an immature psychological need for certainty. To Nietzsche as a physician, a healer of decadence, truth was whatever enhances and affirms human existence: "All is truth to me that tends to elevate man".

After Nietzsche's death his sister addressed the question of what he meant by a Higher Man. She wrote:

> This type must not be regarded as a fanciful figure: it is not a nebulous hope which is to be realized at some indefinitely remote period, thousands of years hence; nor is it a new species (in the Darwinian sense) of which we can know nothing, and which it would therefore be something absurd to strive after. But it is meant to be a possibility which men of the present could realize with all their spiritual and physical energies, provided they adopted the new values.
>
> Elisabeth Förster-Nietzsche,
> Introduction to *Thus Spake Zarathustra,* 1905

A century ago it was of course true that people could "know nothing" about "a new species (in the Darwinian sense)". Today we have enough theoretical knowledge of genetics to be able to imagine such a new form of humanity. Tomorrow, technologically speaking, we will be able to create it. And if our human history teaches us anything, it is that anything that *can* be done *will* be done.

This process has already commenced. Antenatal screening tests are routinely available to mothers in the main countries that make up the Nation of Odin, and as a result, chromosomal abnormalities such as Down syndrome are being eliminated from our gene-pool. Many other diseases will soon disappear from our section of the world's population, simply because it is our nature not to wish suffering on our offspring. If this trend continues, then in perhaps one or two generations, parental love and modern science will have created, for the first time in human history, a human type that is free from the misery of inherited disease. After that, positive steps to improve the gene-pool will be inevitable: among our people, most parents want the very best possible future for their children.

It is likely that modern genetic technology will soon make it possible for a couple to select their most desirable sperm and ova, and even to splice in genetic "patches" to overcome potential illnesses or simply to improve the species. Further possibilities beyond that level of technology may be beyond our current imagining, but as James D. Watson, co-discoverer of the double helix, asked: "if we could make better human beings by knowing how to add genes, why shouldn't we?" [103] And as Stephen Hawking warned: "We should follow this road if we want biological systems to remain superior to electronic ones. In contrast with our intellect, computers double their performance every 18 months." [104]

Perhaps at this stage readers should refer back to Chapter 11. The improvement of our species is an Odinist goal, if for no other reason than that the gods of our people, however you perceive them, have consistently intervened in human evolution for exactly that purpose. Chapter 11 also mentioned a Christian priest and professional "ethicist" who seems to have thought it a good thing (because it was "god's will") that Stephen Hawking suffered from one of the most terrible diseases imaginable. Once again we have a clear clash of values between resurgent Odinism and residual Christianity, as discussed in Chapter 15. One desires joyous and transcendent health, the other makes a spiritual fetish of pain and suffering and disease.

The people Nietzsche called "decadents" will of course oppose the ideal of human improvement as long as they live. At first they used transparent language to voice their anguish, accusing loving parents, and the doctors who helped them, of "playing god". That obviously failed to change our behavior, so at present they mumble darkly that any form of human intervention in our evolution is a "slippery slope", or a "thin end of the wedge". They cannot articulate their fears coherently, for the simple reason that these fears are based on a secularized version of an irrational religion; but that will not stop them.

Nor will it stop us. Even if today's equivalents of Caliban or Saint Cyril manage to use the machinery of our current political system to impose legal sanctions against a whole new generation of Hypatias, it remains a fact that prohibition has never worked. It did not work in the European "witchcraft" trials, it did not work with regard to alcohol in the days of Al Capone, it does not work today as far as illegal drugs are concerned. Anyone who has the means to get around legal prohibitions may do so, and because we are mammals all parents who wish the best for their children will go to great lengths to do so. Therefore planned evolution will happen. And therefore humankind will soon begin to divide into two groups: those who hate themselves enough to wish to perpetuate misery, and those who love humanity enough to wish our children to be more like our revered gods and goddesses.

We are entering an era of confusion, due to the collapse of the Period of Dual Faith. Some people who currently consider themselves Christian will end up on our side, and some people who call themselves Odinists will turn out to have too many residual Christian psychoses to accept the future with an open heart and mind. Time will sort the "nay-sayers" from the "yea-sayers". Meanwhile, it is interesting to note that people who can't be pigeon-holed in one camp or the other are increasingly tilting the intellectual climate in an Odinist direction. One such person was Julian Savulescu, Professor of Practical Ethics at Oxford University, who made these remarks on where we stand, morally, with regard to current genetic technology:

> The genophobe claims it's our environment, or culture, that defines us, not genetics.
>
> A quiet walk in the park demonstrates the power of the great genetic experiment: dog breeding. It's obvious different breeds

of dog differ in temperament, intelligence, physical ability and appearance.

No matter what the turf, a doberman will tear a corgi to pieces.

Of course, you can debilitate a doberman with neglect and abuse. Or you can make him prettier with a bow. But you will never turn a chihuahua into a doberman through grooming, training and affection.

Dog breeds are all genetic – for 10,000 years we've bred more than 150 types of dog from early canids and wolves.

Their characteristics have been created by a crude form of genetic selection – selective mating or breeding.

And we now have additional tools in animal husbandry: genetic testing, artificial reproduction and cloning are all used to create the best farming stock.

Like other animals, selective mating has been occurring in humans since time began. There are many factors that can affect the mating game, even at a subconscious level.

Facial asymmetry can reflect genetic disorder. Smell can tell us whether our mate will produce a child with the best resistance to disease. We compete for partners in elaborate mating games and rituals of display which sort the best matches from the worst.

As products of evolution, we select our mates, both rationally and instinctively, on the basis of their genetic fitness, their ability to survive and reproduce.

Now, with the tools of genetics, we can select offspring in a more reliable way.

The power of genetics is growing. Embryos can now be tested not only for the presence of genetic disorder (including some forms of bowel and breast cancer), but also for less serious genetic abnormalities, such as dental abnormalities ...

Research is going on in the field of behavioural genetics to understand the genetic basis of aggression and criminal behaviour, alcoholism, anxiety, antisocial personality disorder, maternal behaviour, homosexuality and neuroticism.

While at present there are no genetic tests for these complex behaviours, if the results of recent animal studies into hard work and monogamy apply to humans, it may be possible in the future to genetically change how we are predisposed to behave.

Should we take this opportunity to decide what breed of humans to create?

Some people believe children are a gift, of God or nature, and that we should not interfere with nature.

Most people implicitly reject this view. We screen embryos and fetuses for diseases, even mild correctible diseases.

If we are to enhance certain qualities, how should we decide which ones?

Eugenics was the movement early last century that aimed to use selective breeding to prevent degeneration of the gene pool by weeding out criminals, those with mental illness and the poor, on the false belief that these were the result of simple genetic disorders.

The eugenics movement had its inglorious peak when the Nazis moved beyond sterilisation to extermination of the genetically "unfit".

What was objectionable about the eugenics movement, besides its shoddy science, was that it involved imposition of a state vision for a healthy population and aimed to achieve this through coercion.

The eugenics movement was not aimed at what was good for individuals but what benefited society.

Modern eugenics in the form of testing for disorders, such as Down syndrome, occurs very commonly, but is acceptable because it is voluntary, gives couples a choice over what kind of child to have and the aim is to have a child with the greatest opportunity for a good life. The critical question in considering whether to alter some gene-related behaviour is: would the change be better for the individual?

Is it better for the individual to have a tendency to be lazy or hardworking; monogamous or polygamous, or any other range of behaviours?

These questions are difficult to answer.

There will be cases where some intervention is plausibly in a person's interests: manipulating genes to create people who empathise with others, with a capacity to understand oneself and the world around or with a powerful memory.

Or how about that quality most associated with socio-economic success and staying out of prison: impulse control? If it were possible to correct poor impulse control, we should correct it. Whether we should remove impulsiveness altogether is another question.

Our future is in our hands now, like it or not. But by not allowing enhancement and control over the genetic nature of our offspring, we consign a person to the natural lottery, and now, by having the power to do otherwise, to fail to do otherwise is to be responsible for the results of the natural lottery.

We must make a choice: the natural lottery or rational choice.

Where an enhancement is plausibly good for an individual, we should let that individual decide. And in the case of the next generation, we should let parents decide.

To fail to allow them to make these choices is to consign the next generation to the ball and chain of our squeamishness and irrationality.

Julian Savulescu, *New Breeds of Humans* [105]

This issue is about to transform humanity. Genuine Odinists will endorse the future, while genuine Christians, Jews and Muslims will yearn for the past. Those who choose the future will opt for greater health, intelligence, beauty, and a godlike direction for their descendants. Those who choose the past will be condemning their own descendants to a Caliban-like status. Either way, the future will unfold along lines that are already predictable.

Odinists will be joyous that our children can be liberated from the yoke of bad genes. Unlike Nietzsche, we are also aware of the aspects of the Odinist soul that our ancestors believed will survive into the future (see Chapter 13), and we will therefore look forward to our own personal ecstasy, exuberance, passion, fervor, ardor, rapture, delight and bliss – in at least symbolic terms, union with that mighty force that the 21st century calls "Odin".

This coming stage of humanity is in accord with the will of our own gods and goddesses. It is not in accord with many other religions; particularly the "Abrahamic" ones (Judaism, Christianity and Islam), which are essentially competing versions of a death cult. It will result in a complete transformation of how life is and should be lived. Only those who are able to transvalue all the beliefs and values that are genuinely part of the Middle Eastern religions will wish to be part of the future. Those who fail to reject the death cult will achieve their goal: the extinction of themselves and their heirs. Odinists, by contrast, will have no fear of the brave new world that is about to dawn, and will have the courage to assess all the coming moral issues with crystal-clear intellects.

Some of these issues will, however, test our *courage* to the full. For instance, one abiding symptom of our past decadence is a continuing belief in some previous form of politics. Democracy, theocracy, monarchy, aristocracy, socialism, communism, national socialism, anarchism, and all other political systems that humans have previously held dear, were designed for the past, not for the world that is coming. We will be able to take from them whatever is useful for the future, but none of us reading this book at this time can predict what will be found helpful by beings higher than we currently are. The same will apply to art, to literature, to music ... It may be painful *for us* to jettison some of the beauties and glories of our past, especially in the arts; but it will be necessary, in order that *real* art, art that is rooted in the nature and future of our people, may once again be re-born.

It should be remembered that many influential individuals are coming around to our view. One of these is Britain's Astronomer Royal and president of the Royal Society. Martin Rees believes that a "post-human" species will soon emerge. "This is not going to be controlled by Darwinian evolution, but controlled by humans," Lord Rees has been quoted as saying. [106]

Lord Rees has presumably never heard of Odinism, but whether he knows it or not, he is expressing our views. When the Astronomer Royal does that, it is obvious that our religion is making real progress. In the end it doesn't matter whether people whose heritage entitles them to do so choose to wear a Thor's Hammer. What matters is that Odinist values become once again the mainstream values of our people. That is happening now.

Odinists would not wish for a life that was merely "easy". We are the ones uniquely poised to "peer into the dark abyss without vertigo" – in fact, not only without vertigo, but with exhilaration. We seek a new civilization, and a new humanity to create it, and we look forward to a time when even many of the present gods and goddesses themselves will be renewed and surpassed.

43

TOWARD TOMORROW

How much can a human mind bear, how much truth does it dare to face?

- Nietzsche, *Ecce Homo*

O, wonder!
How many goodly creatures are there here!
How beauteous mankind is! O brave new world,
That has such people in't!

- Miranda, in Shakespeare's *The Tempest*

Most people alive today will not and cannot become Odinists. Half of our own people are, sadly, born with an IQ below 100, and therefore could not, at the present stage of the Odinist renewal, understand some of the issues raised in this fairly straight-forward book. Others are above-average in intelligence, but have missed out on a decent education for one reason or another. Yet more are relatively "new" souls, who may need further incarnations before they can address the deeper spiritual issues. Far too many others are merely corrupt (a form of decadence), seeking a small increase of material wealth through service to the forces of entropy – which are personified in our religion by Loki.

We must therefore remember at all times that no-one will ever come back home to Odinism until he or she is ready for it. For the majority of our people, readiness will come naturally when Odinist ideas and moral values have resumed their rightful place at the core of our mainstream culture. At that happy time Odinism will seem both natural and obvious to nearly all of our people.

That is the practical reason why Odinists do not evangelize. But there is also a moral reason for our refusal to try to persuade others of our truths. Many people are, at this stage, simply not ready to confront reality. Some people who are returning to our ancestral faith can grasp only a few aspects of it. Others can see further, but often they will merely waste the time and spiritual energy of the rest of us by asking endless questions that they could resolve for themselves. As Nietzsche's

Zarathustra said: "You had not looked for yourselves: then you found me. That is what all believers do: that is why belief is worth so little. Now I bid you lose me and find yourselves."

Even Odin, the god who best expresses the nature of our people's desire throughout the ages for wisdom, or at least comprehension of the aspects of nature and ourselves that can be understood, does not know everything. That is why the Odinic quest is a search for ever more knowledge and wisdom. We, as mere humans, know less than Odin. We, as Odinists, therefore do not set ourselves up as gurus or rabbis or imams, much less as popes or patriarchs, since we are all in this quest together, all learning, and all sharing our knowledge as best we can.

Unlike the Middle Eastern religions, but like proper science, Odinism has no fixed dogmas. It can therefore never become a cult. That does not mean it has no standards. The ultimate standard is the set of laws that derive from the highest aspects of our own inner nature, derived from the gods – as opposed to the strictures that have been arbitrarily applied against our deepest selves and our most soaring visions by a desert religion that managed to win over the criminal rabble of a Roman Empire collapsing under the weight of massive and inappropriate immigration.

Above all, Odinism is a religion to be *done*, not to be discussed. It is an inspiration for action, not a justification for obscure ritual or for chat-room discussion. It will never become *comfortable* because it is a mature, heroic and impassioned reverence for life itself – and life is uncertain and dangerous.

Those of us who can face this challenge will be the bridge to the future that Nietzsche prophesied. Those who cannot will join the vast majority of species that have existed at one time or another on this planet, and are now extinct.

By way of bidding farewell to readers who have reached this page, let us recall a Norman legend. According to Dudo of Saint-Quentin, when the men ostensibly serving the Scandinavian chief Rollo were engaged in the conquest of Normandy, they were asked the name of their lord or leader. They replied: "None, because we are all equal". [107]

In the brave new world that Odinists are already helping to create, and which our descendants will inherit, there is much yet to be discovered about the spirituality of our ancestors and their insights into the universe. In that sense, we are indeed "all equal". Because of the Christian interregnum, followed by the Period of Dual Faith, our understanding of Odinism is still incomplete. We are still in the stage of Early Modern Odinism. In another generation our knowledge will have increased exponentially. It would be foolhardy for any of us today to claim to have knowledge that will not be surpassed.

Yet at least we now know where to look – in our people's past, in our present intrinsic nature, in the universe of which we are part, and also in our potentially ecstatic future.

NOTES

[1] Described as "one of the key novels of the last century", Stuart Evers, 2010, *The Easton Ellis Generation*, Guardian.co.uk, viewed 7 June 2010: http://www.guardian.co.uk/books/booksblog/2010/feb/11/easton-ellis-generation.
[2] Richard Hoggart, 1975, *The Uses of Literacy*, Chatto & Windus
[3] Pascal Bruckner, 2010, *The Tyranny of Guilt: An Essay on Western Masochism*, Princeton University Press.
[4] Constitution of the Odinic Rite of Australia, 1995, accepted by the Australian Taxation Office
[5] H. M. Chadwick, 1899, *The Cult of Othin*, Cambridge University Press
[6] H. V. Vallois, *The Fontéchevade Fossil Men*, American Journal of Physical Anthropology 7: 339-362
[7] John Geipel, 1969, *The Europeans*, Longmans, London
[8] Robert Silverberg, 1967, *The Morning of Mankind*, New York Graphic Society Publishers
[9] F Clark Howell, 1973, *Early Man*, Time-Life, N.Y.
[10] Stanley Gooch, *Total Man*, 1972, *Personality and Evolution*, 1973, and *The Neanderthal Question*, 1977
[11] Roger Lewin, 1988, *In the Age of Mankind*, Smithsonian, Washington
[12] *Nature*, October, 1987
[13] Desmond Collins, 1986, *Palaeolithic Europe*, Devon
[14] Vincent Gaffney, Simon Fitch, David Smith, 2009, *Europe's Lost World: the Rediscovery of Doggerland*, CBA
[15] J. P. Mallory, 1991, *In Search of the Europeans: Language, Archaeology and Myth*, Thames and Hudson, p. 191
[16] Roger Pearson, 1966, *Race & Civilization*, The Clair Press, London, p. 72
[17] R. Peterson, 1985, *An Atlas of Mankind, volume two, The Classical World*, The Cliveden Press, p. 30
[18] Derick Thomson, 1977, *An Introduction to Gaelic Poetry*, Victor Gollancz Ltd
[19] A. A. Sayce & R. Peterson, 1993, *Race in Ancient Egypt and the Old Testament*, Scott-Townsend Publishers, p. 107
[20] Theodor Poesche, 1878, *Die Arier: Ein Beitrag zur historischen Anthropologie*, Jena
[21] Tenney Frank, 1927, *An Economic History of Rome*, Johns Hopkins Press, Baltimore
[22] Victor Mair & J. P. Mallory, 2000, *The Tarim Mummies: Ancient China and the Mystery of the Earliest Peoples from the West* Thames & Hudson
[23] Sir George Scott Robinson, 1896, *The Kafirs of the Hindu Kush*, Lawrence and Bullen, London; reprinted in facsimile by OUP in 1973 with an introduction by Louis Duprès.
[24] Alfonso Lowe, 1975, *The Spanish: the intrepid nation*, Gordon Cremonesi Ltd
[25] Ninian Smart, 1968, *Secular Education and the Logic of Religion*, New York, Humanities Press, p. 104
[26] For further reading, see Heinrich Stefanik, "Saga and Western", *Parergon*, August 1976, Number 15, pp 55-64
[27] Clifford Pickover, 1999, *Surfing Through Hyperspace*, Oxford University Press
[28] H. R. Ellis Davidson, 1964, *Gods and Myths of Northern Europe*, Penguin

[29] Guy Rundle, "I, lungfish: Richard Dawkins explains the facts of life", in *The Australian Literary Review,* October 7, 2009, pp 12-13
[30] Gabriel Turville-Petre, "The Cult of Óðinn in Iceland", in *Nine Norse Studies,* London, 1972
[31] Eilert Ekwall, 1980, *The Concise Oxford Dictionary of English Place-Names,* Clarendon Press
[32] F. M. Stenton, "The Historical bearing of place-name studies: Anglo-Saxon heathenism", *Transactions of the Royal Historical Society,* 23, 1941, 1-24
[33] Jens Peter Schjødt, 2008, *Initiation between Two Worlds: Structure and symbolism in pre-Christian Scandinavian religion,* The University Press of Southern Denmark
[34] Richard Dawkins, 1988, *The Blind Watchmaker,* Penguin Books
[35] Eliade, M, 1971, *The Myth of the Eternal Return,* Princeton UP
[36] W. D. O'Flaherty, 1981. *The Rig Veda: An Anthology,* Penguin
[37] P. B Taylor & W. H. Auden, 1969, *The Elder Edda: A Selection translated from the Icelandic,* Faber & Faber, London
[38] A. Rey, 1927. *Le Retour Éternel et la Philosophie de la Physique,* Flammarion, Paris
[39] P. J. Bowler, 1984. *Evolution: The History of an Idea,* University of California Press, Berkeley
[40] Fred Hoyle, "World Without End", *New Scientist,* 27/4/96.
[41] Len Hughes, *Laser Cosmology,* Len Hughes International Press, 1995
[42] "Physicist Challenges Big Bang Theory", *The Weekend Australian,* 25-26/5/96
[43] M.I. Steblin-Kamenskij, 1973, *The Saga Mind,* translated by Kenneth H. Ober, Odense University Press
[44] Johannes Brøndsted, 1973, *The Vikings,* Penguin
[45] Rupert Sheldrake, 1981, *A New Science of Life,* J. P. Tarcher, Los Angeles
[46] Rupert Sheldrake, 1988, *The Presence of the Past: morphic resonance and the habits of nature,* Times Books, New York
[47] Jo Marchant, 2009, *Decoding the Heavens: Solving the Mystery of the World's First Computer,* Heinemann
[48] Joachim Kahl, 1972, *The Misery of Christianity,* Penguin
[49] Tacitus, 1970, *The Agricola and the Germania,* trans. H. Mattingly and S. A. Handford, Penguin
[50] Grimm, *Deutsche Mythologie,* Vol. I, ch. 13
[51] Mangasar Mugurditch Mangasarian, "The Female Philosopher of Alexandria", *Rationalist* (Independent Religious Society of Chicago), v. 1-4
[52] Simon Singh, 1998, *Fermat's Last Theorum,* Fourth Estate, London
[53] D. Stannard, 1992, *American Holocaust,* Oxford University Press
[54] B. Hope-Taylor, 1977, *Yeavering,* Department of the Environment Archaeological Reports, London
[55] F. J. Los, 1968, *The Franks: A critical study in Christianization and Imperialism,* tr. John P. Wardle, Northern League
[56] Aryah Grabois (Ed), 1980, *The Illustrated Encyclopedia of Medieval Civilization,* Mayflower, NY
[57] See also Robert Ferguson, 2009, *The Vikings: A History,* Viking
[58] For more information see Niels Lund, *The settlers: where do we get them from – and do we need them?* in *Proceedings of the Eighth Viking Congress,* Odense University Press, 1981

[59] P. H. Sawyer, 1982, *Kings and Vikings: Scandinavia and Europe AD 700-1100*, Methuen, p 101

[60] Gwyn Jones, 1973, *A History of the Vikings*, OUP

[61] Gillian Fellows-Jensen, 1995, *The Vikings and their Victims: the Verdict of the Names*, University College, London

[62] "Pagan Beliefs, Christian Impact and Archaeology – a Danish View", in *Viking Revaluations*, ed. Anthony Faulkes and Richard Perkins, Viking Society for Northern Research, 1993

[63] Roberta Frank, 1994, *Cnut and his Skalds*, in *The Reign of Cnut: King of England, Denmark and Norway*, Ed. Alexander R. Rumble, Leicester University Press

[64] P. H. Sawyer, 1982, *Kings and Vikings: Scandinavia and Europe AD 700-1100*, Methuen

[65] See: Folke Ström, "Poetry as an instrument of propaganda: Jarl Hákon and his poets" in *Specvlvm Norroenvm: Norse studies in memory of Gabriel Turville-Petre*, Odense University Press, 1981

[66] Gwyn Jones, 1973, *A History of the Vikings*, OUP

[67] See Kirsten Hastrup, 1990, *Island of Anthropology: studies in past and present Iceland*, Odense University Press

[68] T.F. Henderson, 1912, *The ballad in literature*, Cambridge University Press

[69] J. A. MacCulloch, 1905, *Childhood of Fiction: a study of folk tales and primitive thought*, John Murray

[70] F. Yorke Powell, 1965, *Corpus poeticum boreale, the poetry of the Old Northern tongue, from the earliest times to the thirteenth century*, New York, Russell and Russell

[71] George MacDonald Fraser, 1974, *The Steel Bonnets: The story of the Anglo-Scottish Border Reivers*, Pan Books

[72] James A. H. Murray, 1873, *The Dialect of the Southern Counties of Scotland: its pronunciation, grammar, and historical relations*, London, Philological Society, p. 18:

[73] G. J. Markus, 1980, *The Conquest of the North Atlantic*, The Boydell Press, Suffolk

[74] ed. T Hearne, 1723, *Hemingi Cartularium Ecclesiae Wigornensis*

[75] Ronald Sheridan and Anne Ross, 1975, *Gargoyles & Grotesques: Paganism in the Medieval Church*, New York Graphic Society, Boston

[76] H. R. Ellis Davidson, 1967, *Pagan Scandinavia*, Thames and Hudson, p. 98

[77] illustrated in H. R. Ellis Davidson, 1967, p. 89

[78] C. S. Lewis, 1958, *The Allegory of Love: a Study in Medieval Tradition*, Galaxy Books, OUP

[79] Kenneth Clark, 1969, *Civilisation*, BBC Books

[80] Augustine, 1972, *Concerning the City of God against the Pagans*, Penguin Books

[81] see for instance Barbara Walker, 1983, *The Woman's Encyclopedia of Myths and Secrets*, Harper, San Francisco

[82] Armaldo Momigliano, ed., 1963, *The Conflict between Paganism and Christianity in the Fourth Century*, Oxford: The Clarendon Press

[83] Gordon Leff, 1958, *Medieval Thought: St Augustine to Ockham*, Penguin

[84] George Eckel Duckworth, 1962, *Structural patterns and proportions in Virgil's Aeneid : a study in mathematical composition*, University of Michigan Press

[85] Christina Hole, 1978, *A Dictionary of British Folk Customs,* Paladin Books, Granada Publishing Ltd
[86] Paul Frodsham, 2008, *From Stonehenge to Santa Claus: the evolution of Christmas,* The History Press, Gloucestershire
[87] E. A. Freeman, 1867-79, *History of the Norman Conquest,* 6 vols, Clarendon Press, Oxford
[88] R. N. Bradley, 1926, *Racial Origins of English Character,* Allen & Unwin, London
[89] Van Wyck Brooks, 1944, *The World of Washington Irving,* E. P. Dutton and Company
[90] Michael Lind, 1995, *The Next American Nation,* The Free Press, NY
[91] Donald Thomas, 1979, *Swinburne: The Poet in his World,* Oxford University Press
[92] Antony H. Harrison, 1988, *Swinburne's Medievalism: a study in Victorian love poetry,* Lousiana State University Press
[93] Robert Graves, 1961, *The White Goddess,* Faber & Faber, London
[94] John Merritt, 1974, *What Shall We Teach?* Ward Lock, London
[95] Paul Hirst, "The logic of the curriculum", *Journal of Curriculum Studies,* 1969
[96] Barbara Winter, 2005, *The Australia First Movement and the Publicist, 1936-1942,* Glass House Books, Australia
[97] A. Rud Mills, 1957, *The Call of our Ancient Nordic Religion,* Melbourne
[98] T. Charman, 1989, *The German Home Front: 1939-45,* Philosophical Library, N.Y.
[99] John Yeowell, 1993, *Odinism and Christianity under the Third Reich,* The Odinic Rite, London
[100] Walter Pater, 1968, *Marius the Epicurean,* Everyman's Library, London
[101] Christina Lee, "Changing Faces: Leprosy in Anglo-Saxon England", in *Conversion and Colonization in Anglo-Saxon England,* eds C. E. Karkov & N. Howe, ACMRS, Tempe, Arizona, 2006
[102] Erich Heller, 1988, *The Importance of Nietzsche,* University of Chicago Press
[103] "Risky Genetic Fantasies", *The Los Angeles Times,* 29 July 2001
[104] "Hawking: it's time for GM people", Severin Carrell, *The Independent,* 2 September 2001
[105] J. Savulescu, 2005, 'New breeds of humans: the moral obligation to enhance', *Reproductive Biomedicine Online*; 10 (Supp 1) 1-9
[106] Leigh Dayton, "Royal Astronomer goes in search of ET", *The Australian,* March 26, 2010.
[107] *de Moribus et Actis primorum Normaenniæ Ducum,* Societé des Antiquaires de Normandie, 1865, p. 154

Printed in Great Britain
by Amazon.co.uk, Ltd.,
Marston Gate.